The Sword
of the Spirit

John R. Knott, Jr.

The Sword
of the Spirit
Puritan Responses
to the Bible

THE UNIVERSITY OF CHICAGO PRESS
Chicago and London

JOHN R. KNOTT, JR., professor of English at the
University of Michigan, is the author of *Milton's
Pastoral Vision*, published by the University of
Chicago Press in 1971.

THE UNIVERSITY OF CHICAGO PRESS, CHICAGO 60637
THE UNIVERSITY OF CHICAGO PRESS, LTD., LONDON

Printed in the United States of America
87 86 85 84 83 82 81 80   4 3 2 1

LIBRARY OF CONGRESS CATALOGING IN PUBLICATION DATA

Knott, John Ray, 1937–
  The sword of the spirit.

  Includes index.
  1. Bible—Criticism, interpretation, etc.—
History—17th century.   2. Puritans—England.
I. Title.
BS500.K6   230   79-23424
ISBN 0-226-44848-7

To my mother and father

*And take the helmet of salvation, and
the sword of the Spirit, which is the
word of God.*

Ephesians 6:17

*For the word of God is quick, and pow-
erful, and sharper than any two-edged
sword, piercing even to the dividing
asunder of soul and spirit, and of the
joints and marrow, and is a discerner of
the thoughts and intents of the heart.*

Hebrews 4:12

Contents

Acknowledgments

A fellowship from the National Endowment for the Humanities and a grant from the Horace H. Rackham School of Graduate Studies of the University of Michigan gave me the opportunity to spend a sabbatical year in England enjoying the splendid resources of Cambridge University. The hospitality of Clare Hall and of many members of the university community helped to make that year a memorable and productive one. I am particularly grateful for the advice and encouragement of Gordon Rupp and H. C. Porter of Cambridge and of Geoffrey Nuttall and Roger Sharrock of the University of London. The Cambridge University Library and the library of Emmanuel College provided a congenial environment in which to work. I am grateful to their librarians and staff, and also to those of the British Library and of Dr. Williams's Library in London and of the University of Michigan libraries closer to home.

I have benefited from discussions with various students and colleagues, among them Russell Chambers, John Bailey, and Russell Fraser. Frank Huntley, Ralph Williams, and C. A. Patrides read the whole manuscript carefully and offered suggestions for revision. I am grateful also for the sympathetic and helpful criticism of Barbara Lewalski and Janel Mueller, who read the manuscript for the press. Mrs. Lewalski was kind enough to let me see chapters of her new book, *Protestant Poetics*, in manuscript. I owe an older debt to Herschel Baker, who first interested me in the English Reformation.

Finally, I am deeply grateful to my wife, Anne Percy Knott, for her patience and her unquestioning support. The dedication expresses my oldest debt, to my father, John R. Knott, and my mother, Wilma Henshaw Knott, who will appreciate the connection between this book and its author's early encounters with "sword drill."

Part of chapter 6 appeared in *English Literary Renaissance* 3 (1973): 443–61 under the title "Bunyan's Gospel Day: A Reading of *The Pilgrim's Progress*." It is reprinted here by permission.

Introduction

Over forty years ago William Haller complained that "literary history in the genteel tradition" had reserved most of its attention and virtually all its praise for the men who represented the Anglican ideal of the church and religious life. Haller himself did much to correct this imbalance with his seminal studies of Puritan writing in the earlier seventeenth century, which bring a different set of men into view and illuminate many of the favorite themes and images of Puritan preaching.[1] Other pioneers such as M. M. Knappen, A. S. P. Woodhouse, and Perry Miller traced the emergence of typically Puritan concerns and modes of thought in England and America.[2] More recently, Christopher Hill has produced his influential books on the economic and social dimensions of Puritanism and the climate of radical opinion in mid-seventeenth century England.[3] With others, like the political scientist Michael Walzer,[4] he has made us more fully aware of the energies of the Puritan movement and of its profoundly revolutionary character. Ben Jonson's stage Puritans—his Tribulation Wholesome and Zeal-of-the-Land Busy with their pious cant—capture only a fraction of the complex of beliefs and activities we have learned to think of as Puritan.

The study of Puritanism has been a recognizable academic industry for some time now. Still, the neglect of the kind of literary study that Haller commented upon remains apparent, despite the appearance of a number of significant works in the past ten years or so.[5] The major Puritan preachers are still relatively little studied (Haller could give no more than a few pages to each), and not until very recently has there been a major effort to place Milton in the context of Puritan and radical thought, most notably by Christopher Hill.[6] Although Bunyan has been the subject of a number of important studies, he still has not received the amount of detailed attention that a figure of his talent and influence deserves.[7] I do not mean to imply that the sermons of a Sibbes merit the full-dress scholarly treatment given Donne's, or that major Puritan poets await discovery. I would suggest, however, that it is reasonable to talk about a Puritan imagination, as Sacvan Bercovitch and others have done in connection with American Puritanism,[8] and to pay more attention than we have given to works that best embody this imagination. If we regard Jeremy Taylor as part of the canon, we should be prepared to admit the claims of Winstanley or Baxter.

My emphasis in the chapters that follow is upon attitudes toward the Bible and uses of Scripture in the work of a group of writers who, taken together, represent the strength and diversity of Puritan prose in seventeenth-century England. Much of the vitality of this prose emerges from the ways in which the Bible acted upon the imaginations of the writers. I am not primarily concerned with Puritan hermeneutics, or with particular writers' use of typology, rather with images and patterns of thought—ultimately biblical or generated by the effort to embody the energy and truth of the Word—that shaped Puritan spiritual life and Puritan visions of a reformed society. I have contrasted Puritan and Anglican approaches to the Bible and to preaching where such contrasts seemed illuminating, recognizing that one cannot regard these terms as applying to fixed and mutually exclusive sets of attitudes. In my first chapter I draw into the discussion figures from the early and middle sixteenth century who cannot accurately be called Anglican or Puritan yet who can be seen as anticipating attitudes and positions that emerged toward the end of the century when major controversies arose.

My broad use of the term Puritan—to include subjects as diverse as Milton and Bunyan, Baxter and Winstanley—requires some explanation. I have followed the modern practice of regarding Puritanism as a movement embracing many kinds of reforming instincts and practices. Contemporary usage of the term, although it admitted some ambiguity, would not have allowed such latitude. The word Puritan gained currency in the 1560s as a name for those who resisted the bishops' efforts to enforce conformity in worship and church discipline and came to be applied to pious people generally, often as a term of abuse.[9] The name was most commonly used, however, to identify those who attempted to reform the established church from within. Others who sought a freer mode of worship outside the structure of the church—Separatists, Anabaptists, Brownists—were not thought of as Puritans.

Insofar as Puritanism became an organized movement for reform, its outlines are clearest at particular times of conflict: the appearance of the Admonitions to Parliament in 1572, the struggle of Thomas Cartwright and others to win approval for a presbyterian system of church government in the 1580s and early 1590s, the confrontation of Puritan leaders with the bishops at the Hampton Court Conference in 1604, the continuing resistance of leading Puritan ministers to the emergence of Arminianism in the church in the 1620s and 1630s. After 1640, when the movement for reform rapidly gained momentum, the term Puritan gave way to more precise names for the contending factions on the Parliamentary side, the most important being Presbyterian and Independent. With Anglicanism in eclipse and sects proliferating the generic term became anachronistic. We may think of Bunyan as the very embodiment of the Puritan temper, but to his contemporaries he was a Baptist.

The difficulties of establishing a definition of Puritanism that will satisfy the claims of historical accuracy are compounded by the fact that the nature of this definition depends upon one's perspective: political, theological, moral, even social.[10] Given these difficulties, some modern commentators have argued for restricting the use of the term, or at least for defining it in narrowly theological ways. Thus C. H. and K. George prefer to think of a "Protestant mind" and to minimize the differences between Puritan and Anglican.[11] From a strictly theological viewpoint, one could argue that there was no significant and lasting division until the Arminian turning away from a Calvinist sense of election in England in the 1620s, with a concomitant emphasis upon the liturgy of the church.[12] Before that time, despite the controversy of Cartwright with Archbishop Whitgift and subsequent disagreement over the strongly Calvinist Lambeth Articles of 1595, the influence of Calvin was pervasive enough to make it relatively difficult to distinguish Puritan and Anglican in doctrinal terms.[13] Yet recent scholarship on Puritanism has demonstrated that valid distinctions can be made, on a number of bases, and that an excessive emphasis upon the unity of English Protestant thought obscures real and important differences.[14]

Modern students of Puritanism have found the term amply justified by the existence of identifiable patterns of thought and behavior, without necessarily agreeing upon a definition. One can think of Puritanism as a "revolutionary ideology," with Michael Walzer, or, more broadly, as a "spiritual outlook, way of life and mode of expression," with Haller. One can speak of a Puritan mind, a Puritan spirituality, or, more generally still, of a Puritan temper or spirit. I find enough evidences of such a spirit in the radical sectarians of the 1640s to want to stretch the term to include them, following the practice of Haller and Woodhouse. The latter characterized as Puritan all the parties to the Army debates of the 1640s, including those of the left, descended from the Separatists and Anabaptists, and encompassed in his broad definition figures at the far reaches of religious radicalism such as Winstanley and the Fifth Monarchists.[15]

The five writers that I discuss can be said to represent different moments in the evolution of a Puritan spirituality and also different aspects of this spirituality. I have chosen them, in fact, partly because of their differences. The writings examined represent a variety of genres: the Puritan sermon (Sibbes), meditation (Baxter), the radical tract (Winstanley), poetry and polemical prose (Milton), spiritual autobiography and religious allegory (Bunyan). The writers themselves differ in numerous respects, including their indebtedness to Calvin, their intellectual backgrounds, and their approaches to the question of how (and whether) the church should be organized. They also illustrate the range of responses to the Bible possible among those who in one way or another resisted the versions of orthodoxy imposed by the Anglican church.

As a leading reformer during a period of growing tension between

Arminian and Puritan factions, Sibbes was the only one of the five who would have been regarded by his contemporaries as unmistakably Puritan. He and his friends found themselves on the losing side of the struggle, but his reforming impulses were not sufficiently strong to drive him out of the church. Baxter wrote his *Saints Everlasting Rest* not long after he had served as a chaplain in Cromwell's New Model Army, near the beginning of a career that reached into the 1680s. Although he liked to describe himself as a "meer Christian"—in his eclecticism and his pursuit of religious unity avoiding identification with any particular church—the latest editor of his autobiography justifiably calls it "the supreme apologetic for the Puritan spirit in Christianity."[16] Winstanley's writings all appeared in a period of a few years around 1650. As a spiritual heir of the Anabaptists and the leader of a sect, the Diggers, who rejected the very concept of an established church, Winstanley is easily the most radical member of my company. His wild allegorizing represents one extreme in the range of responses to the Bible that I discuss. The cautious and learned Baxter can be found at the other. Milton may seem an unlikely choice to those accustomed to thinking of him primarily as a Christian humanist, but I believe that Puritan strains in his thinking, particularly about the Bible, make his inclusion inevitable. I follow some of these through writings spanning most of his career: from the antiprelatical works of the early forties to the major poetry published after the Restoration. Bunyan represents the Puritanism of the Restoration, the period of the "great persecution." As a Baptist and a "mechanick preacher" who defied the prohibition against unlicensed preaching, he exemplifies the dissenting tradition that had become firmly established in English life by the latter part of the century.

These five writers, then, embody the diversity of the Puritan tradition in seventeenth-century England, broadly defined. Their differences will be apparent. Yet the works that I discuss display important continuities and, when juxtaposed, can illuminate each other. Whatever their dissimilarities, these writers were all concerned with recovering the original simplicity of the Word of God and conveying what they perceived to be its extraordinary power to transform the individual and society. A sense of the dynamism of the Word, ultimately the dynamism of the Holy Spirit acting through the Word, animates all five.

These writers all illustrate in some fashion the Puritan commitment to plainness. In their efforts to recover the purity of the Word they were unusually sensitive to the corrupting effects of language that they regarded as pointlessly difficult or given over to rhetorical display. Advocacy of a plain style appears in relatively naive form in the least educated of the writers, Bunyan and Winstanley. Bunyan in the prefatory verses to *Grace Abounding* declares his intent not to "play" in relating his spiritual ordeals and to "be plain and simple, and lay down the thing as it was." Winstanley condemns "fine language," boasting of his "clownish" style, and accuses ministers of all kinds of practicing a "verbal worship." At the other end of the spectrum one finds Baxter's denunciations of witty preaching and Milton's attacks on the mannered prose of the scholastics. Overly elaborate interpretation of the Bible, "darke interpretation" as Winstanley would call it, comes in for abuse, as well as excessive concern for rhetorical effects. Bunyan (in *The Holy War*) and Milton both give demonstrations of Satanic oratory, associating verbal facility with the manipulative strategies of evil.

Puritans had no monopoly on plainness during the period. By the time of the Restoration certain kinds of Puritan preaching had come to seem as excessive in their way as the witty displays of a Lancelot Andrewes did to Puritans. The new norm became the plain, rational preaching exemplified by such prominent Anglican divines as Robert South and John Tillotson.[17] One can find Anglican criticisms of rhetorical excess earlier in the period as well. George Herbert says of his country parson that "the character of his Sermon is Holiness; he is not witty, or learned, or eloquent, but Holy."[18] Daniel Featley, chaplain to Archbishop Abbot under James I and later chaplain to Charles I, praised those prayers and meditations that "shew most affection and least affectation of art, wit, or language."[19] On the other hand, Featley recognized the value of "true eloquence" and put down those who found what he called "pack-staffe plainnesse" the only evidence of "the Spirit, and simplicity of the Gospell."[20]

Discussions of sermon style, particularly among Puritans, were conditioned by an influential passage from Paul's epistle to the Corinthians: "And my speech and my preaching was not with enticing words of man's wisdom, but in demonstration of the Spirit and of power" (1 Cor. 2:4). Whatever area of agreement there might be about avoiding affected eloquence, Puritans were more likely than Anglicans to link plainness with power; in fact, "plain and powerful" became a Puritan formula for describing effective preaching. Both Baxter and Herbert objected to preachers who crumbled a text into pieces, as Herbert put it in *The Country Parson*, but they objected on different grounds. Baxter saw such sermons as devoid of the presence of the Spirit, where Herbert found them lacking in the sense of propriety and the regard for one's audience that informs his advice to the preacher, whom he counseled to declare the meaning of the text plainly and then offer "some choyce Observations drawn out of the whole text, as it lyes entire, and unbroken in the Scripture it self." This way of proceeding was to Herbert "naturall, and sweet, and grave."[21] One is struck by Herbert's respect for the integrity of the text and by his concern with decorum. Baxter's comments on preaching, which I discuss below, are informed by a more urgent sense of the need to convey the Word with "life" and "heat." The writers that I discuss were so insistent upon the need for recovering the original purity of Scripture because they believed that only then could one feel the power of the Spirit operating through it. They might apprehend the truth of the Spirit differently, but all were intensely concerned with perceiving this truth and with finding means of conveying it powerfully.

Most of the writers I discuss show only a modest regard for form. The Puritan sermon, exemplified by those of Sibbes, is more open-ended than its schematic presentation of reasons and uses might seem to imply. The looseness of Baxter's massive work of meditation is apparent from the way it swells to embrace virtually any course of reflection upon spiritual life he cares to pursue. His declared unwillingness to revise his works (he published 130 books) is typical of the Puritan refusal to give undue attention to formal or stylistic considerations. Winstanley's frequently repetitive tracts give the impression of being written at white heat, at the dictation of the Holy Spirit. Bunyan displays a greater sense of conscious artistry, but even in *The Pilgrim's Progress*, his most firmly controlled work, he occasionally allows extended dialogues to dissipate the force of his central metaphor of the journey. In reading these writers one often gets the sense that considerations of form are overwhelmed by a conviction that certain messages must be delivered, or certain voices heard. In some cases this impression is heightened by modulations in tone, especially by eruptions of vehemence.

Milton with his superb sense of form seems an obvious exception. His mastery was such that he redefined virtually every poetic form that he touched. Yet Milton can be seen as adapting or expanding some of these forms to accommodate powerful voices speaking truth, for example, the Lady's in *A Maske* with its "sacred vehemence," the voices in *Lycidas* that interrupt the pastoral vein, the voice of God the Father in *Paradise Lost*. In his prose Milton showed himself capable of venturing into autobiographical self-justification and of assuming the voice of an Old Testament prophet. His antiprelatical tracts disconcerted his antagonists by their vehemence, extreme even by contemporary standards for controversial prose.

Despite their criticisms of abuses of language, the writers that I consider are masters of distinct and memorable styles, in some cases of a variety of styles. Winstanley could proclaim his crudeness and still forge a highly original style by blending colloquialism and free adaptation of biblical phrases. Bunyan found his own ways of accommodating biblical language to the understanding of ordinary people and of creating characters who inhabited allegorical landscapes yet spoke the idiom of the Bedfordshire countryside. In *The Holy War* he demonstrated that he could reach for something approximating a grand style. Those who defended plainness in preaching, such as Baxter and Sibbes, nevertheless believed in using "holy eloquence" to reach their audiences. William Perkins had justified the use of learning and art in both "the matter of the sermon" and "the setting forth of the words" as long as these were concealed: *"Artis etiam est celare artem."* [22] Milton's stylistic virtuosity needs no comment. His criticisms of the misuse of language were those of someone who understood thoroughly the arts of classical rhetoric and could use them to suit his various purposes.

A commitment to plainness was not incompatible with the ability to respond to and exploit the figurative language of the Bible. On the contrary, these writers recognized that the truth of the Spirit often could be expressed only in figurative terms and proved themselves skilled at adapting biblical metaphors. Their use of imagery drawn from the Bible, and of biblical language generally, offers some of the principal evidence for their kinship and reveals a common interest in conveying the energy and influence of the Holy Spirit. Certain familiar motifs recur. They identify frequently with the experience of the Israelites, a common habit in the period. Like other Puritan writers, they typically view this experience collectively, recalling Tyndale and the makers of the Geneva Bible in their vision of an embattled elect working out their destiny with the guidance and protection of God. They tend to see spiritual life as a continuous warfare, whether this involves conflicting impulses within the soul, or the battle of the Christian soldier with those who tempt or assail him, or the larger struggle of the forces of truth and falsehood in society. With the exception of Winstanley, they offer variations on the favorite Puritan theme of life as an arduous pilgrimage toward the heavenly Jerusalem, with its promise of sabbatical rest. Bunyan's *The Pilgrim's Progress* is the supreme literary representation of the journey of the saints; Baxter's famous work of meditation is the most comprehensive and influential exploration of the rest thought to await them.

Most of the biblical images that these writers respond to appear over and over in the literature of the period. They can be found, often brilliantly elaborated, in the work of writers who represent the best of the Anglican tradition: in the sermons of Donne, for example, and the poetry of Herbert and Vaughan. Protestants of all kinds were capable of discovering paradigms in the experience of the Israelites and the spiritual life of David, or of being attracted by the figurative language of Isaiah and the Song of Solomon. Anyone might find in the book of Revelation images of spiritual combat and terms of abuse for the enemies of God. The locusts of hell could be seen coming from any direction, depending upon one's angle of vision. Revelation had greater appeal for those with millenarian expectations, however, as did the story of the Exodus for those who saw themselves as suffering for their religious beliefs. Characteristically Puritan preferences and ways of using the Bible are not hard to find.

The chapters that follow will illustrate some of these patterns of response, as well as some particularly individual responses to Scripture. One larger configuration deserves comment here, the frequent conjunction of images of violence and images of fertility and growth. The same writers who responded to the image of the Word of God as the "sword of the Spirit"

(Eph. 6:17) could just as readily see it as a "seed" (Luke 8:11), in the language of the parable of the sower.[23] The apparent contradiction may be understood by thinking of different manifestations of the power of the Holy Spirit acting through the Word. This can be a destructive force acting upon the enemies of God, or upon the soul of sinful man. Yet it can also be a benevolent influence embodying the restorative action of grace.

The sword of the Spirit could be seen as a weapon wielded by the Christian soldier, as the power of religious truth understood more generally, or as the power wielded by God against his enemies. Bunyan's Christian finally wins his battle with Apollyon through the agency of the "sword of the Spirit," understood to be the Word of God. This "sword" was the weapon with which the Puritan expected to withstand the manifold evils of the world. Milton saw the Word as a spiritual sword that would destroy the twin evils of "Popery and Prelacy."[24] Revelation provided stunning images of the Word as the power of God. John is addressed by a majestic figure whose speech is symbolized by a sword. He sees "one like unto the Son of man," surrounded by seven golden candlesticks:

> And he had in his right hand seven stars: and out of his mouth went a sharp twoedged sword: and his countenance was as the sun shineth in his strength. (Rev. 1:16)

Lucas Cranach rendered the scene in one of his woodcuts for Luther's New Testament (fig. 1). The rider on the white horse of Revelation 19 offered a fiercer vision, this time of Christ militant:

> His name is called The Word of God.... And out of his mouth goeth a sharp sword, that with it he should smite the nations: and he shall rule them with a rod of iron: and he treadeth the winepress of the fierceness and wrath of Almighty God. (Rev. 19:13, 15)

Such an image of the apocalypse appealed to those who, like the separatist Henry Barrow, regarded themselves as one of a triumphant army of saints:

> Yea through the power of his word, they have power to cast down upon Satan like lightning: to tread upon serpents and scorpions: to cast down strongholds, and everything that exalteth itself against God.[25]

The sword of the Spirit could also be seen as the instrument by which God tried the souls of men, on the basis of Hebrews 4:12. The "two-edged sword" described there was understood as a divine force operating to expose one's most private beliefs and inclinations. It could be wielded by God, or by the preacher acting as an agent of the divine. John Preston prayed that through preaching God would make the Word

> lively and mighty in operation, to cut down your lusts, to pierce as a two-edged sword, dividing betweene the bones and the marrow, the joynts and the spirit; that is, that you may know your selves better than you did before.[26]

FIG. 1

Milton characteristically saw the "quick and pearcing word" as dividing the souls of his prelatical enemies and convincing them of their blindness. The metaphor proved a rich one for those who believed that Scripture acted powerfully upon the soul, and they used it in a variety of contexts.

Other biblical images were read as expressions of the irresistible power of God to overwhelm error and perversity in society or in the individual. Images of the Word as light striking through the darkness of ignorance and unbelief pervade English reformation writings.[27] A passage from Jeremiah provided two other images that were widely adapted: "Is not my word like a fire," saith the Lord; "and like a hammer that breaketh the rock in pieces?" (Jer. 23:29) Such images could suggest a force working upon the resistance of the individual sinner or upon the collective ignorance of social groups. Milton pictured Scripture as shattering the idol of tradition. Winstanley speaks frequently of the Spirit as a fire sweeping the land, although he saw it as capable of acting apart from Scripture. In fact, he could understand the sword of the Spirit as the love that would lead men back to their original state of universal harmony.

The restorative power of the Spirit is a fundamental theme of all five writers I discuss, and they draw upon common sources of imagery to express this power. In their emphasis upon the experiential character of religion Sibbes, Baxter, and Bunyan give considerable attention to the process of sanctification. Bunyan is more preoccupied than Sibbes and Baxter with rendering the terrors of the law, and the way these lead to a conviction of sin, but he shares with them an intense interest in representing the fruition of the soul under the quickening influence of the Spirit. All three use the imagery of the Song of Solomon to render the spiritual awakening of the soul and its subsequent flourishing. Isaiah furnished them with imagery of "fatness" by which to describe the delight of the soul capable of experiencing foretastes of heavenly bliss. Other Old Testament descriptions of Canaan provided language with which to represent the pleasures of what Sibbes would call the "spiritual senses." Milton and Winstanley were capable of using similar imagery, as in descriptions of the dawning of the Reformation or of the springtime of the soul, to suggest an imminent renewal of society.

The prose of these writers can become remarkably lyrical when celebrating the spiritual satisfactions of the redeemed soul or the prospect of a harmonious society united by a common vision of truth. The Word stirred hopes of attaining spiritual peace, ultimately the heavenly rest of the saints, and of bringing together all Englishmen, whether in the unified church that Baxter worked mightily to achieve or in the more elusive "unity of the spirit" that Milton and Winstanley pursued in their very different ways. Yet such yearnings and strivings were accompanied by a profound dissatisfaction with the present condition of church and society that fed a sense of life as a state of constant struggle between conflicting impulses and forces. Images of warfare and of peace not only coexist but sometimes appear to engender each other, as if one kind of intensity calls forth its opposite. None of these writers could truly rest in what most of them would have thought of as the wilderness of this world. The absoluteness of their ideals dictated that they work without ceasing to overcome the indifference, ignorance, and corruption they saw around them and guaranteed that they would never be satisfied with the success of their labors. They followed a Christ who could say, with reference to the disruptive effects of the Gospel, "Think not that I am come to send peace on earth: I came not to send peace, but a sword" (Matt. 10:34).

A particular writer might stress the holy violence of the Spirit or its gentler motions, or he might show how one kind of influence succeeds the other, as Bunyan does in rendering the process by which a soul overcome by threats of judgment is subsequently nurtured by promises of salvation. However the writers that I discuss understood the operation of the Spirit, they all regarded it as a powerful agent for change working through Scripture. They saw the dynamism of the Word as requiring a dynamic response from the individual, and they used Scripture to reinforce various kinds of exhortation to action. In Sibbes this is the preacher's insistence upon the necessity for spiritual growth and for the kind of spiritual aliveness, to fear as well as to consolation, that makes such growth possible. Baxter argues the need for struggling with a rebellious heart, in a kind of meditation that he saw as a process of continuous self-examination. Bunyan suggests the most drastic action of all with his image of Christian fleeing the City of Destruction with his ears stopped against the advice of his neighbors and family. The Calvinism of such writers, especially pronounced in Bunyan, helps to explain their need to see Scripture as catalytic. The gulf between God and man was so wide and human sinfulness so persistent that some kind of extraordinary force seemed necessary to precipitate a response.

Milton and Winstanley, at least initially, saw the power of the Word as effecting a reformation of society. Their sense of the inadequacy or corruption of existing institutions stimulated belief in such a power and longing for kinds of simplicity described in the scriptural record, whether of the apostolic church, in Milton's case, or of Edenic harmony, in that of Winstanley. Winstanley's imperative to his followers was to form a new social order by digging the earth and holding its fruits in common. Milton exhorted his readers, even after the millenarianism of his early tracts had waned, to resist all forms of worship and codifications of belief that would bind the Spirit. They saw the Word as demanding a more radical response than the others envisioned, in that they looked for a profound transformation of the English people and, in Winstanley's case, for the birth of a new social and economic order.

All these writers embody the fundamental Puritan conviction that one must always be active, forever striving. What Samuel Butler said of the *"godly-thorough-Reformation"* of Hudibras—that it "alwayes must be carry'd on, / And still be doing, never done"—could apply in some fashion to each of them.[28] Milton emphasized the continuing demands of a "strenuous liberty," Bunyan the need to remain alert to defend against the subtle assaults of sin and despair. They resemble each other, and the other writers that I discuss as well, in their opposition to any kind of stagnation. Sibbes saw the heart of the carnal man as a "standing pool" and argued that man's spirit should always be cleansing itself, like a spring. Milton condemned the "muddy pool" of conformity and tradition and directed his readers to the "streaming fountain" of truth. Winstanley declaimed against all those who would dam the "free running streams of the spirit of life." Milton and Winstanley offer differing versions of the belief in a progressive revelation of truth, Sibbes a variant of the familiar Puritan theme that the process of sanctification must be continuous. Similar images in Bunyan and Baxter represent the spiritual vitality and satisfaction engendered by grace (Bunyan's "river of life") or the gospel promises (for Baxter an "open fountain").

At different stages in the progress of reformation in England one can see a growing awareness of the potential of the reading and preaching of the Word for shaping lives and institutions: in the writings of Tyndale, Jewel, and Cartwright, among others in the sixteenth century. My interest in this complex story, well told by modern historians,[29] is in showing how it illuminates attitudes toward Scripture found in the works that I discuss. In my first chapter I trace the process by which the Bible was made available to the English people, beginning with the translations of Tyndale, and the emergence of a way of approaching Scripture that emphasizes its kinetic qualities. By trying to understand what it meant for some Englishmen to think of the Word as "living" one can develop a better sense of the explosiveness of the Bible and of its impact upon the imaginations of those who were to produce the sermons and meditations, the tracts, the poetry, and the other religious writings that give the best of Puritan literature its richness and power.

1. The Living Word

In January of 1555 John Rogers, a former disciple of William Tyndale, was called before the High Commission to defend himself against charges of heresy. John Foxe reports the following exchange between Rogers and Bishop Stephen Gardiner, Queen Mary's Lord Chancellor:

> L. Chancellor: No, no thou canst prove nothing by the Scripture, the Scripture is dead: it must have a lively expositor.
>
> Rogers: No, the Scripture is alive.[1]

The episode is all the more interesting because Rogers was the man responsible for the Bible issued under the name Thomas Matthew in 1537, the first English Bible to be licensed by the crown, and Gardiner had led the resistance of conservative bishops to the promulgation of the Bible under Henry VIII. At the trial Gardiner insisted that Rogers affirm the authority of the pope. Rogers sought to challenge that authority, and Gardiner's, by appealing to the Bible. Here he is arguing simply that Scripture should be admitted as evidence, but his retort—"the Scripture is alive"—has reverberations that carry far beyond his immediate situation. It could be the motto of any Protestant martyr, of the Reformation itself.

The confrontation of Rogers and Gardiner over the authority of Scripture recalls the classic controversy of Tyndale and Sir Thomas More, himself a fierce hunter of heretics as Lord Chancellor in the early 1530s, and anticipates Bishop John Jewel's vigorous defense of the English church against Rome in the early years of Elizabeth's reign. Jewel initiated the later dispute with his famous "Challenge" sermon, delivered at Paul's Cross in November of 1559. In his subsequent *Apology of the Church of England* (1561) Jewel reminded his adversaries that the early fathers had combated heretics with Scripture alone and defied them to submit all issues "to the trial of God's word."[2] They, he charged, fled the light of the Gospel like owls at sunrise; to preserve their spurious authority they had to reduce the Word itself to "a bare letter, uncertain, unprofitable, dumb, killing, and dead."[3] Had he escaped burning, Rogers no doubt would have endorsed Jewel's argument; he had cited the precedent of early heresy trials himself as a warrant for trying his case by the Word. Protestants who differed about how far reform should be carried found it possible to agree with what became the official position of the English church, as expressed in the sixth of thirty-nine Articles on Religion, that Scripture contained all matters necessary for salvation. They could also accept the Reformation principle that the Bible should be the judge in matters of religious controversy, although they would come to disagree about how far this principle should be carried. It was relatively easy to rally behind the banner that Jewel carried into the battle against the forces of Antichrist.

Jewel argued that the Word, and not an authority vested in the pope, was the key to the kingdom of God, but at the same time he sought to reconstitute the authority of what he saw as the true church by appealing also to the practice of the first six centuries after Christ:

> We have searched out of the Holy Bible, which we are sure cannot deceive, one sure form of religion, and have returned again unto the primitive church of the ancient fathers and apostles.[4]

This appeal to the primitive church would be repeated by Protestants of differing persuasions, including those who, like Milton, would construe it more narrowly to mean the apostolic ideal.

Jewel took no notice of potential opposition on the left in his *Apology* except to register a conventional protest against the pariahs of the age, the Anabaptists (he naively felt that they would be cured of their heresies if only the Gospel were given ample scope). Yet Jewel's "one sure form of religion" was to be challenged in the name of the Word by Englishmen who were unwilling to accept the authority of the English church when this meant strict conformity in matters of worship. The author of the *Second Admonition to Parliament* (1573), speaking for the emerging presbyterian opposition, reasserted the principle of trial by Scripture ("true religion abideth the triall of the word of God") in the course of seeking to enlarge the sphere of its authority.[5] He could claim boldly that the Word was above the established church because he was convinced, as he put it, that his adversaries would not be able to quench the light of the Gospel any more than hay could put out fire. Ironically, Jewel had also represented the Gospel as an irresistible force, in similar terms:

> The flame, the more it is kept down, so much the more with greater force and strength does it break out and fly abroad.[6]

Jewel was as confident as the presbyterians would be that he spoke for true religion, against idolaters, and that the truth he found in the Word would prevail:

> As Dagon fell, and brake his hands and neck, and could not stand in the presence of the ark of the Lord, even so shall all falsehood fall and hide itself in the presence of the truth of God.[7]

Jewel's Catholic opponents, led by his former associate Thomas Harding, asked tough questions about how one could discover the truth of Scripture for himself, especially when Protestants could be seen to differ. Within two decades defenders of the church that Jewel helped to shape would be taking a similar line.

A poem printed with editions of the Geneva Bible beginning in the late sixteenth century suggests that by that time the necessity of regarding Scripture as the sole arbiter of disputes had become an article of faith for Puritans: "Here is the Iudge that stints the strife, / when mens devices faile." Others came to put more stock in "mens devices," and considerably less in the notion of Scripture as "supreme judge," as it came to be described in the Westminster Confession. The policy of the church, as articulated by Archbishop Whitgift in response to Thomas Cartwright's arguments for presbyterianism and subsequently developed by Richard Hooker, became one of sharply limiting the jurisdiction of the Word by reasserting the authority of tradition and making a place for the exercise of reason. This defensive strategy proved notably successful, backed as it was by the power of the church hierarchy to enforce conformity. Hooker regarded the Bible as providing an infallible rule of faith but not binding men in "things indifferent," which included for him the large areas of worship and of church government. The fire of the Word was contained in the last decades of the sixteenth century, yet events of the following century would bear out the truth of Jewel's assertion in ways that would have astonished him.

Foxe had no difficulty sorting out heroes and villains in his massive chronicle of the trials of the faithful, but the issue raised by the exchange of Rogers and Gardiner was to prove more stubborn and complex than it seems in his dramatic rendering of their encounter. What did it mean for a man of the sixteenth century to claim that Scripture is "alive"? What view of the individual's capacity to understand the Word of God does such an assertion imply? Of the manner in which the Word acts upon the individual? Of the way in which it embodies a divine power or energy? These are not questions that one could expect to answer with any thoroughness or finality, even for a single country, but they can serve as useful pointers. My concern in the discussion that follows is with the evolution of attitudes toward the Bible in England, and the questions raised by Rogers's appeal to a living Word are at the heart of the story.

For the ordinary Englishman at the beginning of the sixteenth century Scripture was far from alive in Rogers's sense. He knew the Bible through the ritual language of the Latin mass and through visual images: from stained glass, paintings and carvings in churches, and perhaps the illustrations of the *Biblia pauperum*. Wycliffite translations circulated among the Lollards, but this was a covert and dangerous business, since all such translations lay under a prohibition imposed by Archbishop Arundel in 1409. A man could be reported by his neighbor after being overheard reading a fragment of the New Testament, for which he might have bartered a load of hay.[8] Foxe described the situation that existed before the appearance of Luther in these terms:

> Instead of God's Word, man's word was set up: instead of Christ's Testament, the pope's testament, that is, the canon law: instead of Paul, the Master of Sentences took place, and almost full possession.[9]

William Tyndale told the people for whom he wrote in the late 1520s and early 1530s that they could expect nothing from the church establishment but sophistry, with priests wresting Scripture according to their own purposes and "descanting upon it with allegories...expounding it in many senses before the unlearned laypeople, (when it hath but one simple, literal sense, whose light the owls cannot abide)."[10] He summoned them to take up "the sword of the Spirit, which is God's word" and resist prelates who subdued the people with allegories and "dumb ceremonies," the authority of the fathers, and "the violence of the temporal sword."[11]

Tyndale's New Testament, which first appeared in 1526, was followed by a burst of polemical writings and, in 1530, by his translation of the Pentateuch. As a translator Tyndale worked from Erasmus's version of the New Testament (1516), consisting of a newly edited Greek text and Erasmus's own Latin translation. Erasmus himself was influenced by John Colet, the early humanist and dean of St. Paul's, to undertake an ambitious program of Christian scholarship that was to include an edition of the works of Jerome and paraphrases of the books of the New Testament designed to make them more readily comprehensible to the common reader. Colet's own Oxford lectures on Corinthians in 1496 mark the real beginnings of a new attitude toward Scripture in England. Instead of reducing the New Testament to an array of texts from which a body of dogma might be logically constructed, scholastic fashion, Colet sought to recover the historical Paul and make him speak to the immediate situation of his listeners.[12] Colet broke through the encrustations of centuries of commentary to offer a fresh response to the texts, expressed in a new kind of exegesis, working from Jerome's Vulgate. Erasmus applied himself to the philological problems involved in establishing a sounder version of the text itself. His New Testament was taken up eagerly by all those concerned with recovering a sense of the meaning and force of the original, including Luther.

In the preface to his translation of the New Testament, the *Paraclesis*, Erasmus committed himself to the principle that the Gospel should be made available to all. His ideal was that the farmer should be able to sing parts of the Scripture at his plow. Christ's teachings are accessible to anyone who will seek them out with an open mind and a pure faith, Erasmus argues, but first he must recognize the significance of the Word:

> If anyone shows us the footprints of Christ, in what manner, as Christians, do we prostrate ourselves, how do we adore them! But why do we

not venerate instead the living and breathing likeness of Him in these books?[13]

Why not adorn the Scriptures with gems and gold instead of saving them for statues that represent Christ's body, he asks. In his *Enchiridion* (1503) Erasmus had already insisted that one should approach the Scriptures "reverently, with veneration and humility," driving home the point with the example of Uzzah, struck down by the Lord for laying profane hands on the ark (2 Sam. 6:6–7).[14] One who reads the Scriptures in the proper spirit should be changed by them, he felt, and not simply make a show of allegiance: "the true gospel bearer is the one who carries it in hands and mouth and heart."[15]

Erasmus's *philosophia Christi* has a strong ethical bias. For him Christ was above all a heavenly teacher, whose way was "the way of virtue." To live a godly life, thereby becoming a truer theologian than the man who devotes his time to mastering the syllogism, one should imitate the example of Christ. Erasmus regarded the Bible primarily as the source of the knowledge that makes such a spiritually directed life possible, "the hidden store house of everlasting wisdom."[16] Whereas in the *Paraclesis* Erasmus argued that the Bible offers "the entire wisdom of the world," in the *Enchiridion* and elsewhere he talked about the process of searching out spiritual meanings. The chapter of the *Enchiridion* devoted to the armor of the Christian soldier (including the sword of the Spirit) is remarkable for its lack of militancy; Erasmus spends the greater part of it discussing the need to penetrate the surface of the text. The manna of the Israelites suggested to him the way divine mysteries are concealed in words that are inadequate, the wells and springs of the Old Testament landscape offering an analogy between water hidden in the earth and mysterious truth hidden under the literal sense. Erasmus readily appealed to previous allegorical readings of Scripture, including Origen's, and he recognized that some difficult passages were likely to remain obscure.[17]

This last point was one of many upon which Luther took issue with Erasmus, after welcoming his major contribution to the promulgation and study of the Bible and his telling criticisms of abuses in the church. In the attack by which he signaled that he sided with Rome against Luther, Erasmus took a skeptical view of man's ability to understand and apply Scripture. He distinguished between evident truths, "precepts for the good life" that all men should learn, and others that must remain mysterious.[18] The latter, he argued, "are more properly committed to God, and it is more religious to worship them, being unknown, than to discuss them, being insoluble."[19] He saw unproductive wrangling over Scripture, based upon individual appeals to the Spirit in the face of traditions represented by the fathers of the church, threatening to rend Christendom. Luther met Erasmian eloquence with thundering retorts:

> To wish to stop these tumults...is nothing else but to wish to suppress and prohibit the Word of God. For the Word of God comes, whenever it comes, to change and renew the world.[20]

> The word of God is not bound (2 Tim. 2:9), says Paul, and will Erasmus bind the Word?[21]

For Luther the Word was "an invincible warrior whom none can resist,"[22] neither the individual nor the traditions of the church with which he saw it locked in a battle as inevitable as that of God and Satan. It was hardly a time for restraint: "The Holy Spirit is no Skeptic."[23] Luther could press his case with belligerent confidence because he believed that the Spirit would banish darkness from men's minds and demonstrate the "internal clarity" of Scripture. He acknowledged that some passages were difficult for those who lacked the necessary linguistic skills but at the same time asked, "What sublimer thing can remain hidden in the Scriptures, now that the seals have been broken?"[24] For Luther Scripture was its own interpreter; his new understanding of Christ made its meaning plain.

Luther saw the Holy Spirit as working in and through Scripture, making it the living and authoritative Word of God. He insisted that Spirit and Word acted together, and he denounced the Anabaptists and his colleague Karlstadt for separating the two by appealing to the Spirit alone. Yet he did not take the opposite way, which many of his followers were to pursue, of automatically identifying the Word with the letter of the Scriptures. For him the Word was Christ as revealed in Scripture through the action of the Spirit. He could dismiss the book of James as an "epistle of straw" because its message ("faith without works is dead") did not accord with his sense of the Gospel. The doctrine that everything in Scripture was divinely inspired, down to the pointing of the Hebrew text, developed subsequently, along with a bibliolatry that left Protestants vulnerable to the charge that they had replaced a real pope with a paper one.[25] J. K. S. Reid describes the process as one by which the Spirit became "locked up" in Scripture while the "new insight into the living truth of the Gospel" faded.[26]

Luther's dynamic view of the Word depends upon a refusal to think of Scripture as efficacious apart from the way in which it is received. He was intensely concerned with the *experience* of the Word. Where Erasmus assumed that man should attempt to understand Scripture, insofar as he could expect to, by the exercise of reason, Luther wanted him to remain passive and silent before the Word, ready to be acted upon by God. He saw the soul as being stripped "of its own garment...of all its possessions, and of all its imaginations" and carried away to a previously invisible world which he describes in biblical terms as a wilderness or vineyard or inner chamber (as of the temple).[27] This first stage of the experience entails suffering, "For certainly the Word of the Cross, like a wine press, bruises and humbles the men of the world."[28] Yet those who are regenerated by the Word are nourished and preserved by it. Ultimately the experience is lifegiving; it should enable one to "dance and leap and burn for joy."[29] Luther thought of saving faith engendered by the confrontation of man with the presence of God in the Word as an active, developing state.

Erasmus saw Scripture as the fountain of wisdom and hence the supreme guide to godly living, where Luther regarded it as the medium by which the Spirit of God worked a radical transformation of individuals and whole societies. Both views strongly influenced the attitudes toward the Bible which grew up in England. The two men who did most to shape these attitudes in England in the first half of the sixteenth century are Tyndale, who did the pioneering work of translation and introduced Lutheran ideas of Scripture into England, and Archbishop Thomas Cranmer, who through his advocacy of Bible reading and his work in devising a liturgy firmly established the Bible in the religious life of the English people. Thomas Cromwell as Lord Chancellor played the most important political role in winning acceptance for the English Bible, but this part of the story is not my concern.

As a student at Oxford, and briefly at Cambridge, Tyndale fell under the pervasive influence of Erasmus. He translated the *Enchiridion* and announced his ambition to translate the Scriptures in terms that recalled the *Paraclesis.* Tyndale is said to have boasted that he would cause a ploughboy to know more of Scripture than the priests; ordinary people could know the truth for themselves, he felt, if only they were presented with "the simple plain word of God."[30] This was to give Erasmus's famous wish a decidedly contentious turn. Tyndale did not merely want to give the ploughboy a scriptural song to sing, rather to put a weapon in his hand, the sword of the Spirit.

After Cuthbert Tunstall, the bishop of London, refused to take him in, Tyndale went to the continent to pursue his work of translation and there encountered the Lutheran ideas that were to influence his thinking decisively. Tyndale was attracted to the Luther who translated the New Testament into vigorous, colloquial German and who provided a new understanding of the force and significance of the Gospel. He argued in Lutheran terms the need for understanding that all the Scriptures "flow unto Christ ...the way's end and resting-place."[31] In *A Pathway unto the Holy Scriptures* (1525), an expanded version of the prologue to his New Testament, he hammered away at the message that the Gospel is the means to salvation:

Then cometh the evangelion, a more gentle pastor, which suppleth and suageth the wounds of our conscience [inflicted by the Law] and bringeth health. It bringeth the Spirit of God; which looseth the bonds of Satan, and coupleth us to God and his will, through strong faith and fervent love, with bonds too strong for the devil, the world, or any creature to loose them.[32]

Tyndale insisted the Scripture be seen as "the touchstone that trieth all doctrines,"[33] and he roughly threw out the traditions that Erasmus sought to reconstitute: "And when they cry, 'Fathers, fathers,' remember that it were the fathers that blinded and robbed the whole world, and brought us into captivity."[34] Like Luther, he regarded the Bible as justifying itself ("the Scripture is the cause why men believe the scripture")[35] and communicating the truth of the Word through the action of the Spirit. Tyndale saw the literal sense of Scripture as "spiritual" for the believer who could find there "spirit and life and edifying."[36] As for Luther, experience rather than method was the key to interpreting Scripture aright. One must "feel the power of faith, and the working of the Spirit in the heart" and not trust to "blind reason and foolish fantasies."[37] The critical word here is "feel." Tyndale insisted that "where the Spirit is, there is feeling"[38] and talked of the need for a "feeling faith." Such a faith is "a lively thing, mighty in working, valiant, and strong, ever doing, ever fruitful,"[39] and it leads inevitably to a godly life. In his later writing, possibly because of his involvement in translating the Old Testament,[40] Tyndale placed more emphasis upon learning to keep divine laws and upon regarding God's promises as a contract with man, but he continued to see the activity of the Spirit as fundamental, making the law "a lively thing in the heart."[41]

Foxe reports that Tyndale cried out "Lord! open the king of England's eyes" while being burned at the stake in Belgium, his last European refuge. John Rogers's "Matthew" Bible was licensed two years later, and in 1539 the Great Bible was issued with the full authority of church and state behind it. Tyndale's Pentateuch and his New Testament, revised by Miles Coverdale, formed the bulk of this first official version of the Bible.[42] There is considerable irony in the triumph of Tyndale's language and in the fact that the English church came to accept the Lutheran understanding of the supremacy of Scripture and the principle of justification that he had advocated. In the 1520s Cuthbert Tunstall had made bonfires of Tyndale's New Testament at Paul's Cross. A proclamation that he issued in 1526 accuses unnamed translators of seducing the common people by introducing "heretical articles, and erroneous opinions" and of attempting "to profanate the majesty of the Scripture, which hitherto hath remained undefiled, and craftily to abuse the most holy word of God, and the true sense of the same."[43]

A decade later Cranmer, more concerned with making the Bible available to the people than with preserving the majesty of Jerome's Vulgate, was trying without success to prod his bishops into completing a translation that could replace Tyndale's still controversial one.[44] The official Bible that Cranmer finally settled for was the one that Miles Coverdale saw through the press in 1539. When the first copies of the Great Bible appeared in April of that year, they were adorned with an engraved title page showing Henry VIII handing copies inscribed "Verbum Dei" to his archbishop Thomas Cranmer and his lord chancellor Thomas Cromwell, who in turn hand them down to representatives of the clergy and laity (fig. 2). At the bottom of the page people of various estates listen to a preacher proclaiming the Word and cry "Vivat Rex." At the top the Almighty spreads his hands over the scene and offers a scriptural blessing, in the Latin of the Vulgate. The frontispiece effectively glorifies Henry as head of church and state and affirms the hierarchical nature of the society over which he presides at the same time that it celebrates the coming of the open Bible to England.[45] Royal proclamations of 1539 and 1541 decreed that this Bible be set up in the churches and urged all the people to read it. Cranmer contributed a preface for the second edition. A few years later the Council of Trent would uphold the Vulgate against vernacular translations and emphasize the necessity for lay obedience.[46]

Cranmer's preface, reprinted along with a new preface by Archbishop Parker in the Bishop's Bible of 1567, strongly endorsed the private reading of Scripture and sought to establish guidelines for this reading. Cranmer himself was a serious student of the Bible in the original languages and regarded it as the supreme authority in matters of doctrine and the source of all things necessary to salvation. With other reformers, he saw the Holy Spirit as revealing the truth of God embodied in Scripture and engendering a "true and lively faith" in the hearts of believers. A renewed interest in the Holy Spirit was characteristic of Protestants generally.[47] In the three homilies commonly attributed to him Cranmer elaborates upon the fundamental Reformation principle of justification by faith and argues that a lively faith is inevitably "fruitful in bringing forth good works."[48] Cranmer's discussions of faith here and elsewhere have much in common with Tyndale's, although they lack Tyndale's intense emphasis upon the experience of the Word. Cranmer differs more sharply from Tyndale in his tendency to appeal to "the old and ancient authors, both Greeks and Latins," to buttress his references to Scripture. In his preface to the Great Bible, as in his other writings, Cranmer sought to rehabilitate the tradition established by the early fathers in what he viewed as the "golden time" of the church.[49]

Both Cranmer and Tyndale played key roles in establishing the open Bible and the central principles of Reformation doctrine in England. Both earned places of honor in Foxe's chronicle of Protestant martyrs. Yet the sober prose of Cranmer's preface reveals a way of approaching Scripture that differs significantly from Tyndale's. In his ethical bias, his regard for tradition, and his moderation Cranmer is much closer to Erasmus than to Luther.[50] Tyndale was able to value Scripture for its ethical guidance, perhaps in some measure because of his early interest in Erasmus, yet his emphasis on the action of Scripture upon the individual is essentially Lutheran. Cranmer's preface charts a middle course between extremes, addressing on the one hand reluctant readers who neglect the Scriptures and, on the other, the overly eager ones who are too ready to speculate and dispute; he took a similarly moderate stance in explaining why he retained some ceremonies in the Book of Common Prayer.[51] To convince his disparate audience Cranmer relied heavily upon the weight of patristic authority: Chrysostom to show the value of Scripture, chiefly as armor against temptation and a salve for spiritual wounds, and Gregory Nazianzen to suggest the hazards of reasoning from it "out of measure and good order."[52] Cranmer carefully balances Chrysostom's exhortations to all people to read the Scriptures against Nazianzen's arguments against speculation by the unworthy ("it is dangerous for the unclean to touch that thing that is most clean").[53] Thus he follows praise of the "largeness and utility of the Scripture" with instruction in the proper way to approach it:

> Wherefore I would advise you all, that cometh to the reading or hearing of this book, which is the Word of God, the most precious jewel and most holy relic that remaineth upon earth, that ye bring with you the fear of God, and that ye do it with all due reverence, and use your knowledge thereof not to vainglory and frivolous disputation but to the honour of God, increase of virtue, and edification both of yourselves and other[s].[54]

Edification, in the sense of moral and spiritual education, is Cranmer's central concern. In amplifying Chrysostom's arguments he presents the Bible as a comprehensive source of "instruction" in godly living:

> Herein may princes learn how to govern their subjects; subjects obedience, love, and dread to their princes: husbands how they should behave them unto their wives, how to educate their children and servants; and contrary, the wives, children, and servants may know their duty to their husbands, parents, and masters.[55]

Tyndale had made much the same point near the beginning of *The Obedience of a Christian Man* (1528) in characterizing Scripture as providing "rules" for the obedience of children, servants, wives, and subjects. The argument from social utility was in fact a common prop for Reformation defenses of Scripture. Heinrich Bullinger, for example, in a treatise published in 1538, claimed that Scripture taught "all kinds of vertues."[56] In *The Obedience of a Christian Man* Tyndale used this argument to counter criticism that reformed religion was undermining the authority of the state, yet he could go on to characterize the Bible in Lutheran terms as a galvanizing spiritual force. While Henry approved of Tyndale's new concern with obedience, More was not so trusting. For him Tyndale was the prince of English heretics, hopelessly tainted with Lutheranism, and his book a "holy

FIG. 2

book of disobedience."[57] More argued that Tyndale's New Testament, like the Wycliffite Bible, deserved burning for its heresies.[58]

For Cranmer the Bible was a textbook of morality and, as it had been for Chrysostom, a place where one might seek spiritual nourishment ("In the Scriptures be the fat pastures of the soul").[59] His cautious approach mirrors that of Cromwell in the injunctions of 1538, which urge the people to seek out the sense of the Bible with an "honest sobriety," avoiding contention and seeking the help of the learned with obscure places.[60] The royal proclamation of 1541 makes very plain the official assumption that the Bible-reading Englishman should be a virtuous and dutiful subject, mindful of his place in the social and political order. It announces to the people that in reading the Bible they may see for themselves God's justice and mercy and learn thereby

> To observe God's commandments, and to obeye theyr soveraygne Lorde and hyghe powers, and to exercyse Godlye charite, and to use themselves, accordynge to theyr vocations: in a pure and syncere christen lyfe without murmure or grudgynges.[61]

The contrasting attitudes of Tyndale and Cranmer reflect in some measure their very different situations. Cranmer wrote as primate of the English church, conscious of the hazards of making the Bible available to people unused to hearing or reading it in their own language. His influence can be seen in the official justifications of Scripture in the prefaces to the Bishops' Bible (1567) and the Authorized Version of 1611, the successors to the Great Bible in the parish churches. Tyndale, on the other hand, wrote as an exile acutely aware of the difficulties of pursuing his personal vision. He appealed most strongly to those who saw themselves as suffering for the truth in opposing the religious establishment of their day, sounding a theme that was to reverberate for more than a century: the affinity of the elect with the Israelites.

At the same time that Tyndale defied the prelates as enemies of the truth of the Word he sought to comfort the people for whom he did his work of translation by identifying them as God's own. God's truth brought the Israelites out of Egypt, Tyndale says in the preface to his *Obedience*, and the promises recorded in Scripture guarantee that all the faithful will be delivered from temporal afflictions. Trials are the Spirit's way of purging us:

> We must needs be baptized in tribulations, and through the Red Sea, and a great and fearful wilderness, into our natural country...therefore let us arm our souls with the comfort of the scriptures.[62]

This theme was to reappear in the Geneva Bible, along with Tyndale's sense of the Word as a force capable of transforming the individual and regulating society, and Foxe would make it a motif in his memorial to Protestant martyrs.

The greedy reception of the Word by the people suggests something of the explosive potential that Cranmer feared. They read from the chained Bibles during services, loudly; they became disputatious; they expounded texts.[63] One John Porter was thrown into Newgate, where he died, for reading and allegedly commenting on the Bible in St. Paul's to crowds that gathered to hear him.[64] And in 1543, as a result of agitation by Stephen Gardiner and other conservative bishops, an act was passed forbidding the reading of the Bible by women, artificers, apprentices, and others of insufficient status. Only noblemen and gentleman householders were allowed to keep a copy at home for the use of their families.[65] The act is symptomatic of a major shift of opinion within the church against the English Bible in the late years of Henry's reign, as those who wished to check the progress of reformation gained the upper hand. It was not until the accession of Edward VI in 1547 that Cranmer was able to resume his campaign to educate the laity in the Word.

Cranmer's great legacy to the church of England was the Book of Common Prayer, published in its first version in 1549. Through his masterly work in fashioning an English liturgy from various Latin orders for services he firmly established the Bible in the religious life of the people. The preface of the first prayer book, probably written by Cranmer, claims to revive the practice of the early fathers by ensuring that the whole Bible be read through in the course of the year, so that the ministers might be roused to godliness and the people to a love of religion.[66] Public reading of Old and New Testament lessons, accompanied by the congregational singing of psalms, played a major role in reinforcing the rhythm of worship set by the church calendar and created a context for preaching on any given occasion. By incorporating Scripture in the ceremony of worship Cranmer regulated its public use and at the same time ensured that it would be regarded with reverence. It was, as Cranmer had written in his preface, the "most holy relic that remaineth upon earth."[67] For him the handsome folio Bible standing open upon an eagle lectern would have symbolized the restored primacy and dignity of the Bible in the church.

During Edward's brief reign Cranmer also supervised the issuing for use in the churches of the first book of homilies, which begins with an exhortation to read the Scriptures. This first homily, if not Cranmer's work surely a reflection of his views, shows the same balance that characterizes the preface. The first part praises the Bible as a "well of life" containing all doctrine necessary to salvation, a source of comfort and instruction in religion and moral duties, and, in language drawn from the Psalms, "a more excellent jewel or treasure than any gold or precious stone"[68]—while the second part shows how one may read without error. Scripture has high mountains as well as valleys and plain ways, the homily cautions. One must be content with ignorance of the darker mysteries of the Word until God is pleased to open them.

In this same period of resurgent support for lay reading of the Bible, Erasmus's paraphrases of the New Testament books were translated into English and ordered to be placed in the parish churches. Nicholas Udall's prefaces to these are important signs of increased Protestant militancy. He describes the English Bible as "the consuming fyer of Goddes worde," the only weapon able to confound the pope.[69] In his idealized version of Reformation history Henry is the English David who hurled the stone of the Word at Rome (Erasmus in the *Enchiridion* had used a similar figure, but the enemy was Satan).[70] Edward is the boy king Josiah, a common comparison in the period, as well as a Joshua leading his people into the promised land and a Solomon building the temple of true religion. In his readiness to invoke the history of the Israelites, and especially the examples of such reforming kings as Josiah and Hezekiah, Udall anticipated the spirit of the Geneva Bible. Yet the way of reading Scripture that he recommends to his readers is close to what Cranmer offered.

Udall simply ignored Erasmus's loyalty to the pope, accepting him as a witty and eloquent critic of abuses in the church and the best of teachers. The *Paraphrases* served the didactic purpose of simplifying Scripture for the "unlearned multitudes" and, by preserving the best of patristic commentary, furnishing them with the equivalent of a good library of divinity. Luther had denounced the *Paraphrases* for coming between the people and the Word. Like Cranmer, Udall was concerned with potential abuses of Scripture. He describes the project of translating the *Paraphrases*, in a preface to its sponsor the dowager Queen Katharine Parr, as designed for people who thirst

> for the simple and plain knowledge of God's word: not for contentious babbling, but for innocent living: not to be curious searchers of the high mysteries, but to be faithful executors and doers of God's biddings.

But the dominant note of Udall's prefaces is a humanistic confidence in the power of the Bible, supplemented by such aids as the homilies and the newly translated paraphrases, to work a moral reformation in England. This emphasis on the ethical utility of Scripture is essentially that of Erasmus, as manifested in his own preface to the paraphrase of Matthew. Udall, however, expressed the temper of the English reformation at a particular moment. He saw Christ beginning to dwell among the English, as the light of the gospel burned away the mist of "popish trumpery," and a new love of virtue and hatred of vice springing up in the land.[71]

The view of Scripture that I have associated chiefly with Cranmer persisted, with some modification, in justifications of the Bible by spokesmen for the church. In 1567 Archbishop Matthew Parker introduced the Bishops' Bible, an authorized translation designed to replace the Great Bible in the churches, by reprinting Cranmer's preface and adding one of his own that contrasted the early fathers' advocacy of Bible reading by the people with the Roman Catholic position that to translate Scripture into vulgar tongues was to invite heresy and dissension. At approximately the same time Jewel was citing Chrysostom and Clement of Alexandria against Harding to make the point that Scripture was not dark but clear and plain.[72] Harding went so far as to suggest that Hebrew lacked vowels in order "that among the people of Israel the seventy elders only could read and understand the mysteries of the holy books that we call the bible." The "vulgar people" were kept from such reading "by special providence of God," according to Harding, "that precious stones should not be cast before swine...as being for their un-reverent curiosity and impure life unworthy."[73] Jewel countered by going to the opposite extreme: "Oftentimes the unlearned seeth that thing that the learned cannot see."[74]

For Parker God's Word was "the incomparable treasure of his Churche," preserved despite such hazards as library fires "to our singular comfort and instruction." Parker placed greater emphasis than Cranmer on the need to read the Scriptures with the aim of finding out Christ (perhaps influenced by Calvin's insistence upon this point) and demonstrated more confidence in their perspicuity. He assured his readers that Christ would open the sense of the Scriptures to "the lowly and contrite in heart." Parker's preface suggests that the initial fears of the abuses of Bible reading had subsided, along with the need to justify it as a means of preserving order in the state. What remains is a concern with the central place of the Bible in the tradition of the church and a sense of Scripture as a treasury of sacred wisdom, to be approached with reverence and humility, rather than a force acting on the believer.

These emphases continue in the lengthy preface to the Authorized Version of 1611, the successor to the Bishops' Bible that came to be known as the King James Bible. Its authors demonstrate their sense of the continuity of the church by placing the latest version of the Bible historically in a long line of translations and by invoking a battery of fathers (Augustine, Jerome, Cyril, Tertullian, Justin Martyr, Basil) to buttress claims for the merits of the Word. These claims have become more extravagant by 1611; Scripture is not only a treasury of costly jewels and a fountain of pure water but "a Pandect of profitable lawes," "a whole paradise of trees of life."[75] Jewel had set a precedent for such hyperbole in a remarkable series of sermons published in 1570 as *A Treatise of the Holy Scripture*. Jewel himself was self-consciously following the example of the early fathers in praising Scrip-ture. For Jewel the Bible is, among other things, "the true manna," "the store house of wisdom," a lodestar to guide one through life's tempests. The effect of his copious praise is to enforce the lesson that Scripture is the great stay of Christians in this world:

> So constant is he that hath learned the word of God, and hath set his delight upon it, and is through it assured of the will of God. Heaven shall shake; the earth shall tremble; but the man of God shall stand upright.... Such a ground, such a foundation, such a rock is the word of God.[76]

Praise of this sort, inspired for the most part by scriptural metaphors, became commonplace in characterizations of the Bible by Protestants of various persuasions. The poem incorporated in the Geneva Bible, "Of the incomparable treasure of the holy Scriptures," sounds many of the same notes that Jewel did. Yet apologists for the established church tended to place more emphasis on the sanctity of the text and the reverence with which it should be regarded. Jewel's technique of heaping up praises, repeated in the preface to the Authorized Version, was a way of establishing the holiness of the Word itself. The Scriptures are the "registry of the mysteries of God," Jewel says at one point, "the holy place in which God sheweth himself to the people, the mount Sion, where God hath appointed to dwell for ever."[77] The preface of the Authorized Version speaks of the translators as putting aside the curtain, "that we may look into the most holy place."[78] For all of his claims about the intelligibility of divine truths, Jewel was cautious enough to warn that one should not be curious and seek to know more of the mysteries than God has revealed.[79] Jewel himself is more venturesome than Cranmer, yet all insist in their various ways that one must tread reverently in the presence of God. The example of Uzzah remains in the background; one must not handle the mysteries with unclean hands.

The authors of the 1611 preface show themselves much more disposed to trust in the capacity of the "vulgar" to profit from Scripture than Cranmer was, both by their enthusiastic praise of the Word and by their readiness to believe that the Holy Spirit will make it comprehensible and effective. Still, they demonstrate much the same concern that Cranmer did with charting a middle course between extremes, in this case the "scrupulositie of the Puritanes" and the "obscurities of the Papists."[80] Catholic translators are seen as darkening the sense of the text with their Latinisms and the Puritans as distorting it by doctrinal bias, as when they substitute "congregation" for "church" in the Geneva Bible. The bishops claim to offer a Bible that will speak "like it selfe, as in the language of Canaan,"[81] and for itself, without the strongly Calvinistic notes of the Geneva version that James found so offensive.

The kind of moderation that the Authorized Version represents becomes more apparent when it is set beside a contemporary edition of the Geneva

Bible. In presenting a text unencumbered with doctrinal notes the translators were simply following a precedent established by the Great Bible, but the action had particular significance because of the immense popularity of the Geneva Bible. The latter had established itself almost immediately as the Bible of the people when it first appeared in 1560 in a convenient quarto format, printed in roman type and augmented by such aids as maps and tables. It went through 140 editions, 60 of them after the printing of the Authorized Version in 1611.[82] The last appeared in 1644. The Geneva notes were still controversial enough in the 1650s for Peter Heylyn to upbraid Thomas Fuller for suggesting in his *Church-History of Britain* that they were not entirely bad. Heylyn reminded Fuller that James had found them seditious and challenged him to defend the identification of the locusts of Revelation (9:3) as bishops and archbishops (as well as monks and cardinals). In response Fuller conceded that far too many of the notes were indeed factious and dangerous.[83]

In 1611 editions of the Geneva Bible were still reprinting the preface from the original 1560 edition, which presents a strikingly different view of history and the church from that of the committee of bishops responsible for the Authorized Version. Its authors, Englishmen who sought refuge from Mary in Calvin's Geneva, represent themselves and the English people as spared God's judgment "after so horrible backsliding and falling away from Christ to Antichrist, from light to darkness, from the living God to dumme and dead idoles" and now mercifully called "to the marveilous light of his Gospel." In a dedicatory epistle to Elizabeth that appeared in 1560 the exiles present a triumphant view of recent events as ordered by divine providence. Having preserved Elizabeth that she might govern England, God now seemed to be reanimating the church by the wind of the Spirit. Yet they betray their nervousness about Elizabeth's future course by the strenuousness with which they exhort her to be zealous in the struggle against the agents of Satan, who include "worldlings" and "ambicious prelates" as well as the ubiquitous papists. They argue not from historical precedent but, by analogy, from the examples provided by Scripture, the sole authority that they will acknowledge, urging Elizabeth to emulate the zeal of such reforming kings as Jehosaphat, Hezekiah, and Josiah in establishing the Word of God and rooting out all evidences of idolatry. Her great work should be to build the spiritual temple, the church of Christ, as Zerubbabel rebuilt the material one.

The habit of identifying with the experience of the Israelites, by an essentially ahistorical leap to the truth of the Word, pervades the Geneva Bible. It can be seen in notes on the book of Isaiah remarking on God's power to punish the wicked and to deliver the faithful, and, most noticeably, in the woodcut printed on the original titlepage, which reveals the Israelites on the shore of the Red Sea with the pursuing Egyptians behind them and a pillar of fire on the other side (fig. 3). The same woodcut appears at the beginning of the fourteenth chapter of Exodus with a gloss explaining that the afflictions suffered by the church and its ministers in this world are sent as trials of faith and patience and that God is most ready to offer succor when the dangers are greatest. If the makers of the Geneva Bible thought that the deliverance of the English church that they envisioned was at hand, they were quickly disillusioned, but the experience would not have invalidated the biblical parallel, only a particular reading of it. Setbacks could only give a fuller resonance to the lesson pointed by a verse quoted on the titlepage: "Great are the troubles of the righteous, but the Lord delivereth them out of all" (Ps. 34:19).

By invoking the Pauline figure of the living temple of believers the authors of the epistle to Elizabeth portrayed the church as a dynamic fellowship of the elect. They saw this church as founded ultimately upon the common experience of the saving power of the Word. Puritan writers in the late sixteenth and early seventeenth centuries recovered the Pauline understanding of the process of "edification" as involving a living, growing house of God:[84]

> Now therefore ye are no more strangers and foreigners, but fellow citizens with the saints, and of the household of God; and are built upon the foundation of the apostles and prophets, Jesus Christ himself being the chief corner stone; in whom all the building fitly framed together groweth unto an holy temple in the Lord: in whom ye also are builded together for an habitation of God through the Spirit. (Eph. 2:19–22)

To insist upon regulating such "things indifferent" as vestments and ceremonies in the manner of Whitgift and Hooker was to impose an external kind of order and to deny the vital nature of the church, to see it as static rather than as continually developing under the influence of the Spirit. For such defenders of the establishment edification was a matter of imparting doctrine which could be deduced from Scripture and codified by the church.

Various attitudes toward Scripture that Hooker was to challenge emerged in the Geneva Bible, among them an intense concern with the individual experience of the Word. According to the epistle:

> It [the Word] is the trial of the spirits: and as the Prophet saieth, It is as a fyre and hammer to breake the stonie hearts of them that resist Gods mercies offred by the preaching of the same. Yea it is sharper then any two edged sworde to examine the very thoughtes and to judge the affections of the heart, and to discover whatsoever lyeth hid under hypocrisie and wolde be secret from the face of God and his churche. So that this must be the first fundacion and groundworke, according wherunto the good stones of this building must be framed, and the evil tried out and rejected.

THE BIBLE

AND
HOLY SCRIPTVRES

CONTEYNED IN
THE OLDE AND NEWE
Teſtament.

TRANSLATED ACCOR
ding to the Ebrue and Greke, and conferred with
the beſt tranſlations in diuers langages.

WITH MOSTE PROFITABLE ANNOTA-
tions vpon all the hard places, and other things of great
importance as may appeare in the Epiſtle to the Reader.

FEARE YE NOT, STAND STIL, AND BEHOLDE
the ſaluacion of the Lord, which he wil ſhewe to you this day. Exod.14,13.

THE LORD SHAL FIGHT FOR YOU·THERFORE
holde you your peace, Exod. 14, verſ.14.

AT GENEVA.
PRINTED BY ROVLAND HALL
M·D·LX.

FIG. 3

To seize upon these particular biblical metaphors—the Word as fire, hammer, sword[85]—was to express a conviction about the supernatural force acting through Scripture and the need to submit to it. This kind of trial by the Word, of individuals rather than of doctrines, was the beginning of the process of edification.

Scripture was seen as continuing to play a central role in the life of the godly society. If the Israelites appointed priests to instruct the people in the knowledge and fear of God and judges "to minister justice according to the worde," we should conclude that God "willeth that nothing be attempted before we have inquired thereof at his mouth." The Genevan theocracy had shown how a society might be governed by the Word. The emphasis of the 1560 edition on the need to consult the Word was eventually translated into a table, "How to take profit in reading of the holy Scripture," included in later editions for the benefit of the ordinary reader. This comprehensive guide tells one not only how to read the Bible but how often to read it (twice daily, at regular times) and breaks its contents down into broad categories of instruction: in matters of religion, of government, of family life, of private life, and of social behavior. It expresses in diagrammatic form (and occasionally by means of Ramistic dichotomies) what came to be a typical Puritan emphasis on applying the Bible systematically to every aspect of daily life. One could never give too much attention to Scripture. As the Puritan preacher Richard Greenham counseled, "Evermore be musing, reading, hearing, and talking of Gods word."[86]

Although Anglicans would agree that Scripture should be the rule of faith and a guide to holy living, they did not apply it so relentlessly. The preface of the Authorized Version presents the Bible chiefly as a means of salvation and of enriching one's spiritual life: "Happie is the man that delighteth in Scripture, and thrice happie that meditateth in it day and night."[87] Hooker voiced an attitude that may underlie this comparative reticence when he commented:

> The meanness of some things is such, that to search the Scripture of God for the ordering of them were to derogate from the reverend authority and dignity of the Scripture.[88]

Hooker wrote out of a sense of decorum and reverence: one should not seek to regulate the petty business of life by the "Scripture of God." His attitude arises from a principle spelled out in the *Laws*, that "the end of the word of God is to save."[89] Hooker felt that scriptural injunctions should be interpreted literally, and obeyed strictly, only in matters pertaining to salvation. He saw the "venerable books" of the Bible as offering an "infinite variety of matter"—prophecies, exemplary histories, meditations of piety, among other things—but he valued them chiefly for revealing "the principal necessary laws of God,"[90] necessary, that is, to salvation.

The argument between Anglican and Puritan was on one important level an argument over how much scope the Bible was to be allowed and the inseparable issue of how it was to be interpreted, and by whom. The authors of the *Second Admonition* accused the church hierarchy of trying to stop the spread of the Gospel in England:

> It is so circumscribed and wrapt within the compasse of suche statues, suche penalties, suche injunctions, suche advertisements, suche articles, suche canons, suche sober caveats...that in manner it doth peepe out from behinde the screene.[91]

Cartwright charged that Whitgift injured the Word by pinning it in "so narrow room."[92] He boasted that the "glorious light of the gospel" would prevail, as the "sun of truth" had in apostolic times, arguing that the time was ripe for building the temple.[93] The authors of the Marprelate tracts put the case more vigorously and claimed that the pride of Canterbury would soon be humbled "if the Word had free passage," echoing a verse that Coverdale had quoted on the title page of the translation of the complete Bible that he published in 1535: "Pray for us, that the word of God may have free passage, and be glorified" (2 Thess. 3:1).[94] They invoked Tyndale and his contemporaries Barnes and Frith as the "first planters of the Gospel among us."[95] Canterbury, in the person of Whitgift, raised the specter of the Anabaptists and accused Cartwright of making of Scripture a "nose of wax," repeating a figure used by Catholic apologists in arguing that Protestants distorted the meaning of the Bible to suit themselves.[96] Hooker subsequently attacked what he characterized as an "earnest desire to draw all things under the determination of bare and naked Scripture."[97] The figure betrays an uneasiness at the prospect of seeing human authority displaced by scriptural, as well as a fear of what the "vulgar sort," trusting to the urgings of the Spirit, would make of the text. Although Hooker acknowledged that one needed the aid of the Spirit in reading Scripture, he stressed the role of reason. He could accept the scriptural claim that the gospel is a two-edged sword only by qualifying it, "but in the hands of reasonable men."[98]

Cartwright posed a clear threat with his insistence that "the Word of God containeth the direction of all things pertaining to the church,"[99] especially since he saw Scripture as dictating a presbyterian form of church government which would substitute the two offices of pastor and deacon for the elaborate Anglican hierarchy and would grant considerable autonomy to individual congregations. Whitgift and Hooker exaggerated the degree of Cartwright's reliance upon Scripture, however, and modern commentators have often accepted that exaggeration. Cartwright did not insist that all church practices be explicitly authorized by Scripture but that they be tested against four Pauline directives.[100] He did, however, refuse to accept the

Anglican defense of established practices in the name of reason and tradition, even when these could be shown to be "not repugnant to" Scripture.[101] Because of his sense of the overwhelming importance of the Bible, the Calvinistic Cartwright felt that all forms of worship and church government had to be derived somehow from the Scripture; they could not be regarded merely as "things indifferent" to which scriptural precepts did not apply.

The distinction is a subtle but crucial one. As Coolidge has shown, Hooker's magisterial argument seems unanswerable because he reduced the Bible to a "doctrinal instrument,"[102] to be understood rationally as a collection of spiritual laws. He criticized the habit of identifying with the children of Israel, associating it with the Anabaptists,[103] and repeatedly attacked claims made in the name of the Spirit. To establish his position Hooker had to dam one of the major currents of Reformation thought. Puritan claims for the authority and force of Scripture, although not necessarily for its universal applicability, had their own theoretical justification in the doctrine that Scripture is self-authenticating, or *autopistos*. Calvin articulated this doctrine,[104] and William Whitaker provided its fullest expression in English in his *A Disputation on Holy Scripture* (1588), written as a response to Cardinal Bellarmine. Tyndale had reiterated Luther's argument that Scripture interpreted itself, through the agency of the Holy Spirit. Whitaker, following Calvin, was able to provide a fuller account of the workings of the Spirit. His argument rests upon the assumption that one is persuaded of the truth of Scripture by "the internal testimony of the Holy Spirit" (a translation of a key phrase of Calvin's):

> The sum of our opinion is, that the scripture is *autopistos*, that is, hath all its authority and credit from itself; is to be acknowledged, is to be received, not only because the church hath so determined and commanded, but because it comes from God: and that we certainly know that it comes from God, not by the church, but by the Holy Ghost.[105]

Whitaker argued, as Calvin and other reformers had before him, that the Scripture generates its own light for believers; it is a lamp whose light can be beheld only by those who look with the "eyes of faith."[106] Whitaker insisted also that Scripture possesses "great force and virtue in itself...to infuse into us an intimate persuasion of its truth."[107] The Word of God is like a seed: "it springs up, and breaks forth, and manifests its energy."[108] The power of Scripture to persuade, presumably observable in his own experience and that of other believers, was itself proof for Whitaker that Scripture was *autopistos*.

Calvin had also stressed the power of the Word: "The Word of the Lord constrains us by its majesty, as by a violent impulse, to yield obedience to it."[109] He saw it as being given a hidden energy by the Spirit. The conception of the Word as *autopistos* implied an inherent power by which Scripture could convince one of its truth, make itself plain, and act upon the heart. Luther had believed in such a power, without explaining it so systematically as Calvin did, and so had other early reformers. Zwingli argued that "the Word of God is so alive and strong and powerful that all things necessarily have to obey it."[110] Like Luther, Calvin was careful not to make the letter of Scripture sacrosanct. For him the Word became authoritative and efficacious only through the operation of the Spirit.[111]

In seeking to extend the claims of Scripture the Puritan opponents of the Elizabethan church were more concerned with following the letter than the early reformers had been. The assertion of the author of the first Admonition that nothing should be done "but that which you have the expresse warrant of Gods worde for"[112] suggests the rigidity that biblicism could assume. Cartwright, although he did not demand a specific scriptural warrant for all the practices of the church, could construe the Old Testament judicial laws to be literally binding and argue that blasphemy and adultery should be punished by death. Still, the more radical Protestants could seek to derive a church discipline from Scripture and to regulate conduct by it without losing their sense of the dynamic interaction of Spirit and Word. Their claims of inspiration were of course vulnerable to the arguments of a Hooker, yet their sense of the importance of the Spirit was much closer to that of the major reformers than was Hooker's. He denied that Scripture was self-authenticating[113] and sought to minimize the role of the Spirit in illuminating it and spreading its influence. One cannot imagine him conceiving of the Word as a seed in the sense that Cartwright did, or as a fire, or as a sun banishing the darkness of past errors.[114] Hooker was defending an order that he believed in, as the product of tradition and rational consideration by judicious men, against a conception of the church as a developing communion of believers brought together by the action of the Word.

Hooker established a foundation for Anglican discussions of Scripture in the next century that strengthened the authority of the church. Although Archbishop William Laud, arguing with a Catholic opponent, gave somewhat more attention than Hooker did to the action of the Spirit, his position is close to that of the *Laws*. Laud's three primary grounds for believing Scripture divine are the tradition of the church, the light of nature, and the light of the text itself. Scripture persuades "with the help of the ordinary grace and a mind morally induced and reasonably persuaded by the voice of the church."[115] This institutional voice was even more important in guiding the interpretation of Scripture. As Donne put it, "The *Word* is the *Light*, but the *Church* is the *Lanthorne*."[116] Joseph Hall described the Bible as a well from which not everyone could draw: "There is no Christian that may not enjoy God's book, but every Christian may not interpret it."[117] Jeremy Taylor wrote eloquently on the danger of believing any particular interpretation to be absolutely valid in *The Liberty of Prophesying* (1647), arguing against doctrinaire positions and for tolerance on the grounds of the obscurity of much of Scripture and the difficulties of interpretation. Taylor's argument is eminently sensible and has the appeal of being less polemical than Hooker's, yet the inheritors of the Puritan tradition that I have described would have found it irrelevant to their spiritual needs. What mattered to John Goodwin, writing in the same year as Taylor, were the evidences of the miraculous power of the Word to transform lives:

> The world now for many generations together, hath had a full experiment of this great power we speak of, breaking out of the Scriptures in the ministry of them, like fire or lightning out of the cloud, by which their hearts and souls have been reviv'd, quickned, and rais'd, as it were, from the dead: yea and sometimes taken up into the heavens. I make no question but that our own ears have heard, and some of our fathers, yea and some of our children, and many of our friends have told us, many of these *magnalia,* these great and wonderful works of the Scriptures in them, and upon them.[118]

The gulf that we saw opening between Erasmus and Luther has widened significantly here. They at least were engaged in the common enterprise of making the Bible more accessible to the people. Taylor and Goodwin, although as Protestants they would presumably agree on many points of doctrine, at times scarcely seem to be talking about the same work. Taylor was convinced of the sacredness of the Bible, but he approached it intellectually, as a difficult and extremely various text that had to be interpreted warily. Goodwin, on the other hand, experienced Scripture as a field of force. His concern was not with the limits of interpretation but with the signs of the Word's influence upon those who were open to it. It could be a "rod of iron" working "great and terrible effects in the inner parts" or a source of waters of life that could make an Eden of the "dry and barren wilderness" of the soul.[119]

I do not mean to imply that Puritans paid no attention to the problems of interpretation. The most influential Puritan theologian, William Perkins, recognized the need for learning, especially knowledge of the original languages of Scripture, and accepted the generally held principle that no interpretation should be contrary to the "analogy of faith." Augustine was the common source of this concept for Puritans and Anglicans.[120] In Perkins's formulation the analogy of faith was "a certain *abridgement* or *summe* of the Scriptures, collected out of the most manifest and familiar places" and having two parts, faith and love.[121] He would have readers consider the circumstances from which a particular verse arose and compare other passages that might illuminate it; the table of instruction printed with the Geneva Bible offers similar advice. Such guidelines allowed a reasonable amount of freedom in interpretation. For all the talk of the literal sense from Tyndale onwards, there was widespread recognition that this could often be extended legitimately to include figurative or "spiritual" meanings. The practice of reading the Old Testament typologically, as foreshadowing the New, was widespread and sometimes carried to extraordinary lengths—but I am not concerned here with illustrating the practice.

The contrasting attitudes toward the scope and force of the Bible that I have traced underlie a fundamental disagreement over the importance of preaching that intensified as Puritan attitudes became more widespread. Those of Goodwin's general persuasion felt that the power of the Scriptures broke out in the ministry of them; the Spirit most commonly worked through the preaching of the Word. While there were great preachers who were comfortable within the confines of the established church—John Donne and Lancelot Andrewes are obvious examples—the Anglican emphasis upon liturgy tended to limit the role of preaching in the worship service. Laud aggressively promoted the concept of the beauty of holiness by refurbishing churches and restoring traditional rites wherever he could and opposed the altar to the pulpit: "For ther 'tis *Hoc est corpus meum*, this is my body. But in the pulpit 'tis at most but; *Hoc est verbum meum*, this is my word."[122] The Eucharist was indeed the heart of the Anglican service, and Laud reinforced its importance by insisting that the communion table be positioned altarwise, railed to separate it from the parishioners. Laud also acted upon his view of the subordinate role of the sermon by mounting a vigorous campaign to enforce existing rules governing preaching, regularly summoning offending ministers before the High Commission. The struggle to regulate preaching was by this time an old one.[123] The Canons of 1604, deeply resented by Puritans, had tightened provisions for licensing preachers and established stricter sanctions for nonconformists. James's *Directions Concerning Preachers* (1622) had attempted, with little success, to limit the scope of preaching by restricting ministers to subjects related to the Thirty-nine Articles and the Book of Homilies and by specifying that Sunday afternoon lectures be replaced by catechising. Laud's severity, which resulted in a greater number of suspensions, made life more difficult for Puritan ministers, but even his harassment did relatively little to reduce their effectiveness. The enthusiasm for what came to be called spiritual preaching, like the enthusiasm for unrestricted reading and interpretation of the Bible, was too powerful a force to be contained.

Efforts to restrict preaching had obvious political implications, given the fact that the pulpit was the most effective forum for the expression of dissent, but they also reflected a belief that the truth of Scripture could be conveyed with sufficient force by public reading. The basic religious issue can be seen in the dispute between Hooker and Cartwright. Hooker asked, reasonably, why the Word had to be preached to have saving power and argued the advantages of exposing the people to the lessons prescribed by the Book of Common Prayer. Cartwright had not objected to the public reading of Scripture, conceding that it could be efficacious on occasion, but he felt that faith was far more likely to be aroused by hearing the Word preached:

> As the fire stirred giveth more heat, so the word as it were blown by preaching flameth more in the hearers than when it is read.[124]

Hooker asked hard questions (What kind of preaching? Are we to regard the preacher's words as inspired?) that reflect a basic unwillingness to take seriously Cartwright's claims for the importance of the Spirit. For Cartwright the formal reading of Scripture was apt to be a lifeless business, as the reading of officially sanctioned homilies that passed for preaching in the Elizabethan parish churches certainly was. The letter of Scripture had to be animated by the Spirit, and the Spirit was most likely to be conveyed by lively preaching. Such preaching was at the time being encouraged by clandestine "prophesyings," meetings of reform-minded ministers to share interpretations of Scripture, and would eventually spread with the growth of a system of privately endowed lectureships.

Hooker of course did more than read homilies in the pulpit, and he was prepared to acknowledge that preaching was a "worthy" part of the service (although he could extend the meaning of the term to include the public reading of Scripture).[125] Yet he did not feel that Scripture needed to be cut in order to be nourishing or bruised like spices to bring out its savor, to use Cartwright's metaphors. It was enough to think of the Bible as a "treasure," whose riches—chiefly those principles that pointed the way to salvation—were discoverable by "the industry of right discourse."[126] In putting down Cartwright on the subject of preaching Hooker considerably diluted if he did not altogether reject an important Reformation doctrine formulated by Bullinger, that the preaching of the Word is the Word: *"praedicatio verbi Dei est verbum Dei."*[127] Luther had insisted that God spoke through the minister: "True, the voice is his: but my God is speaking the Word which he preaches or speaks."[128] Others stressed the role of the Spirit in enabling the minister to convey the living Word. Bucer commented on the need for the minister to pray that his words, and deeds, "may have the energy and force of the Spirit."[129] Perkins exhorted the preacher so to behave that his hearers may judge "that it is not so much he that speaketh, as the Spirit of God in him and by him." He must have a "fiery tongue," and "the fire of [his] zeale must be kindled by God's spirit."[130]

Calvin read 1 Corinthians 3:6 ("The letter killeth, but the Spirit giveth life") as a commentary on the difference between "dead" and "spiritual" preaching:

By the word *letter* Paul means preaching which is external and does not reach the heart; by *Spirit* he means teaching which is alive, which works mightily in the souls of men by the grace of the Spirit.[131]

Such an emphasis upon preaching by the aid of the Spirit led naturally to a concern with the godliness of the minister. Whatever his rhetorical skills, he must have the gift of the Spirit or his preaching will be ineffectual. Thomas Hooker, writing in 1640, saw the right conditions for preaching as existing only "when there is a kind of spiritual heat in the heart, when there are holy affections."[132] Then the preaching of the Word can truly be powerful:

> Now is there come a great rain, and a mighty wind with it, especially a whirlwind, it carrieth all before it...and overturns all things with the violence of it. The doctrine and truth which the ministers deliver, is as the rain: now the holy affection wherewith it is delivered, is like the whirlwind. When the truth of God is delivered with a holy violence, and hearty affection by God's servants, evermore it makes way, it beats down, and breaks all before it.[133]

Hooker's exhortations to "holy violence" suggest the direction in which a concern with spiritual preaching would lead.

Spiritual preachers were expected not only to display "holy affections" themselves but to know how to work on the affections of their audiences. Perkins instructed preachers in the different kinds of auditors they might encounter and showed how they could reach them by skillful application of doctrines.[134] Richard Bernard described four affections the preacher should seek to arouse (love, desire, hope, and fear) and distinguished a further stage, the personal application of the use: "This home-speaking is the sharpe edge of the sword, the word of God."[135] The presbyterian divines who constituted the Westminster Assembly advised preachers to search out the "most needful and seasonable" uses for their flock and apply comfort in such a way as "to answer such objections as a troubled heart and afflicted spirit may suggest to the contrary."[136] Clearly, the affective dimension of preaching was regarded as critically important.

All English Protestants would agree that in some sense the Bible expressed the "living" Word of God. They were people of the book who took their stand on Scripture in rejecting the authority of Rome and who continued to practice a strongly scriptural religion, whether this was given its shape by the Book of Common Prayer or by the vigorous preaching of the Word. Yet the Bible was much more alive for some than for others, in the sense that they felt themselves dramatically changed through confronting the Word, both by reading it for themselves and by hearing it preached, and were convinced that the energy of the Spirit was manifesting itself in a continuing Reformation. A sense of the divine presence in Scripture led many of them to pay minute attention to the details of the text and to allow its authority to extend to virtually every aspect of their lives.

It would be misleading to insist that the contrasting attitudes toward Scripture that I have outlined constitute two clearly defined traditions. They overlap at various times and in various people. Sometimes they are virtually inseparable, as in the case of a complex figure such as Bishop Jewel, a former Genevan exile who could write eloquently of the power of the Word and complain to friends on the Continent about the slow progress of the reformation in England and yet force recalcitrant clergy to wear the surplice when Elizabeth decided that conformity in vestments was essential to the unity of the church. Jewel could see the truth of the Gospel breaking out in England, as he contested with Catholic adversaries, yet insist upon the authority of his own church and the need for reverence and restraint in lay reading of Scripture. Still, these attitudes did begin to diverge early, as the contrasts between Tyndale and Cranmer demonstrate, and their opposition became pronounced in the last decades of the sixteenth century when battle was joined over the issue of vestments and the charges made by the authors of the Admonitions. When the governance of the church was at stake, spokesmen for the ecclesiastical establishment had to find ways to confine the power for disruption implicit in Scripture. Those who believed strongly in the kinetic quality of the Word sought to extend its authority. Their position was the more difficult to maintain, yet they and not Hooker, who erected such seemingly impregnable defenses, were riding a current that would eventually prove impossible to withstand. So strong was this current, in fact, that when the presbyterian system advocated by Cartwright and others had hardened into orthodoxy in the 1640s, this system was resisted effectively by those who claimed the right to follow the Spirit in their own ways.

The living temple was an elusive yet irresistible ideal. To achieve it those who felt the power of the Word most strongly, shaping them to take their places in the communion of the elect and perfecting the Reformation in England, seized upon texts that pointed the way to their particular version of the ideal with a zeal that appalled the more reasonable and temperate. Donne saw those who controverted or allegorized Scripture as violating the text by tearing it apart:

> So do they demolish Gods fairest Temple, his Word, which pick out such stones, and deface the integrity of it.... In the Temple was admitted no sound of hammer, nor in the building of this great, partriarchal Catholick Church, of which every one of us is a little chappel, should the word be otherwise wrested or broken, but taken intirely as it is offered and presented.[137]

Donne could admire the Bible, as he could a cathedral, for the harmony of its parts; the beauty was in the structure. His figure implies that one should be able to recognize the fundamental unity of the church, like that of the Scriptures, and not press individual differences. Yet this impressive vision of order assumes a willingness to settle for agreement on basic doctrinal issues and not contend over the shape of the church itself. Those who did not want to accept the particular form of Donne's church would have been no more willing to see the Word as a completed temple. Such a structure would have seemed to them lifeless. The immense difficulties of building a living temple out of radically disparate elements would become evident in the Commonwealth period. And the sense of the Word as a temple to be approached with reverence would persist through it. Thus Robert Boyle, the father of modern chemistry and a stalwart Anglican, on the other side of the divide:

> I use the Scripture, not as an Arsenal...but as a Matchless Temple, where I delight to Be, to contemplate the Beauty, the Symmetry, and the Magnificence of the Structure, and to Encrease my Awe, and Excite my Devotion to the Deity there Preached and Ador'd.[138]

This is where Cranmer's sense of Scripture as "the most precious jewel" (Boyle calls it "a Sacred Jewel") was to lead. In Boyle reverence mingles with aesthetic appreciation for a structure seen to embody the incomparable design of God. He might need the aid of the Spirit to comprehend this design, but its power seems unlikely to break forth from a specific text for one who views the Bible in this fashion, as an object of holy admiration.[139]

2. Richard Sibbes and Spiritual Preaching

So much critical attention has been given to the sermons of John Donne in recent years that one might be forgiven for thinking that he was the only popular preacher whom educated Londoners went to hear in the early decades of the seventeenth century. Richard Sibbes is another who, though not capable of Donne's dramatic effects and verbal ingenuity, deserves notice as one of the chief exemplars of a kind of preaching that rivaled Donne's. Sibbes's works have been quarried regularly by scholars of Puritanism, but he has not received the kind of sustained attention that a preacher of his skill and importance deserves.[1] While Donne was first gaining attention at Lincoln's Inn, Sibbes was building a devoted following at Gray's Inn, attracting by his preaching "besides the learned lawyers of the house many noble personages, and many of the gentry and citizens."[2] Donne and Sibbes exemplify two radically different styles of preaching, which their contemporaries would have identified as witty and spiritual (we would be likelier to call them metaphysical and plain). The conceits and the brilliant wordplay of a Donne or a Lancelot Andrewes can dazzle a twentieth-century reader who would be bored by the earnest simplicity of Sibbes or his good friend John Preston, Donne's successor as lecturer in divinity at Lincoln's Inn. Yet, as William Haller has shown, spiritual preaching was the dominant kind in its day.[3] Its practitioners were the most influential figures in the pulpits of London and Cambridge, the great nursery of Puritanism, and in numerous provincial towns.

Sibbes, a member of that Cambridge-educated spiritual brotherhood whose interlocking relationships Haller has traced, left a body of sermons that exercised a continuing influence in England and America. He became a fellow and subsequently preacher of his college, St. John's, then in 1610 assumed a lectureship created for him by the people of Trinity parish.[4] In 1615 Sibbes was removed from this position, which he had made into one of the most important in Cambridge, by a royal prohibition against new lectures,[5] but shortly thereafter found a more prestigious and influential pulpit as lecturer at Gray's Inn. Sibbes returned to Cambridge as master of Catherine Hall in 1626, retaining his post at Gray's Inn by special dispensation. John Preston's time was similarly divided between London and Cambridge, where he had become both master of Emmanuel and Trinity Lecturer. Until Preston's premature death in 1628 the two friendly rivals

gave Cambridge some of its most memorable preaching, appearing frequently at the University church, Great St. Mary's, as well as in their own
pulpits.

Sibbes flourished at a time when moderate Puritans still felt it possible to
function within the established church. He was evidently a gentle and
peaceable man, renowned for his "Christian humility,"[6] who for the sake of
unity tolerated practices with which he disagreed. In a letter arguing against
separatism, probably addressed to Thomas Goodwin, he asked:

> Must we therefore separate for Ceremonies, which many think may be
> lawfully used. But admit they be evils, must we make a rent in the Church
> for Ceremonious Rites, for circumstantiall evils? That were a remedy
> worse than the disease.[7]

Yet Sibbes felt the pressure that could be applied to ministers identified as
Puritans during this period, a pressure which intensified as William Laud
gained power, first as bishop of London and then as primate. Early in his
career at Gray's Inn he had to fight off an attempt by Laud to remove him
from the lectureship. Later, his participation in efforts to raise funds for
"godly preachers" of the Palatinate ("cast out of their house and homes, out
of their callings and countreys, by the furie of the mercilesse papists" [1:lix])
earned him a summons to appear before the Star Chamber, where he was
reprimanded along with the other influential Puritan ministers with whom
he had collaborated in this venture (William Gouge, Thomas Taylor, and
John Davenport).

Sibbe's most significant encounter with authority resulted from his activities as one of twelve Feoffees (a group composed of four ministers and a like
number of lawyers and merchants) engaged in buying up impropriations in
order to appoint qualified preachers to lectureships throughout England.
This important Puritan enterprise was dedicated to finding support for
"good and faithful preachers of the truth of the Gospell."[8] Not surprisingly,
it was perceived as a threat to the authority of the church, and the Feoffees
were brought to trial before the Court of Exchequer in 1632 for behaving as
a corporation without being licensed as one. They had in fact met frequently since 1626, keeping extensive records and establishing canons
governing the appointment and supervision of lecturers. This activity,
which the Feoffees defended as a "pious work," was denounced as a dangerous conspiracy that usurped the power of the king. In early 1633 the
court dissolved the group and took control of the considerable funds that
had been raised.

As an influential preacher and one so active in the effort to promote
spiritual preaching, Sibbes was bound to come into conflict with the hierarchy of the church. Such conflict, however, was something that Sibbes and
others like him were prepared to accept. What he said of the inner life of

Christians he could as well have said of the life of the church: "Where there is no conflict, there is no Spirit of Christ at all" (1:22). One had to struggle for the continuing reformation of the church as for the salvation and spiritual health of individuals. Struggle of this sort, against external as well as internal forces, could only heighten the sense that preaching must be an energetic and utterly serious business. Sibbes believed—with Calvin, Perkins, and a host of others—that preaching could be vital only if animated by the Holy Spirit. The preacher must possess "spiritual heat" and find means of conveying the power of the Spirit to his hearers.

Witty preaching was suspect to such men because of its extraordinary concern with language. Richard Baxter, who was strongly influenced by Sibbes, made perhaps the most trenchant case against such preaching. Displays of "phantastick wit" and "rhetorical jingling" were to him self-indulgent and irresponsible, trivializing the divine message:

> When I read such a book as Bishop Andrew's [sic] Sermons, or heard such a kind of preaching, I felt no life in it: methought they did but play with holy things.[9]

In the course of arguing that God's "serious" commands require a "serious" response, Baxter soberly remarks that "There is no Jesting in Heaven, nor in Hell."[10] Andrewes's delight in verbal play was to Baxter a sign that he lacked the seriousness essential to powerful preaching. Power was inseparable from plainness for Baxter. Andrewes's sermons were all glittering surface, "like beautiful Pictures:" "Life, or heat, or motion there is none."[11] Sermons lacking this inner dynamism in Baxter's view could not possibly express the workings of the Holy Spirit.

Sibbes shared the common conviction that "motion" and "life" in preaching were signs of the presence of the Spirit, but he was not as apt as Baxter, or Thomas Goodwin, to deliver the truth of God with a "holy violence." Sibbes sought rather to convey the gentler motions of the Spirit, with the primary aim of quieting the doubts and fears of his hearers. He was above all a preacher of assurance. As such, he offers a particularly telling example of the concern with the capacities and the spiritual well-being of the hearer that is a distinguishing feature of spiritual preaching. This concern emerges most clearly in the numerous comments by Puritan divines on the necessity to seek a plain, unembellished style in order to convey the truth effectively. In *The Bruised Reed and the Smoking Flax*, his most famous collection of sermons, Sibbes cautions that preachers should be careful "that they hide not their meaning in dark speeches, speaking in the clouds," then offers an analogy that is an index of his solicitude:

> Christ came down from heaven, and emptied himself of majesty in tender love to souls; shall we not come down from our high conceits to do any soul good? (1:53–54)

Sibbes's appeal goes beyond pragmatic considerations of how best to communicate. He asks ministers to emulate the "spirit of mercy" that Christ showed in taking on "our familiar manner of speech" by abasing themselves "for the good of the meanest." Before putting on the disposition of Christ, Sibbes counsels, "we must put off ourselves first." This insistence that ministers be self-effacing is one sign of a concern with reducing the distance between the preacher and his congregation that pervades Sibbes's work. Donne's sense of the mysteriousness and elevation of the priesthood offers a striking contrast:

> What a Coronation is our taking of Orders, by which God makes us a Royal Priesthood? And what an inthronization is the coming up into a Pulpit, where God invests his servants with his Ordinance, as with a Cloud.[12]

Sibbes liked to describe the minister in terms of the Song of Songs as a friend of the bride whose role was to bring together Christ and his spouse. Such a conception suggests both a sense of intimacy with his audience and a desire to present Christ as the embodiment of a divine love that accepts human frailty.

In his skillful diagnoses of spiritual illness in *The Bruised Reed* Sibbes follows the advice he gives to ministers to "put upon" the condition of those they address. Sibbes was not the only one to describe the church as "a common hospital, wherein all are in some measure sick" (1:57), but his use of the figure seems particularly appropriate. One quickly becomes aware of Sibbes's unusual sensitivity to the spiritual needs of his hearers. His aim was to bring them to accept their condition, and to understand that they are "bruised" by God for a purpose. At the same time he encouraged them to take hope by regarding themselves as "burning flax" containing the sparks of grace.[13] They are led gradually to a state of confidence in the power of God to reclaim his people, based upon an understanding of how the Spirit acts upon them:

> God's people feel a powerful work of the Spirit, not only revealing unto us our misery, and deliverance through Christ, but emptying us of our-selves as being redeemed from ourselves, and infusing new life into us, and strengthening us, and quickening of us when we droop and hang the wing, and never leaving us till perfect conquest. (1:95)

The characteristic use of "us" ("we" and "our" also appear frequently) strengthens the sense of identification between Sibbes and his hearers, as does the simple language intended to remove any barriers of learning or wit that might come between them. His homely figure, "when we droop and hang the wing," has the effect of domesticating theological language and catching the reader up in an effective image of his human condition.

Sibbes followed, at least loosely, the common Puritan practice of dividing a text into profitable doctrines, supporting these with reasons, then applying the doctrines to the lives of his hearers in a series of uses. The logical structure of his sermons, with arguments that progress by sequences of numbered points, reflects the same concern with communicating divine truths simply that informs his style. Yet however many markers he may have set out to guide the understanding of those who heard, or read, his sermons, Sibbes saw the process by which they apprehended the truth as a complex one involving much more than rational comprehension.

Until recently most discussion of Puritan sermons, following the influential lead of Perry Miller, has emphasized their rationality. Miller relied heavily upon such manuals as Perkins's *The Arte of Prophesying* and Richard Bernard's *The Faithfull Shepherd* in developing a conception of the Puritan sermon as essentially a legal brief. In his view the Puritan preacher first flattened his text in the process of expounding it, then proceeded methodically through the prescribed sequence of doctrine, reason, and use.[14] Whatever truth there may be in Miller's characterization, it is inadequate as an explanation of the way a sermon by one of the more imaginative Puritan preachers such as Sibbes actually works. It does not allow for the skill of a Sibbes in playing on the affections of his hearers or sufficiently recognize the importance of figurative language, often drawn from the Bible, to the effects he sought.

One must recognize, first, that however fixed the basic structure of a Puritan sermon may be, it permits considerable flexibility in developing an argument. Sibbes may introduce a list of "trials" or "encouragements" or a sequence of objections and answers that takes the form of a sustained dialogue. He may subdivide a "use" several times as he pursues a theme worth elaborating. Like many preachers, Sibbes gave much more space to uses, intended to stir up the affections, than to doctrines and reasons, aimed at the understanding. Sometimes it is difficult to draw the line between reason and use. The former may consist of biblical illustrations and analogies drawn from common experience that shade into an application. The movement of a sermon from point to point is generally more complicated than one would suspect from looking at a table of contents or the detailed procedures offered by the manuals.

Perhaps the most important thing to recognize is that the logical skeleton of a Puritan sermon may give an imperfect or even misleading impression of the way the preacher sought to bring his hearers to an apprehension of divine truths. The danger of overemphasizing structure is that one may assume that all Puritan preachers sought to do was to rectify the understanding by setting forth clear, rational arguments. For Sibbes and others like him *how* one knew was the key to *what* one knew. Sibbes speaks disparagingly of those who see heavenly things "by a human light, notionally:" "Alas! there is a veil over their soul, that they do not know them, or not experimentally. They have no taste or feeling of them" (2:462–63). The distinction between notional and experimental knowledge was a critical one for Puritan thought. It was not enough to exercise the reason; one had to learn to experience divine truth, to "taste" it.[15]

Sibbes shared the common Reformation assumption that Scripture was *autopistos,* sufficient in itself to convince one of the truth of its message. We know the Word to be true, Sibbes argues, "by the powerful work of it in the heart, by the experience of this blessed truth."[16] Yet to experience the power of the Word, whether it worked to terrify the unconverted or to "pacify the soul amidst all troubles" (2:494), one had first to be properly receptive. The Spirit had to frame the heart to be "suitable to divine truths," to create "answerable affections." It was the place of the minister to do all he could to cultivate such affections by facilitating the work of the Spirit.

Sibbes spoke of the necessity of preparing the heart to be acted upon by the Spirit, using one of the favorite idioms of later Puritan preachers. He instructed his hearers how they might examine their hearts, "stir up" their hearts, in order to have "hearts prepared" for every occasion. Such preparation was necessary not only for conversion but for the continuing work of sanctification, the growth in holiness that was the business of all Christians. Norman Pettit has traced the emergence of a concern with what could be done to prepare the heart for grace as Puritanism moved beyond the early Reformation emphasis on the suddenness of conversion through the overwhelming power of the Spirit to a sense that the Spirit worked its transformations by degrees.[17] The subtlety of Sibbes's discussions of the workings of the Spirit suggests how complex the Puritan sense of spiritual life could become, and it helps to explain why for a Sibbes "edification" involved more than setting forth doctrine in rationally comprehensible terms. He would have understood the word as implying a dynamic process of growth, for the individual as for the emerging church, through the agency of the Spirit.[18]

Unlike the Quakers and other followers of an inner light who sprang up later in the century, Sibbes saw the Holy Spirit as acting upon the reason as well as upon the will: "For though God work upon the will, it is with enlightenment of the understanding at the same time" (4:225). Yet the knowledge he advocated, as I have shown, was a knowledge inseparable from feeling, and he describes this as a kind of spiritual perception.[19] Sibbes represented the desire for heavenly things in terms of the senses. One must develop a spiritual appetite, Sibbes insists:

> The soul must first be brought to relish, before it can digest; there must be first an holy harmony between our nature and truth. (7:189)

Sibbes claims that in the heavenly feast all the senses are satisfied, and refers frequently to the need to "feel" divine truths, but he most often invokes the senses of taste and sight, linking the two:

> The Spirit of God must work in us spiritual senses, sight and taste, that we may see, discern, and relish heavenly things. (2:415)

Sibbes refers to sight as the noblest of senses and speaks of learning to see God with a "spiritual eye" or the "eagle-eye of faith."[20] One must work to clear the eye of the soul, he urges, in order to look upon God's glory in the "glass of the Gospel." In heaven this spiritual sight will become "immediate and perfect," and the taste possible in this life will be succeeded by "fullness." In the meantime one should develop one's spiritual senses, stimulated by the "sweet" and "savoury" language of the Bible. Sibbes found in the concept of spiritual senses a way of describing the conditioning of the affections that he saw as necessarily involved in the life of faith. They constitute a part of the language that he helped to develop for talking about the complex motions of the heart.

Sibbes was as wary of enjoying the physical senses as were most Puritans, describing "outward things" as "dead" and "not fitted to the spiritual nature of the soul" (1:219). Yet in commenting on the figurative language of the Song of Songs he recognized that "it pleaseth *Christ* to vaile heavenly matters with comparisons fetchd from earthly things, that so he may enter our souls the better by our senses" (2:32). Sibbes could speak of the "beauty of holiness" to be found in the church and in God's ordinances and describe sacraments as intended "to help our souls by our senses, and our faith by our imagination" (1:219, 1:185). If the senses could be used in worship, they could also contribute to the preacher's art. Sibbes justified the use of figurative language in sermons by appealing to the rhetorical effectiveness of "the putting of lively colours upon common truths" (1:184). As William Madsen has pointed out, Sibbes was anticipated by Tyndale and others who saw the value of using "similitudes."[21] One regularly finds advocates of plain style commending the use of tropes and figures to express spiritual truths in a lively fashion, typically citing the Bible as a warrant for such practices.[22] Sibbes offered an unusually full defense of the "holy use of imagination" and showed in his sermons how it can work on "sensible things" to represent heavenly ones.

Figurative expression was consonant with the fundamental Puritan ideal of simplicity, as one can see not only from sermons but from the Puritan habit of praising biblical style for being both eloquent and simple. Puritans tended to stress the simplicity of the Bible because they felt that this made it accessible to ordinary men. They found in this simplicity the key to the extraordinary power of Scripture to affect individuals. The Baptist preacher Benjamin Keach, a contemporary and rival of Bunyan, used a formula that exemplifies Puritan attitudes toward scriptural style:

> There simplicity is joyned with Majesty, commanding the veneration of all serious men; more than the Elaborate flourishes and long winded periods of Tully.[23]

Milton's praise of the "majestic unaffected style" of the prophets in *Paradise Regained* (4.359), opposed to "the orators of Greece and Rome," implies a similar tendency to join majesty with simplicity. For Keach the "grave, lively, and venerable Majesty of the Prophet Esaias stile" could be set against the puerility of Cicero's. The opposition of biblical eloquence to classical oratory goes back at least to Augustine, whose *Christian Doctrine* Keach cites as authority. Augustine had linked wisdom and eloquence, arguing that the persuasiveness of biblical writers arises from the truth of their message. Their eloquence was not calculated, in his view, but flowed naturally, like a river, and he demonstrated that it could be found in the speech of someone as uneducated as Amos, a "rustic turned prophet." The power of biblical language depended for him upon the attitude of the writer, as this comment on Jeremiah indicates:

> O eloquence more terrible that it is pure, and because it is genuine more powerful! Truly a "hammer that breaketh the rock in pieces!"[24]

Keach followed Augustine in praising biblical style for its gravity and its genuineness, but his praise of simplicity takes an extreme form characteristic of the Puritanism of his time:

> But what if in that *humility* of stile in Scripture, there be more *height* and *loftiness*, and more profoundness in its *Simplicity*, more *beauty* in its nakedness, and more vigor and *acuteness* in its seeming *rudeness*, then in those things we so praise and admire?[25]

In his discriminating analysis of biblical language Augustine had seen Paul as employing different styles according to his purpose: the low or subdued style to teach, the moderate style to praise, and the grand style to exhort. He describes the moderate style as "adorned with verbal ornaments" and the grand style as "forceful with the emotions of the spirit;" one employs "splendid" words, the other "vehement" words. Puritan discussions of biblical style tend to collapse these distinctions, banishing ornament altogether and, by joining majesty and simplicity, providing a basis for finding vehemence virtually anywhere in the Bible.

Calvin contributed significantly to a shift of emphasis from the words themselves to the force behind them. While he was sensitive to variations in biblical style, his primary concern was with a sense of majesty that he saw as pervading Scripture:

> But whether you read David, Isaiah, and the like, whose speech flows sweet and pleasing, or Amos the herdsman, Jeremiah, and Zechariah, whose harsher style savors of rusticity, that majesty of the Spirit of which I have spoken will be evident everywhere.[26]

This majesty was evident, for Calvin, because of its great power to move the reader or hearer, a power that he found lacking in classical oratory for all its elegance. The fact that simple language could have such force was to him proof that the words of Scripture mattered less than the Spirit that informed them: "The truth of Sacred Scripture is manifestly too powerful to need the art of words."[27] A sense of the majesty of biblical style became an important criterion for establishing the authority of the Bible. Sibbes makes this affective standard one of his proofs,[28] and the Westminster Confession offers "the majesty of style" as a reason for declaring the divinity of Scripture.[29] The ultimate warrant for this position was biblical: "The voice of the Lord is powerful, the voice of the Lord is full of majesty" (Ps. 29:4).

Perkins urged Puritan ministers to make their speech "simple and perspicuous, fit both for the peoples understanding and to express the Majestie of the Spirit."[30] Such majesty could best be conveyed, in other words, by a style that did not obscure it by unnecessary rhetorical complication. Biblical writers were seen as offering models for such a style, not only Paul and Jesus, both valued for speaking the language of ordinary men, but the prophets as well. The majesty of God shines through their writing, according to commentary of the sort that I have quoted, because this writing is genuine, "unaffected," to use Milton's term. For the Puritan preacher seeking to attain the simplicity that Perkins counseled the first task was to avoid the kind of ostentatious artifice that would reveal his own virtuosity rather than the majesty of the Spirit.[31]

One finds a different sense of biblical eloquence in Donne, who was attracted by what he called the "inexpressible texture and composition" of the Word. Donne rejoiced in the stylistic virtuosity of "a figurative, a metaphorical God:"[32]

> The Holy Ghost in penning the Scriptures delights himself not only with a propriety, but with a delicacy and harmony, and melody of language; with height of Metaphors, and other figures, which may work greater impressions upon the Readers, and not with barbarous, or triviall, or market, or homely language.[33]

He makes his case for the majesty of Scripture by arguing that the style of the Holy Spirit cannot be called "low," at one point characterizing it as "a diligent, and an artificial style."[34] Where Augustine had stressed the naturalness of biblical eloquence and shown that even an Amos was capable of it, Donne concentrated on the idea of God as supreme artificer. He could recognize the power of the Spirit acting through Scripture, as in the "holy vehemence" of some of Paul's language, but he could at the same time approach the Bible as a rich and various poem, with styles ranging from plain to "curious" and "harmonious." He praised it as "this Mosaick, this various, this mingled work."[35] Such delight in the complexity of the Bible no doubt owes something to Augustine's appreciation of the uses of different biblical styles, but Donne shows a fascination with texture and a preference for the curious over the simple that go beyond anything in *Christian Doctrine.*

Puritans are notorious for reducing the figurative language of the Bible to the flattest kind of expository prose. Richard Bernard, while urging ministers to imitate biblical similitudes in their preaching, paraphrased psalms and transformed them into diagrams starkly laying out the doctrines that he had extracted.[36] This kind of relentless clarification gives the impression that Puritan preachers, unlike Donne, saw the poetry of the Bible simply as hard matter that had to be "made fit" for their hearers. Yet, as Haller has shown, the best of these preachers drew extensively upon the imagery of the Bible to create what he called "the Puritan epic of wayfaring and warfaring."[37] Haller's brief discussions of many of the leading spiritual preachers suggest how their use of "lightsome similitudes" enabled them to give color and force to their renderings of spiritual struggle. A closer look at the sermons of Sibbes reveals how one of the more imaginative of these preachers could exploit figurative language to work upon the affections of his auditors.

Sibbes displays a typically Puritan reluctance to attach excessive importance to the language of the Bible. Those who lack grace, he says, may know the grammar of Scripture, the logic and rhetoric of Scripture, but fail to see "the things themselves:" "They stick in the stile" (2:462). Sibbes was careful, like Calvin, to preserve the distinction between the text and the Word itself, insisting that Scripture is but the "modus" for conveying the Word (1:197). One could get beyond the "shell," Sibbes felt, only through a spiritual awareness that would yield experimental knowledge of the things within. Such fear of sticking in the style, or stile (Sibbes seems to have intended both senses), did not have to mean that the words were husks, to be discarded to get at kernels of meaning. It did, however, preclude the kind of absorption in the text that one finds in Donne.

Sibbes's sermons offer abundant evidence of that instinct for communicating spiritual truths by means of similitudes drawn from daily experience that is one of the hallmarks of Puritan preaching. To illustrate his point that Christ will not break the bruised reed, Sibbes offers commonplace examples: a surgeon who will lance but not dismember, a mother who will not cast off a "sick and froward child" (1:45). The need to impress his hearers with the fact of original sin occasions a homelier similitude: "The mortar wherein garlic hath been stamped, will always smell of it" (1:62). Sibbes's handling of biblical images shows a similar regard for speaking to the experience of his readers. He took the metaphor of the bruised reed as an invitation to show his audience how to see their inevitable "bruising" as a positive spiritual state, a discipline in humiliation, and to join God in this work of bruising. By pointing out that Christ was "bruised for us," in the language of Isaiah, Sibbes provided a readily comprehensible image of divine love. The effect of his elaboration of the metaphor is to apply it to his hearer's condition, in familiar terms, with the end of arousing them to respond to a merciful Christ:

> Art thou bruised? Be of good comfort, he calleth thee; conceal not thy wounds, open all before him, keep not Satan's counsel. (1:46)

In *The Soul's Conflict*, a series of sermons that rivaled *The Bruised Reed* in popularity, Sibbes adapted the popular image of life as a sea to dramatize his sense of the tension of man's spiritual condition. Beginning with a traditional use of the image ("Here we are in a sea, where what can we look for but storms?" [1:141]), Sibbes proceeds to suggest that storms are God's way of raising a "right grief." Tumult is to be expected, even welcomed as a sign of spiritual life, although one should pray to Christ to "walk upon our souls, and command a calm there" (1:147). The ideal is perfect calm, a constancy above all storms sought by the heavenly minded soul, but Sibbes holds out little hope for achieving it in this life. In fact, he seems to have been attracted to the image of the sea because it expresses so well the dynamism of man's spiritual state. Affections are for him "the wind of the soul," a positive force that must nevertheless be regulated. The soul is properly active when it is neither "becalmed" nor "tossed with tempests to move disorderly" (1:159). Spiritual motion is essential, and Sibbes pictures this as a constant beating forward, against unfavorable wind and tide, toward the desired haven.

Again, the contrast with Donne is instructive. In the *Devotions* Donne asks God why he has so often presented afflictions "in the name of waters, and deep waters, and seas of waters" and then answers himself:

> Thou hast given a remedy against the deepest water by water; against the inundation of sin by baptism.... All our waters shall run into Jordan, and thy servants passed Jordan dry foot; they shall run into the red sea (the sea of thy Son's blood), and the red sea, that red sea, drowns none of thine.[38]

Such leaps of the imagination, from "deep waters" to the water of baptism and from the Red Sea to Christ's blood, reflect Donne's acute sense of the symbolic potential of biblical language. He counters the threatening waters of the Old Testament with appropriate symbols of redemption from the New. Although I have quoted from a work of meditation, the technique demonstrated here can be found in the sermons.[39] These amply display Donne's sensitivity to the interrelationships among widely scattered verses. He could lead his hearers through the intricacies of the temple of the Word because he was so able, and eager, to perceive its essential unity. As he puts it, in a variation on the old figure of the Bible as mirror,[40] "The Scriptures are as a room wainscotted with looking glass, we see all at once" (3:57).[41]

Janel Mueller has argued that for Donne the words of the Bible were "means of revelation." This attitude toward Scripture helps to explain the kind of spinning out of biblical images that one finds frequently in the sermons. According to Mueller, "in Donne's preaching the stress is on the figuring, imaging, signifying force of Biblical language in order to make it memorable in the special Augustinian sense."[42] Donne's aim, as she notes, was to bring the auditor by way of types and figures "to him that is *Logos* it self, the Word; to apprehend and apply Christ himself."[43] Although Sibbes would not have objected to Donne's purpose, his restrained handling of figurative language reflects a fundamentally different emphasis, upon understanding the interior world of the Christian and the stages of regeneration. Sibbes typically elaborates biblical metaphors and develops figures of his own, to illuminate the various spiritual states that Christians may expect to encounter. He is less concerned with typology than Donne, much more concerned with exactly how the "divinity in the word of God" (1:186), "powerfully unfolded" by the preacher, can work upon the soul. His sermons make one more conscious of the nature of spiritual experience than of the mysteries of the text.

Sibbes derived some of his most effective imagery for describing the regenerate soul from the Song of Solomon. His very attraction to this most lyric and sensuous book of the Bible belies the stereotype of the Puritan preacher as someone intent on setting forth doctrine in the plainest fashion possible. The Song of Songs was commonly read as an allegory of the "Love, Union, and Communion betwixt Christ and the Church, and consequently betwixt Him and every believing soul," as Sibbes puts it in the subtitle to a series of twenty sermons published as *Bowels Opened*. Bernard, whom Sibbes cites several times, and numerous commentators after him took the remarkably erotic imagery of the Canticles as God's way of showing the intimacy possible between a loving Christ and a redeemed soul; this was frequently seen as leading to a state of mystical union with Christ for the believer.[44] By comparison with much of this commentary Sibbes's use of the imagery of the Song of Songs seems restrained, yet it served him effectively as a way of exploring the relationship between Christ and the soul in sensuous language that would appeal to his hearers as straightforward exposition of doctrine could not.

Sibbes at one point defines preaching as "the lifting up of the banner of Christ's love," citing the Canticles as an illustration of this love and its appeal: "When the beauty of Christ is unfolded, it draws the wounded, hungry, soul unto him" (2:232). He was able to see the imagery of the Song of Songs as a revelation of this love and beauty because, as he puts it,

> Christ is the object of all the senses. Beloved, he is not only beauty to the eye, but sweetness to the smell, and to the taste. (2:152)

Thus he can declare the presence of Christ, or the manifestation of Christ in the ordinances of the church, to be "delectable as spices and flowers." Sibbes used biblical language to give Christ's wooing of the soul a vivid immediacy:

> He that knocks and stands knocking, while his locks are bedewed with the drops of the night, doth he delight in strangeness, that makes all this love to a Christian's soul? (2:58)

Yet he can suggest the tenderness of Christ, and the delights of the responsive soul, without transmuting eroticism into spiritual ecstasy in the manner of a Bernard or a St. John of the Cross. For him Christ is less a lover than a "loving Shepherd" seeking the "sweetest pastures" for his flock (2:188).

Sibbes found friendship in some ways a better term than marriage for the relationship of Christ and the soul; marriage itself was to him "conjugal friendship," the "sweetest" kind. The friendship exemplified by the Song of Songs involves mutual sympathy, mutual comfort, and perfect liberty: "Christ openeth his secrets to us, and we to him" (2:37). It is a communion in which Christ and the soul delight in each other. Sibbes stresses the active participation of the soul in this relationship. One must labor "to be such as Christ may delight in," he says, because "where he tastes sweetness he will bring more with him" (2:29). At the same time Sibbes sees the grace of Christ as a necessary stimulus, the myrrh that calls forth myrrh from the soul. As he puts it in a memorable image in *The Bruised Reed* drawn from the Canticles:

> The heart of a Christian is Christ's garden, and his graces are as so many sweet spices and flowers, which his Spirit blowing upon makes them to send forth a sweet savour. (1:75)

The moral that Sibbes goes on to point—keep the soul open for the Spirit to bring in "fresh forces to subdue corruption"—underscores the fact that for him this interaction was part of the continuous process of sanctification. He was more interested in the prospect of spiritual growth, and in the vital relationship that he saw as engendering it, than in any possibility of mystical rapture. The communion that he sought was not a contemplative state but an active one affecting every aspect of daily experience: "*A Christian life should be nothing but a communion and intercourse with Christ*, a walking in the Spirit" (2:87).

One of Sibbes's fundamental purposes was to teach his hearers to recognize and obey what he liked to call the "sweet motions" of the Spirit, and to do this he sought figurative means of describing these mysterious motions, deriving his illustrations primarily from the Bible. He describes the Spirit as working "like new wine, enlarging the spirit from one degree of praising to another" (1:254) and compares its operations with those of fire, anointing oil, and wind. Sibbes tends to analyze his metaphors, breaking them down into various senses. Thus he will list six ways in which the graces of the Spirit are like anointing oil or ointment. Such oil is sweet and delightful, it strengthens, it heals, it makes nimble the joints of the soul, and so forth (3:443–46). If Sibbes did no more than enumerate possible implications of a metaphor, as Benjamin Keach does in his *Tropologia*, one might accuse him of squeezing all the imaginative life out of it. But in fact he skillfully plays upon its connotations as he applies a particular sense to the state of his hearers, drawing upon a few texts to illustrate his central point. He cites texts showing the fragrance of ointment, for example, to suggest that grace makes one delectable to God and sweet to the church. Other texts establish the corollary, that men in a state of nature are unclean: "swine and goats, stinking creatures" (3:444). Sibbes's explication is given coherence by his clear, well-focused aim: to explain the action of grace upon the soul.

One finds in Sibbes a more explicit and detailed explanatory framework than one does in Donne. Sibbes uses the customary devices of the Puritan sermon—numbered reasons and uses, interspersed with observations, objections, questions and answers—to show the auditor how a particular metaphor might apply to his experience. When he sets out to explain the operations of the Holy Spirit, he does this by leading the auditor by a series of well-marked steps to recognize their complexity. Like the wind, the Spirit blows where it lists; it can bring fragrance to bear down all before it. The related image of the soul as garden is developed in similar fashion to show the dependence of the Christian upon the wind of the Spirit: "We ebb and flow, open and shut, as the Spirit blows upon us" (2:12). Central images take on a cumulative force in Sibbes's hands. Having shown the power of the "quickening" wind of the Spirit to make the "barren wilderness" of the heart fruitful, he explores the nature of this fruitfulness and how to sustain it. Although Sibbes's applications may seem mechanical at times, he shows a considerable gift for exploiting the rich vein of biblical imagery that he found in the Song of Solomon, Isaiah, and elsewhere to suggest the gentleness and power of the grace conveyed by the spirit and the intense satisfactions to be found in responding to it. His favorite word, "sweet," takes on many of the connotations of these images. The frequency with which Sibbes uses it suggests a basic confidence that the interactions of God and man will be productive, that the garden will bloom and spices flow forth as a benevolent Spirit releases the sweetness to be found in man.

Another side of Sibbes emerges in *The Soul's Conflict*, his most ambitious effort to describe the turbulence of spiritual life and show how it might be stilled. In this series of sermons, as in *The Bruised Reed*, he addressed himself to the troubled and tempted in an effort to comfort the "perplexed soul." Sibbes took his text from a psalm thought to represent the self-questioning of David in his period of exile:

Why art thou cast down, O my soul? and why art thou disquieted within me? hope thou in God; for I shall yet praise him, who is the health of my countenance, and my God. (Ps. 42:11)

Sibbes saw this psalm as offering a moving image of David's "unruly grief" ("*the passionate passages of a broken and troubled spirit*" [2:130]) and at the same time proof that a spiritual victory over the heart was possible through trust in God. His procedure was to use the humanly engaging example of David to explore the nature of grief and to offer a model by which one could learn to deal with the soul's tempestuous inner weather.

The Psalms were commonly regarded as a storehouse of spiritual comfort and instruction and, as Calvin phrased it, "An Anatomy of all the Parts of the Soul."[45] Sibbes calls them "the anatomy of a holy man" and, like Calvin, sees the psalms as calling one to self-examination and a recognition of inward corruption. While Protestants generally agreed that David's experiences could be taken to represent that of all Christians,[46] they might examine this experience more or less closely and make different uses of it. For example, Donne was drawn to the penitential psalms whereas Sibbes was not. In a series of Lenten sermons on Psalm 32 Donne develops the themes of penitence and mortification and devotes one sermon to what he calls the "mystery of Confession."[47] The sermons published as *The Soul's Conflict* are concerned primarily with David's "wrestling with God" and with the stages of his progress toward reconciliation. Sibbes's analysis presents David as the archetypal "holy man," a hero of faith with the tenacity to persevere until he subdues the "unquietness of his spirit": "David must bid his soul trust, and trust, and trust again before it will yield" (1:200).

Donne and Sibbes both saw David's spiritual struggles as exemplary and found in the psalms abundant occasions for discussions of human sinfulness and divine grace; yet their interests and techniques diverge in significant ways. In his sermons on the psalms Donne distinguishes three kinds of meaning, summarized in this comment upon Psalm 38:4: "*Historically, David; morally, we; Typically, Christ* is the subject of this text" (5:97). While both preachers gave most of their attention to the moral application of the text to the lives of their hearers, Donne proved more interested than Sibbes in reading the psalms typologically and less interested in analyzing David's spiritual state. With the psalms, as with other texts, Donne proceeds by way of an intense scrutiny of key words. Of three sermons upon Psalm 38:4 ("For mine iniquities are gone over my head, as a heavy burden, they are too heavy for mee"), one focuses upon the meaning of "heavy," another upon the meaning of "burden." Donne saw himself as unfolding mysteries implicit in the language of the text: "How exact and curious was the holy Ghost, in *David*, in choice of words?" (2:93). The mysteries themselves may have to do with the nature of original sin, or of divine power, among other large subjects. Their explication has the general effect of illustrating man's dependence upon God's mercy.

Donne's sermon on Psalm 38:2 ("For thine arrowes stick fast in me, and thy hand presses me sore") offers a good example of his method. Donne takes the arrows of the text as a metaphor for the temptations and tribulations of all men. The metaphor enables him to enumerate characteristics of temptations (unexpected, swift, invisible) and to demonstrate that they come from the hand of God, seen as directing the arrows and limiting their pain. Remedies are to be found in the promises of Scripture, ultimately in the experience of Christ, whose sufferings, like David's, are described by the metaphor. Donne gives relatively little space to the process of dealing with spiritual wounds (pulling out the arrows). In *The Soul's Conflict* Sibbes focuses more sharply upon the condition of the sinner and specific means for improving it, devoting many pages to the causes of spiritual disquiet, numbered and subdivided into kinds.

Sibbes's discussion of what it means to "cast down" the soul will illustrate his method. In his analysis of this particular cause of disquiet, Sibbes begins by fixing the blame for the condition, generalizing from the example of David:

> It was not the troubled condition that so disquieted David's soul, for if he had had a quiet mind, it would not have troubled him. But David yielded to the discouragements of the flesh, and the flesh, so far as it is unsubdued, is like the sea that is always casting mire and dirt of doubts, discouragements, and murmurings in the soul. (1:142)

He observes that it is the nature of sorrow to cast down ("Grief is like lead to the soul, heavy and cold") and that such sorrow weakens the soul. The first step toward recovery is to recognize the source of the problem, the sin of pride, and the progenitor of that sin, Satan:

> No creature under heaven so low cast down as Satan, none more lifted up in pride, none so full of discord. The impurest spirits are the most disquiet and stormy spirits, troublesome to themselves and others; for when the soul leaves God once, and looks downward, what is there to stay it from disquiet: Remove the needle from the pole-star, and it is always stirring and trembling, never quiet till it be right again. (1:143)

The remedies offered by Sibbes are to question oneself about the causes of discontent and to charge oneself to trust God, recognizing that there is no good reason to be discouraged. He anticipates his final "use," "labour for a calmed spirit," by insisting that until the Spirit "meekens" the soul it is not quiet enough to receive "the seed of the word": "It is ill sowing in a storm; so a stormy spirit will not suffer the word to take place" (1:143).

The psalms offered Sibbes a record of experience that he could draw upon to instruct his hearers on such topics as how to strike at the roots of sin and how to recognize and respond to the "holy motions" of the Spirit. The crises of David, as he describes them, would have seemed familiar to a Puritan of the early seventeenth century: "David was very watchful, yet we see here he was surprised unawares by the sudden rebellion of his heart" (1:177). Many of the themes that he elaborates are recognizably Puritan, for example, the need for "waiting upon God" and the ways of recognizing "signs" of the Spirit's action. Sibbes's focus upon the inner life of the believer is characteristic of spiritual preaching and reflects a common belief in the importance of recognizing the impact of God upon human experience:

> If we were well read in the story of our own lives, we might have a divinity of our own, drawn out of the observation of God's particular dealing with us. (1:277)

The primary use of memory for Sibbes is not to recall a text but to draw upon the treasury of experience to meet the world's assaults: "The use of a sanctified memory is to lose nothing that may help in time of need" (1:277). Scripture served him as an instrument with which to analyze experience such as David's, that he might show others how to understand their own.

Sibbes presented David's dealings with his soul as a model for the kind of self-examination he and other Puritan preachers consistently encouraged: "Let us see more every day into the state of our own souls" (1:165). One should cite the dejected soul before the court of the heart and press it to give an account of itself, according to Sibbes. He saw such a trial, in which conscience is to act as both accuser and judge, as a process of reasoning with oneself, a process that leads to understanding: of the temptations posed by Satan, of one's sin or predisposition to it, and of the grounds for trusting in God. Such an emphasis upon calling the soul to a "reckoning" is to be expected in a Puritan preacher, though Sibbes offers particularly detailed instructions for conducting the desired inner dialogue, which he sometimes describes as a "soliloquy" aimed at awakening the soul. David's psalm was to him an admirable example of such a soliloquy. Sibbes is uncommonly subtle and persistent in showing "all the turnings and windings and byways of our souls" of which one should seek to be aware. His analyses of the causes of disquiet, including a long section on the disorders of the imagination, reveal him to be an unusually discerning spiritual doctor.

Sibbes's insistence upon the active character of the search for spiritual peace is worth comment. Soliloquies not only awaken the soul but,

> keep it in a holy exercise, by stirring up the grace of faith to its proper function. It is not so much the having of grace, as grace in *exercise*, that preserves the soul. (1:199)

There was no relaxing for Sibbes, or for Puritans generally, because of the sense that exercise, "motion," was essential to spiritual health. This attitude meant that "seasonable grief" could be welcomed as a stimulus to holiness: "Troubles stir up David; David being stirred, stirs up himself" (1:199). For Sibbes the soul "without action" was like "an instrument not played," or, in the terms of a more common image, like a ship idled in the harbor. He used the image of a spring to suggest the ideal action of the soul:

> The spirit, as a spring, will be cleansing of itself more and more. Whereas the heart of a carnal man is like a standing pool, whatsoever is cast into it, there it rests. (1:202)

> Our praising God should not be as sparks out of a flint, but as water out of a spring, natural, ready, free, as God's love to us is. (1:255)

In Sibbes's view the motions of the Spirit should call forth answering motions in the soul of the Christian; anything less than a dynamic response was regarded as spiritual stagnation.

The end of all this activity was the rest that Sibbes felt, with Augustine,[48] could be found only in God. In *The Soul's Conflict* Sibbes imagines this rest as a kind of spiritual peace to be found through rational self-examination followed by the exercise of a faith that will quiet the tumult of the soul.

> The way, then, whereby faith quieteth the soul, is by raising it above all discontentments and storms here below, and pitching it upon God, thereby uniting it to him, whence it draws virtue to oppose and bring under whatsoever troubles its peace. (1:213–14)

The "perfect rest in God" to which the soul should aspire is attainable only in heaven; in the meanwhile one is supported by "sanctifying and quieting graces."

Quieting the soul was for Sibbes a matter of recovering insofar as one could the communion with God destroyed by the fall.

> The soul was created in that sweet harmony where there was no discord, as an instrument in tune, fit to be moved to any duty; as a clean, neat glass, the soul represented God's image and holiness. (1:173)

> When passions are subdued and the soul purged and cleared, there is nothing to hinder the impression of God's Spirit; the soul is fitted as a clean glass to receive light from above. (1:211)

The ideal of order was inseparable from those of peace and harmony with God ("the God of peace, is the God of order" [1:168]). Sibbes sought to persuade his hearers of "the beauty of a well-ordered soul," suggesting that one attains this by keeping the affections "in due proportion." His comments about the role of reason in ordering the soul may seem to suggest a classical ideal of temperance, but one must remember that for him the Spirit was the necessary catalyst for any real progress of the soul. It is in statements about the power of the Spirit that Sibbes strikes his most distinctive notes:

> The soul without the Spirit is darkness and confusion, full of self-accusing and self-tormenting thoughts. If we let the Spirit come in, it will scatter all and settle the soul in a sweet quiet. (5:452)

In *The Soul's Conflict* Sibbes showed himself to be acutely conscious not only of the inner conflict between grace and nature, spirit and flesh, but of the imperfect state of the church in his time. Sibbes saw in the situation of David in exile, hunted by Saul "as a partridge in the wilderness" (1:105), an emblem of the sufferings of Christians in a world in which the enemies of the church flourished. His use of such stock terms for Rome as "antichrist" and "Babylon" suggests that he was thinking of the Catholics, but he probably meant to include as well the antagonists of the Puritan movement in England and "carnal people" generally. Although Sibbes could find some signs that the church was beginning "to lift up her head again" he did not look to the speedy completion of the Reformation in England, as Milton would in 1641. He saw the church as not yet prepared for "a full and glorious deliverance," lamenting the quarrelsomeness of Christians and their "coldness and indifferency in religion" (1:261). Still, in "these times of Jacob's trouble and Zion's sorrow," he could take comfort from God's promises of deliverance for his people and emulate David's posture of "patient waiting."

In concluding *The Soul's Conflict* Sibbes once more characterizes man's "conflicting state" and insists upon the need for assurance that whatever God does is for man's ultimate benefit, posing possible questions (*"But why then doth God appear as a stranger to me?"*) and answering them. His procedure in the final section reflects an overwhelming concern with making his message clear: by summary, variations upon important themes, and an imaginary dialogue with his hearers. Sibbes uses biblical verses sparingly, weaving them into the fabric of his prose rather than descanting upon images or words in the manner of Donne. As in his sermons generally, he hammers away at his main points in sentences that are simply phrased and tend to be short, even aphoristic ("If trouble be lengthened, lengthen my patience"). The style is modest, eschewing witty effects and elaborate rhythmic patterning. It does not build to climaxes, yet Sibbes's concluding paragraph speaks with authority, even resonance:

> Thus we see that discussing of objections in the consistory of the soul settles the soul at last, faith at length silencing all risings to the contrary. All motion tends to rest, and ends in it. God is the centre and resting-

place of the soul, and here David takes up his rest, and so let us. Then whatsoever times come, we are sure of a hiding-place and sanctuary.

The deliberateness of this conclusion is characteristic of Sibbes. It is not meant to work the hearer up to a pitch of devotion, rather to consolidate the assurance that he has been given in sermons stretching over many weeks. Sibbes's summarizing comment suggests that he has led his hearers through a reasonable kind of proceeding, a "consistory of the soul" in which objections could be raised and calmly dealt with, and that he is confident of having settled their fears. Such settling, or quieting, of the soul was one of the fundamental aims of Sibbes's preaching. He had first to arouse the soul, to stir it to "motion," then to speak to intensified spiritual needs: by offering instruction in the delights of sanctification and guidance through storms of doubt. In concluding *The Soul's Conflict* Sibbes leads his hearers skillfully back to one of the central themes of his sermons, that God is "the resting-place of the soul." He speaks his consoling words plainly and with an assurance that they will serve as remedies against troubles in the church as well as in the soul, "whatsoever times come." In the simplicity of the language and in the conviction that it carries there is a kind of quiet strength peculiar to the best of the spiritual preachers, those most finely attuned to the needs of their hearers and best able to draw upon the resources of biblical language to speak to them.

3. Richard Baxter and the Saints' Rest

In a long and hectically active life Richard Baxter produced enough works of controversial and practical divinity to fill twenty-three volumes in a nineteenth-century edition, but he remained best known in his own time for his early devotional treatise, *The Saints Everlasting Rest* (1650). This unwieldy work of over eight hundred quarto pages went through twelve editions in Baxter's lifetime, the first eight of these appearing in the 1650s.[1] Like Baxter's immense history of his life and times, *Reliquiae Baxterianae*, *The Saints Everlasting Rest* is likely to be read now only in a drastically abridged version, if at all, but it makes serious claims on the attention of anyone interested in the seventeenth century. It is a compelling statement of some of the central themes of Puritan spirituality, strongly colored by Baxter's immediate experience of the chaos of civil war as a chaplain with the Parliamentary army.

By the force and quantity of his writings and by the sheer persistence of his efforts to promote unity in the church Baxter made himself one of the most important religious leaders of the century. When he wrote *The Saints Everlasting Rest* in 1647, during his recovery from an illness that terminated his career as an army chaplain, most of the accomplishments for which he is remembered lay before him. Baxter returned to Kidderminster to take up the position of lecturer which he had held briefly before the war and enjoyed remarkable success in reforming the unpromising inhabitants of that town. In the course of his ministry he established the Worcestershire Association, a model for regional organizations of ministers concerned with establishing church discipline. Baxter was sufficiently well known to be summoned to London in 1655 to help frame the articles of religion in the Instrument of Government. At the time of the Restoration he emerged as the leading spokesman for non-Anglican ministers in their unsuccessful efforts to reach an accommodation with the new ecclesiastical establishment. After declining a bishopric and refusing to take the oath required by the Act of Uniformity, Baxter persisted in trying to preach, in a variety of circumstances, and found himself harassed and frequently prosecuted for his efforts. At the age of seventy the "Bishop of Nonconformity," as Baxter came to be known, went to jail because he was unable to pay a stiff fine.

One must go to the *Reliquiae Baxterianae* to get a sense of the complexity of the man and of the frustrations he experienced in attempting to chart a moderate course in an intensely factional age. As that work reveals, he pursued the tasks he set himself with an energy and determination that are extraordinary even in a time when everyone seems to have been writing furiously. The very bulk of Baxter's writing suggests how keenly he felt the need to set right the errors and attack the spiritual deficiencies that he saw everywhere. In the preface to *The Christian Directory*, a virtual encyclopedia of advice concerning every aspect of Christian life, Baxter replied to critics who suggested that he wrote too much by pointing to the immensity of his task:

> And as to the *number* and length of my Writings, it is my own labour that maketh them so, and my own great trouble, that the World cannot be sufficiently instructed and edified by fewer words.[2]

This attitude helps to explain the prolixity of *The Saints Everlasting Rest*; it was difficult for Baxter to stop.

Baxter's dramatic rendering of the circumstances in which he began *The Saints Everlasting Rest*, in a letter dedicating the whole work to the people of Kidderminster, suggests that he wrote it as a spiritual stay against fear of his own impending death:

> Being in my quarters far from home, cast into extream languishing (by the sudden loss of about a Gallon of blood after many years foregoing weakness) and having no acquaintance about me, nor any Books, but my Bible, and living in continual expectation of death, I bent my thoughts on my Everlasting Rest: And because my memory through extream weakness was imperfect, I took my pen, and began to draw up my own funeral Sermon; or some helps for my own Meditations of Heaven, to sweeten both the Rest of my life, and my death.[3]

The work that resulted quickly outgrew Baxter's original plan. It consists of four substantial parts, each with a separate dedication, divided into chapters and subdivided into sections. Baxter began with a text, "There remaineth a Rest to the people of God" (Heb. 4:9), and proceeded to develop arguments by means of a numbered series of reasons, occasionally distinguishing uses. His systematic approach to his subject suggests the organization of a Puritan sermon, but the subject itself exerts a centrifugal pull against his efforts to contain it. He must deal with hindrances to a heavenly life as well as with helps, with the ways the soul clings to the world as well as with the promises of heaven. Because a belief in the validity of those promises is critical to the whole undertaking, he gives one entire part, the second, to arguments establishing the authority of Scripture. Baxter shows some regard for the form of the work in checking a tendency to engage in controversy ("but I forget myself in thus digressing"), but one finds him enlarging the second edition by two chapters (one an excursus on the signs of justification), a long preface to the second part, and a postscript answering a critic. Finally, form mattered less than the demands of his seemingly all-inclusive subject.

Those critics who have discussed *The Saints Everlasting Rest* have tended to consider the fourth part by itself, as a treatise on formal meditation.[4] The looseness of the overall structure of the work seems to invite such an approach. The second and the fourth parts, at least, appear detachable, and some sections or clusters of sections within the four parts constitute meditations that could stand alone. In such a meditation Baxter may develop variations on a particular theme, linking them by repeating a key adjective ("seasonable") or imperative ("Consider"), or he may attempt to convey a particular state ("joy") that he associates with the rest of the saints. These sections function as part of a larger argument, but they grow into meditations as Baxter warms to his subject and seeks to work his reader up to a pitch of desire. The table of contents reveals their place in the design of *The Saints Everlasting Rest* but not their force or the way the vigor of Baxter's prose ebbs and flows in the work as a whole. In fact the formal organization of *The Saints Everlasting Rest* is not the best indication of the kind of coherence the work possesses. This has more to do with the sense of urgency that animates Baxter's prose and with the way he keeps returning to his fundamental preoccupations. Meditation on heaven was for Baxter less an occasional activity than a way of energizing one's spiritual life. He could not talk about it without exploring the nature of the rest that for him was the most compelling subject for meditation and arguing, at great length, the necessity for becoming "heavenly-minded." It takes him until the middle of the fourth part to get to the point of offering "Directions" for meditation. While some of his concerns seem more immediately relevant to the method of meditation that he outlines than others, it is difficult to understand this method without considering attitudes that inform the entire work and the way these were shaped by the particular circumstances in which Baxter wrote.

Baxter's approach to meditation was unusually eclectic for someone writing in the mid-seventeenth century for a predominantly Puritan audience. He was able to assimilate influences of widely varying kinds: Puritan divines, church fathers, Bishop Joseph Hall, George Herbert (whose poetry he quotes), Jean Charlier de Gerson (fifteenth-century chancellor of the University of Paris and the author of influential devotional works). Louis Martz saw Baxter as consciously imitating devotional practices of the Counter Reformation which had been neglected, in Martz's view, because of a Calvinistic preoccupation with looking for evidences of grace. He appealed to Catholic tradition to explain Baxter's use of the senses to recreate biblical scenes and his emphasis upon the need to arouse the affections, especially the love of God. It has since been demonstrated, primarily by U. Milo Kaufmann and Barbara Lewalski, that it is necessary to speak of a tradition of Protestant meditation in England antedating Baxter.[5] Kaufmann has suggested that *The Saints Everlasting Rest* belongs to an emerging Puritan tradition of heavenly meditation. He shows that previous Puritan writers had appealed to sensuous experience as a way of anticipating the delights of heaven, citing Lewis Bayly, Thomas Adams, and particularly Richard Sibbes, who goes to some lengths to justify the "holy use of imagination" to heighten one's faith.[6] Kaufmann's discussion of heavenly meditation gets at an important aspect of Puritan thought that deserves further exploration. To understand how broadly Baxter conceived heavenly meditation, and how seriously he regarded its claims, one must at least consider such questions as how a pervasive concern with heavenly-mindedness shaped Puritan writing and why this concern is so central to Puritan spirituality.

Baxter's marginal citations reveal his openness to Catholic influences, and his attraction to the work of the moderate Anglican Hall suggests another channel by which some of these influences might have reached him.[7] Baxter's awareness of writers in the Catholic tradition is not unusual among learned Puritans. References to the fathers adorn the margins of such men as Robert Bolton, John Preston, and Sibbes, all of whom appear in the select list of "old solid Divines" (with Perkins and Dod) that Baxter counsels his Kidderminster flock to read (in the general dedication). Baxter's references to later writers such as Nicholas of Cusa and Gerson might have been more surprising to his readers. He can exclaim of Gerson, in the course of attacking the indifference of Antinomians to meditation, "Read this you Libertines, and learn the better way of Devotion from a Papist" (*The Saints Everlasting Rest*, p. 662). Baxter cites both Nicholas of Cusa and Gerson on the love of God and the latter on the need to meditate and to purge oneself of sin beforehand. He also cites Gerson on the role of the Holy Spirit in meditation, an emphasis that had previously attracted Luther. Yet there is no real need to believe, as Martz suggests, that Baxter learned to meditate on the Passion from the pseudo-Bonaventura or that he knew the techniques of Ignatius and François de Sales; one can account for his practice otherwise. Baxter refers far more frequently to the fathers, especially to Augustine and Cyprian, than to medieval and later Catholic writers. Their descriptions of heaven and of the state of the blessed clearly sparked his imagination, and he repeats their appeals to abjure the world and cultivate a love of God. Baxter goes all the way back to Gregory and Augustine to justify comparing the delights of heaven with actual sensuous experience. His sense of the pleasures of heaven and of the importance of imagining them owes much to these writers; yet such influences do not alter the fundamentally Puritan emphases of Baxter's work.

Protestant meditative writing proved capable of absorbing elements of

Catholic tradition without necessarily imitating the methods of Counter Reformation writers. Frank Huntley sees Joseph Hall's meditations as imbued with the spirit of the Augustinian monks of Windesheim and notes that Hall invokes Augustine, Bernard, and Bonaventure for "their emphasis upon the heart rather than the brain."[8] Irvonwy Morgan has suggested that Puritan preachers during Elizabeth's reign practiced a "discipline of godliness" that consciously recalled medieval monasticism while remaining steadfastly in the world rather than withdrawing from it to seek perfection.[9] Protestants concerned with spiritual discipline and the practice of meditation inevitably shared the concern of their predecessors with purging the affections and schooling the Christian in ways of approaching God. They drew upon what they found useful and inoffensive in Catholic tradition while developing characteristic methods and emphases of their own.

Barbara Lewalski singles out a focus on the Bible and a special kind of application to the self as characterizing Protestant meditation.[10] My discussion assumes that it is useful to distinguish Puritan emphases within the broader tradition, especially in attempting to understand the character of Baxter's work. One can find pronounced variations in the ways different kinds of Protestants approached the Bible and in the manner in which they applied it. The intense concern of Puritan writers with rousing the affections is particularly noticeable. This concern frequently generates extensive directions for overcoming "lets" to meditation and for "debating with ourselves about our mortalitie and corruption," as Richard Rogers put it.[11] Such attention to the motions of the heart springs from a considerably darker view of human nature than one sees in Hall. Rogers exclaims:

> How doth it [meditation] make us acquainted with the manifold rebellions of our nature: with our blindnes, securitie, earthlines, and infinit other loathsome filthinesses.[12]

The dour Rogers presents an extreme version of an attitude that underlies the preoccupation of Baxter with the dialogue with the self, or *soliloquy,* as it was called. For all his eclecticism, Baxter strongly resembles the older Puritan divines such as Rogers and Robert Bolton in the spirit in which he approached meditation.

Puritan writers do not show much concern with systems of meditation, at least until they begin to assimilate the one introduced by Hall, but they continually exhort their readers to meditate, and some offer what can be called treatises on meditation as parts of larger works on. godly living. Baxter's Puritan audience would not have been surprised at being offered a "Directory for the getting and keeping of the Heart in Heaven" by the practice of "Heavenly Meditation." Meditation was commonly described as "heavenly" or "divine" (the terms are virtually interchangeable) and seen as a means of raising the heart to heaven. Paul had urged the Christian, "Set your mind on things above, not on things on the earth" (Col. 3:1), and had declared, in a verse that Baxter quotes on the title page to part 4, "our conversation is in heaven" (Phil. 3:20). It was generally assumed that the faithful should strive for familiarity with God through meditation, prayer, and public worship that would accustom them to thinking heavenly thoughts. Baxter's originality lay in focusing exclusively on the "rest" of the saints, normally one of a number of possible subjects for meditation, and in placing unusual emphasis upon the imaginative re-creation of celestial scenes as a means of achieving "heavenly-mindedness."

Baxter's view of the scope and importance of heavenly meditation, encouraged by Sibbes and a host of others, has deep roots in Protestant theology.[13] In the *Institutes* Calvin argues that one should learn to meditate on heaven by cultivating a contempt for the world.[14] He took the need for such meditation for granted:

> So the only prop for our faith and patience is to disregard the state of our present life and direct our minds and senses to the last day, and pass through the world's hindrances until the fruit of our faith at last appears.[15]

The underlying figure here is the familiar one of Christian life as a journey through a hostile world toward the New Jerusalem. Calvin affirms that meditation on judgment and the ultimate reward of the saints is necessary to sustain the faith that makes the journey possible. Thoughts of the end not only motivate one to think of life as a journey but also serve as a preservative against sin.

Calvin gives little indication of the form meditation might take, other than to suggest that it is "a true and holy thinking about Christ which forthwith bears us up into heaven."[16] The figure that Calvin uses here, in picturing meditation as enabling one to ascend "forthwith" to heaven, is a commonplace one that a number of Puritan writers before Baxter employ. Arthur Dent in the *Plaine Mans Path-way to Heaven* (1601) has his spokesman Theologus say that the Christian should attempt to "soare aloft as the Eagles" in order to see the world in a proper perspective:

> I beseech the Almightie God, give us his holy spirit, whereby we may be carried above this world, into the mountains of Myrrhe, and the mountains of Spices. For how happie a thing it is, to have our conversation in heaven! that is, to have an inward conversation with God, by much prayer, reading, meditation, and heavenly affections.[17]

Robert Bolton, writing two decades later, gives an indication of the form that such soaring might take. In a passage that strikingly anticipates Baxter's sustained efforts to realize the experience of soaring to heaven Bolton meditates on Christ and the glory of the saints:

Let thy sould full often soare aloft upon the wings of faith, unto the glory
of the Empyrean Heaven, where God dwelleth, and bathe it selfe beforehand with many a sweet meditation in that everlasting blisse above.[18]

Bolton goes on to advise the reader to "looke" upon the glorious body of
Christ, the brightness of the place, the fellowship of the saints, and, finally,
Jehovah, the object of beatific vision. He talks about the need to arouse the
affections to a love of God and the possibility of achieving "a very reall
fruitfull fore-taste of eternall joyes."[19] Like Baxter, Bolton frequently cites
Augustine (an Augustinian injunction to ascend frequently to heaven
appears in the margin next to the passage quoted above). He places particular stress on achieving a state of "heavenly-mindedness," seen as enabling
one to walk with God.

To understand the place of *The Saints Everlasting Rest* in Protestant
meditation it is necessary to look at the influence of Joseph Hall in more
detail. Kaufmann makes a case for two contrasting traditions of Puritan
meditation, a "line of Hall" dominated by the logical categories and the
systematic procedure for arousing the affections that Hall adapted from the
scala meditationis, and a tradition of heavenly meditation culminating in
Baxter. His distinction is useful, in calling attention to divergent strains in
Puritan meditation, but it has the disadvantage of implying that these can
be regarded as distinct, when in fact they sometimes coexist in a writer. It is
perhaps more accurate to speak of various tendencies in Puritan meditation
than of definable lines or traditions.[20] Hall himself talks of the need to
"Soare up to heaven in Meditation" and suggests that we "see our Saviour
with *Steven,* we talke with God as *Moses,* and by this we are ravished with
blessed Paul into Paradise; and see that heaven which wee are loath to
leave."[21] Hall illustrated his method by showing how one might meditate on
the glory of the saints, in the process imagining scenes of heavenly bliss that
bear comparison with Baxter's, although the latter are far more sustained
and dramatic. While Baxter developed a method that differs in crucial ways
from Hall's, he may well have been influenced by Hall's treatment of this
subject and by his illustration of the technique of imagining the pleasures of
heaven by comparing them with those of this life.[22] Baxter responded to
biblical instances of visionary experience that attracted Hall and like him
used the device of imagining human life as antlike when seen from a
heavenly prospect. In his late *Soliloquies,* published in 1651, Hall urges the
importance of cultivating a "heavenly conversation" with God and of
imagining the glory of the saints in a heaven "visible to our faith."[23] Baxter's
marginal references to a number of these soliloquies in the second edition of
The Saints Everlasting Rest make it clear that he responded to Hall's
heavenly-mindedness.

This side of Hall tended to be neglected by those writers who adopted his
convenient format for discussing meditation (with chapters on such topics

as the circumstances of meditation and the differences between occasional and deliberate meditation) and his schematic method. Hall prescribes a series of logical operations for the intellect. One must describe the subject, divide it, consider its causes and its effects, enumerate its qualities, contrast present misery with heavenly pleasure, and finally consider the testimonies of Scripture. The process of rousing the affections follows a series of distinct stages, beginning with an effort to "taste" what has been conceived, continuing with a sequence which includes an inward recognition of dullness and a wish that the heart might be carried to heaven, proceeding to a confession of weakness and a prayer for success, and culminating in an act of submission and thanksgiving to God.

John Downame's A Guide to Godlynesse (1629) and the abridgment of Richard Rogers's Seven Treatises (1603), published in 1618 as The Practice of Christianitie, provide two early and striking instances of the way Hall shaped Puritan discussion of formal meditation. The fact that Rogers's editor would rewrite the section on meditation in a popular handbook on Christian living to conform to Hall's method suggests the high regard in which The Arte of Divine Meditation had come to be held. Downame praised Hall as "one who in his kind leaveth all others farre behind him"[24] and took over the substance of his method. Isaac Ambrose in Media (1654) and Edmund Calamy in his Art of Divine Meditation (1680) also borrowed significantly from Hall, as Kaufmann has shown.[25] Yet these influential Puritan divines could take over Hall's method and still convey a very different impression of the ends and possible uses of meditation. Rogers, Downame, and Ambrose present meditation, in the course of long treatises on Christian life, as one of a number of private aids to godliness (along with watchfulness and self-examination) by which one's daily life may be ordered. In Downame's view,

> It [meditation] purifieth the minde...it governeth the affections, it directeth the actions, correcteth excesse, composeth our manners, orderly amendeth and graceth our lives, and finally, conferreth experimentall and feeling knowledge, both of things divine and human.[26]

Downame actually distinguishes meditation from contemplation, reserving the latter to the great practitioners who can, like eagles, "as weary of the earth, raise up their soules, and renew their wonted flight."[27] He and other Puritan writers on the subject represent meditation in homelier terms, sometimes as a means of chewing and digesting divine truths. Their primary concern was with the state of the believer and the way meditation could contribute to the continuous process of sanctification. Thus they surrounded discussions of method with lists of hindrances to meditation and advantages to be gained by meditating. Downame's choice of regeneration, rather than the glory of the saints, as the subject for a sample meditation, suggests how radically his orientation differed from Hall's.[28]

Baxter is unusual in combining an extraordinary capacity to soar with the characteristic Puritan concern with the state of the soul that is so pronounced in a Downame or a Rogers. He gives considerably more attention to hindrances to meditation and the means by which these may be overcome than to the actual process of meditation. He also assumes the need for self-examination, making this a crucial part of meditation rather than treating it separately, and raises the Puritan concern with watchfulness to a feverish level. Baxter differs from Downame and others primarily interested in showing how life may be reduced to a godly order in his recognition of the inherent drama of the life of faith. Meditation is for him a highly dynamic process, a constant internal struggle to attain a state of heavenly-mindedness. If the heart resists, he advises, echoing the account in Genesis (32:24–29) of Jacob's wrestling with the angel, "wrestle with it, till thou hast prevailed, and say, I will not let thee go, till thou hast answered" (The Saints Everlasting Rest, p. 429).

Baxter's discussion of formal meditation in the fourth part of The Saints Everlasting Rest follows the format popularized by Hall and his Puritan imitators and owes some specific debts to Hall, but the method that he presents is remarkable for its originality. Where Hall emphasizes the soul's orderly progress up the mount of contemplation ("by certain staires and degrees") Baxter concentrates on the critical activity of pleading with the heart.[29] His acute sensitivity to the defects of the "lazy loytering heart" meant that the affective side of meditation received a disproportionate amount of attention. While he gives the reason an active role to play in the "consideration" of the subject, his real emphasis is on the "acting" of a series of "affections:" love, desire, hope, courage, and joy. He insists that the reader must work at "winding up" the affections until he has "pleaded" his heart "from Earth to Heaven; from conversing below, to a walking with God" (p. 798).

For Baxter the task of reason was not to analyze the subject by logical categories but to shock the soul into an awareness of the claims of Scripture and to present the arguments for their validity. He saw the beginnings of the meditative process, in which reason calls up the subject from memory and then presents it to judgment, as involving a strenuous effort to overcome natural resistance. He imagines reason gradually coming alive, "till it rowse up it self as Sampson, and breaks the bonds of sensuality" (p. 720).[30] This resurgent reason acts upon the heart as "the powerful motion of the wind" (p. 727) or a stone from David's sling. Judgment is a matter of deciding between the claims of glory, set forth by reason, and those of the world and arriving at a state of "holy admiration." Baxter dramatized the importance of belief in the scriptural promises of rest by making this the business of a third stage, which he called "faith." He demanded that his readers confront the Word directly and experience a sense of its power. Faith in the efficacy of the Word makes it possible to stimulate the affections, from love to joy, by summoning visions of heavenly scenes and following them with provocative questions. For example, the reader, instructed by Baxter, might arouse joy by imagining himself joining the heavenly choir and drinking of the river of pleasure and then asking himself, "Why is not my life a continual joy? and the savor of Heaven perpetually upon my spirit?" (p. 747).

The fluidity and drama of the meditative process as Baxter conceived it can be seen from his sample meditation on the text upon which he based the whole of *The Saints Everlasting Rest*. This meditation loosely follows the procedure that I have outlined—opening the text to suggest the various wonders of the saints' rest, contrasting its superior claims with those of the world, urging the truth of the Word, and "acting" at least some of the affections (marginal notes point to love and joy)—but in reading it one is less conscious of separate stages than of the surges of Baxter's prose as he alternately represents scenes of celestial bliss and exhorts his "drowsie soul" to rouse itself. There is no assumption of steady progress, rather a sense that faith can ebb at any moment. The meditation goes on for almost fifty pages, in which Baxter never loses the sense of a tension between the glories promised by the Word and the recalcitrance of the heart, even in the sustained prayer with which he concludes.

Instead of dividing meditation into intellective and affective parts, Baxter saw three separate but closely related "actings of the soul" as characterizing the whole meditative process: cogitation, soliloquy, and prayer. Cogitation describes the action of the reason in propounding truths and duties, soliloquy the pleading with the heart that is necessary if these truths are to be applied. Baxter urges that prayer be interspersed with cogitation and soliloquy in the manner of David's ejaculations. Of these three meditative modes by far the most important is soliloquy, which Baxter saw as a "Preaching to ones self" (p. 750). Comments that Baxter made subsequently in his *Christian Directory* (1673) suggest why he was so attracted to this form of preaching to the self:

> In thy Meditations upon all these incentives of Love, preach them over earnestly to thy Heart, and expostulate and plead with it by way of soliloquy, till thou feel the fire begin to burn. Do not only think on the Arguments of Love, but dispute it out with thy Conscience, and by expostulating earnest reasonings with thy heart, endeavour to affect it. There is much more moving force in this earnest talking to our selves, than in bare cogitation, that breaks not out into mental words.[31]

Most of Baxter's illustrative meditation on the rest of the saints can be described as soliloquy. Even when, theoretically, he should be opening the nature of the rest for judgment to consider, he carries on a spirited argument

with himself in a continuous effort to bring the soul to a state of spiritual
vitality in which the joys of heaven will seem immediate. What one chiefly
remembers about the meditation is the insistent voice of Baxter, preaching
to himself.

Baxter cites the example of David's pleading with his soul in the Psalms,
as well as the meditations of Augustine and Bernard, to justify his use of
soliloquies. The technique was so widely used, in various forms, that it is
pointless to talk about sources, but it can be said that Baxter gave the
soliloquy a special importance and brought it to a new level of intensity. He
suggests that soliloquies can be ordered as a sermon would be, proceeding
by explication, confirmation, and application, followed by a series of uses
(information, instruction, examination, reproof). This is the most systematic that Baxter becomes; he even incorporates some of the logical categories that Hall uses into the process of self-examination, as means of
discovering signs of one's spiritual condition. In practice Baxter's soliloquies
develop by a pattern of interrogation and exclamation that is less structured
than his sermon outline would suggest. He typically presents self-examination as a dramatic rather than a calmly analytical procedure:

> Get alone, and question with thy self; bring the heart to the bar of tryal;
> force it to answer the interrogatories put to it; set the conditions of the
> Gospel, and qualifications of the Saints on one side, and thy performance
> of those conditions and the qualifications of thy soul on the other side;
> and then judg how neer they resemble: thou hast the same word before
> thee, to judg thy self by now, by which thou must be judged at the great
> day. (P. 671)

To account for the dynamic quality of Baxter's meditation one must
understand his voice and the assumptions and conditions that shaped it,
and to do this it is necessary to consider his view of preaching. As Barbara
Lewalski has shown, Protestant meditation shares many of the aims and
techniques of Protestant preaching.[32] This is especially true of Baxter's
meditation. As Baxter abandoned his original plan of writing a sermon, or
sermons, on the rest of the saints, he adjusted his manner to suit the aspects
of his subjects, such as the authority of Scripture, that he felt compelled to
take up. But the voice of the preacher keeps returning: didactic, solicitous,
anguished, urgent, depending upon the intensity of the concern that Baxter
felt at any given moment.[33] Where Herbert saw the minister as "the Deputy
of Christ for the reducing of Man to the Obedience of God,"[34] Baxter
imagined him as a "messenger of the Lord of hosts" charged with the most
serious and difficult task conceivable: "to stand up in the face of a Congregation, and deliver a Message of salvation or damnation, as from the living
God, in the name of our Redeemer."[35] The sense of urgency with which
Baxter regarded this task burns through his exhortations to his fellow
ministers in The Reformed Pastor:

Let us therefore rowse up our selves to the work of the Lord, and speak to our people as for their lives, and save them as by violence, pulling them out of the fire: Satan will not be charmed out of his possession: we must lay seige to the souls of sinners which are his garrisons, and find out where his strength lyeth, and lay the battery of Gods Ordinance against it, and ply it close till a breach be made.[36]

Baxter goes on to urge that they come "as with a torrent" upon the understandings of the hearers and "bear down all before us...that they may be forced to yield to the power of truth."[37]

This view of preaching as a kind of warfare to be carried to the hearer with the greatest force one can muster demands an extraordinary commitment on the part of the minister, as Baxter clearly recognized: "What have we our time and strength for, but to lay it out for God? What is a candle made for, but to be burnt?"[38] But energy by itself is insufficient. To achieve a "communion of souls" the minister must himself be spiritually alive. Nothing is more indecent, Baxter says, "than to be a dead preacher speaking to a dead people the living truth of the living God."[39] He characteristically looks beyond the language of a sermon to the spiritual condition of the preacher:

A Sermon full of meer words, how neatly so ever it be composed, while there is wanting the light of [Scripture] Evidence and the life of Zeal, is but an image or a well drest carkass.[40]

Baxter was acutely aware of the inadequacies of language, as Joan Webber has shown.[41] He recognized the imperfections of his own work, written for the most part in great haste, and was willing to let them stand. He regarded even the language of Scripture as reflecting the infirmities of its human authors and argued the need for looking beyond the letter: "The words are but the Dish to serve up the sense in."[42] Baxter's famous assertion that "Truth loves the Light, and is most beautiful when most naked"[43] implies a radical devaluation of language. The simile that he goes on to develop, comparing "painted obscure Sermons" to "the painted glass in the windows that keeps out the light," suggests that what he is really objecting to is the personal coloration that some preachers give to their sermons by the use of rhetorical figures. Yet it is dangerous to take Baxter's own words as setting up absolutes. Other pronouncements suggest that he was by no means indifferent to the effective use of language. He could advocate a "grateful holy eloquence"[44] and urge preachers to be masters of the people's affections, "as potent in your divine Rhetorick as *Cicero* in his Humane" (*The Saints Everlasting Rest*, p. 512). What Baxter shows here is an awareness that seriousness by itself is not enough; the light must be transmitted by some effective means. This concern with mastery does not mean that the preacher should complicate or embellish his prose unnecessarily but that he must learn to convey the truth forcefully. Baxter did this in his own vigorous prose, with such effectiveness that it is difficult to imagine him as he pictured himself, a mere "pen in God's hand."[45]

Baxter was not sufficiently concerned with the workings of language to write anything approaching a formal rhetoric for preachers. He urged them to speak to the capacities of their hearers and to heed Paul's advice (2 Tim. 2:15) to "study to become a workman that needeth not to be ashamed, rightly dividing the word of truth." Insofar as he suggests a method of his own, it is based upon a mixture of questioning and exhortation. Sermons should be "frequently interlocutory,"[46] challenging the reader and forcing him to attend to the message. This could be a description of Baxter's own technique in *The Saints Everlasting Rest*, in which he writes, as I have suggested, essentially as a preacher. The technique can be seen in its purest form in the catechising of families which was so central a part of Baxter's ministry at Kidderminster. In the illustrations of this catechising that Baxter gives in *The Reformed Pastor* the questions sometimes expand into miniature sermons, but without losing their immediacy. Baxter's questions must have assumed familiar patterns, but he could not rely upon the set questions, and set responses, of the Anglican catechism. He had to create his own kind of "communion" with his auditors.

Baxter was ultimately less concerned with the medium in which truth was expressed than with the spiritual condition from which he felt it had to proceed. To be alive in Baxter's terms one must have experienced "the transforming renewing work of the Spirit" (*The Saints Everlasting Rest*, p. 482) and must continue to act "in the Spirit." As he puts it in *The Reformed Pastor*, "all our work must be done spiritually, as by men possessed by the Holy Ghost" (p. 128). Such a statement could have come from any number of Puritan divines, but Baxter can be distinguished by the urgency with which he felt the necessity of communicating God's truth. His own chronic ill health sharpened his conviction of the need to act immediately to redeem the time, and it provided him with a ready emblem of human mortality: "Yet a few days, and we shall be here no more...many hundred diseases are ready to assault us" (*The Saints Everlasting Rest*, p. 352). Baxter seems genuinely to have felt that he was on the brink of death many times in his career (he even published his *Dying Thoughts* at one point), but it is fair to say that he knew how to realize the dramatic potential of his condition. He saw the effectiveness of picturing himself preaching "as a dying man to dying men."[47]

The sense of urgency that pervades *The Saints Everlasting Rest* owes a great deal to Baxter's firsthand experience of war. His voice belongs to a specific moment in history in a way that the voice of Joseph Hall in his meditative writings and that of John Donne in the *Devotions* do not. Having seen towns burning and under siege, he can readily talk about breaching the souls of sinners with "God's Ordinance" and bring a new sense of concreteness to the biblical imperative to snatch souls from the fire. He can offer a startling typological reading of Parliamentary victory, comparing it with the triumphant appearance of "the Conquering Lion of the Tribe of *Judah*...with all the Hoasts of Heaven:"

> I have thought on it many a time, as a small Emblem of that day, when I have seen our prevailing Army drawing towards the Towns and Castles of the Enemy: Oh with what glad hearts do all the poor prisoners within hear the news, and behold our approach? How do they run up to their prison windows, and thence behold us with Joy?... How do they clap each other on the back, and cry, *Deliverance, Deliverance!* (P. 49)

Baxter was not willing, like Cromwell, to hail victories as proof of divine support of the Parliamentary cause. On the contrary, he saw in the carnage of battle a pouring out of divine wrath on the sluggish people of England:

> Christ hath been pleading with England these fourscore years and more by the word of his Gospel, for his worship and for his Sabbaths, and yet the inhabitants are not perswaded. Nay, he hath been pleading these six yeers by threatnings, and fire, and sword, and yet can prevaile but with very few...he hath (as it were) stood in their blood with the sword in his hand, and among the heapes of the slain hath he pleaded with the living, and said, What say you? Will you yet worship me, and fear me, and take me for your Lord? (P. 343)

Here Baxter assumes the stance of an Old Testament prophet (he quotes Isaiah on the judgment of the Israelites) to insist that God has entered history and is demanding an immediate response from his people—not Jehovah, as one would expect in a more conventional handling of the biblical materials, but a militant Christ. The war was to Baxter a terrible warning that the work of reformation was far from complete. It intensified his conviction of the need for haste: "The spur of God is in our sides, we bleed, we groan, and yet we do not mend our pace" (p. 346). Baxter introduced into meditative writing a sense of crisis born of a particular time. His evangelical appeals are rooted in his experience of civil chaos and reflect a peculiarly strong conviction that the time in which to seek salvation is forever "posting away."

Baxter did not search Daniel and Revelation for keys to future events or the historical books of the Old Testament for justifications of present ones as many writers and preachers were doing in the 1640s. He tried rather to give meaning to the lives of his readers by persuading them to read their own experience in terms of the pattern established by Hebrews: as a journey of the faithful, the children of Abraham and the people of God, toward the New Jerusalem. In part 1 Baxter urges the desirability of the rest promised the saints by presenting the conditions from which they would be released in unusually concrete terms. He appeals to the people in terms of their particular experience:

> The names of Lollards, Hugonots, Puritan, Roundheads, are not there used...there are no Bishops or Chancelors Courts; no Visitations, nor High Commission Judgments. (P. 114)

Would not rest be "seasonable," Baxter asks, to those "weary of their Taxes, weary of their Quartering, weary of Plunderings, weary of their fears and dangers" (p. 93). Baxter had to convince his audience of the reality of a Canaan at the end of the "hazardous and grievous Wilderness" and at the same time warn them that they must journey on if they expect to reach it: "There is no singing the songs of Zion in the land of your thraldome" (p. 273). This Calvinist emphasis on the necessity of perseverance is strong in Baxter, as one might expect. He repeatedly urges the reader to continue traveling, fighting, sailing (the old figure of life as a sea is perhaps his favorite), bringing to these elaborations of the Exodus motif the same intensity with which he says that one must keep lashing on one's heart in meditation.

As the passages that I have quoted should indicate, Baxter turned habitually to the Bible for images of crisis and for assurances of deliverance from it. His uses of figurative language derived from the Bible are characteristically Puritan. Yet his approach to the problem of the authority of Scripture, set forth in the second part of *The Saints Everlasting Rest,* is unusually rational and conservative. The standard Puritan position (established by Calvin and developed by Perkins, Sibbes, and others) was that the surest proof of the validity of the Word was the testimony of the Spirit. Baxter rejected this view and chose to consider only proofs from reason, which involve him in arguing from such evidence as miracles and possession by evil spirits. He also took the unpopular line of emphasizing that the text of the Bible depends upon tradition. The original words, themselves savoring of the humanity of their authors, had to be transmitted and then translated for the benefit of most readers. Baxter accepted the common Protestant view that the Scriptures contained everything necessary for salvation but took a skeptical view of the ability of the untutored individual to interpret Scripture for himself. Ministers had a central role to play:

> Why els are Ministers called the eyes and the hands of the body? Stewards of the Mysteries, and of the house of God? Overseers, Rulers, and Governors of the Church? And such as must give the children their meat in due season? (Pp. 211–12)

In his writing Baxter carried on a running battle with the Quakers and anyone else who made excessive claims for the witness of the Spirit. He took an extremely cool view of the millenial fever raging around him: "We may rather wish then hope, that all the Lords people were Prophets" (p. 211).

Baxter could describe faith as "a rational Act of a rational Creature" (p. 176), by which he meant that whatever the soul entertains should be approved by the understanding before engaging the heart. He was careful to argue that the Spirit does not destroy reason but rather rectifies it, acting through the Word to remove darkness from the understanding. Yet, as Nuttall points out, while Baxter gives reason what he regards as its due place, he never gives it primacy.[48] The character of his faith emerges more clearly in his conviction of the reality of heaven, which he felt driven to communicate, and in what Nuttall calls "an overwhelming sense of God's presence" than in his defenses of rationality. Although Baxter saw part 2 of *The Saints Everlasting Rest* as a vital link in his argument, the rational discussion of the claims of Scripture that he offers there gives only a partial indication of its real importance to him. To appreciate this one must look to his comments on the way man should use the Word and to his imaginative responses to particular texts.

Baxter went to the Bible for doctrine and for moral examples; yet he valued it chiefly for revealing the promises of glory: "God hath set open Heaven to us in his Word" (p. 556). These are the "soul" of the Gospel for him, because they force one to consider the end of all human activity. He speaks of the Gospel as a "looking glass" in which men may discover the state of their souls.[49] The images of heaven that we see in this glass are imperfect, accommodated to our limited understandings, but they are expressed in "phrases of the Spirit" intended to "quicken our apprehensions and affections" (p. 758). Baxter stresses the active role of Scripture in the process of spiritual regeneration (he can describe conversion as being "touched to the quick with the Word" [p. 58]), though he insists that the Spirit, rather than the letter of the Word, acts as the instrumental cause in the work of regeneration.[50]

Baxter saw the promises of heaven not only as a power for bringing spiritually dead souls to life through the operation of the Spirit but as an inexhaustible source of spiritual nourishment for the regenerate soul, "an open fountain flowing with comforts day and night" (p. 769). He found the consolation of the Word chiefly in the "foretastes" of heavenly joys offered by Old Testament descriptions of the experience of the Israelites. He imagines his readers as living "where the Gospel groweth, whose heaven is urged upon us at our doors, and the Manna falls about our tents" (p. 340). Many writers used manna as a symbol of the riches of the Word, seen in generalized terms; Baxter sought to make his readers identify with the immediate situation of the Israelites in the wilderness. Canaan became a symbol of the joys that they could anticipate on earth by meditation but only experience to the full in heaven:

> Thou camest to spie out the Land of Promise; O go not back without the bunch of Grapes, which thou maiest shew to thy Brethren, when thou

comest home, for their Confirmation and Encouragement; till thou canst tell them by experience, that it is a Land flowing with Wine and Oyl, with Milk and Honey. (P. 788)

While Herbert instinctively made the bunch of grapes into a Eucharistic symbol (the juice becomes the wine that is the blood of Christ), Baxter, like so many Puritan writers, took the Old Testament promises of Canaan as an earnest of the satisfactions to be found by the faithful in heaven.[51] Meditation for him necessitated learning to desire these satisfactions and to imagine them in sensuous terms suggested by the Old Testament. Baxter pictures the "experience" of the promises in terms of Old Testament imagery of feasting. He imagines Christ as spreading a table with the food of angels and saints:

He hath prepared thee all the ingredients in Heaven, onely put forth the hand of Faith, and feed upon them, and rejoyce and live; The Lord saith to thee, as he did to *Elias, Arise and eat, because the journey is too great for thee, I Kings 19:7.* (Pp. 710–11)

On another occasion Baxter brings his readers up to the actual process of meditation as to the "feast of fat things" described by Isaiah (Isa. 25:6):

All this hath been but to get thee an appetite; it follows now, That thou approach unto the Feast; that thou sit down, and take what is offered, and delight thy soul, as with fatness and marrow. (P. 718)

Baxter's loose "All this" could refer to his comments about the circumstances of meditation in the preceding chapter, or to the whole first half of his fourth part, or indeed to all of *The Saints Everlasting Rest* up to this point. The process of preparing for meditation encompasses much more for Baxter than the traditional stage of purging the soul of worldly thoughts (although he does give several pages to this specific kind of preparation, perhaps following Hall). Before Baxter could bring his readers to the feast he had to convince them of the validity of the promises of glory and the need to meditate upon them. They had to experience the regenerative power of the Word before they could taste its delights.

Baxter demonstrates early in part 1 that the "Rest" of his text is attainable only by an elect, called by God and sanctified by the blood of Christ and the "Spirit of Grace," and later devotes a chapter to the spiritual regeneration that distinguished this "Peculiar People." An early chapter on the "four great Preparatives" to the rest illustrates the way Baxter sought to further this regeneration by bringing the power of the Word to bear on his readers. To persuade them to accept these "Preparatives" (the second coming of Christ, the resurrection of the dead, the last judgment, and the glorification of the saints) Baxter attempts to convince them of the reality of these future events. He invokes relevant passages from Scripture, less as proof texts than as aids to the imagination and the affections, attempting in each section to work the reader up to a state of intense expectation. He questions, exclaims ("O Terrible! O Joyful Day!"), and exhorts in order to make the scenes vividly present: "Triumph now, O Christian, in these promises" (p. 55).

Such a whetting of the reader's spiritual appetite is an essential aspect of the preparation for meditation. In demonstrating meditation itself, particularly in describing the acting of the affections, Baxter gives the fullest indication of how one can experience a "foretaste" of heaven. The heart of his advice is to "Bring down thy conceivings to the reach of sense" (p. 759). Baxter makes ample use of the traditional technique (practiced by Hall and long before him by Augustine) of using remembered sensuous experience as a means of imagining the greater delights of heaven. But the "conceivings" that he refers to here are the emotionally charged scenes that he creates for the reader at various places in *The Saints Everlasting Rest*:

> Suppose thou hadst heard those Songs of *Moses*, and of the Lamb; or didst even now hear them praising and glorifying the Living God...I would not have thee, as the Papists, draw them in Pictures, nor use mysterious, significant Ceremonies to represent them.... But get the liveliest Picture of them in thy minde that possibly thou canst; meditate of them, as if thou were all the while beholding them, and as if thou were even hearing the *Hallelujahs*, while thou art thinking of them; till thou canst say, Methinks I see a glympse of the Glory! methinks I even stand by *Abraham* and *David*, *Peter* and *Paul*, and many more of these triumphing souls! methinks I even see the Son of God appearing in the clouds, and the world standing at his bar to receive their doom; methinks I even hear him say, *Come ye blessed of my Father!* and even see them go rejoycing into the Joy of their Lord! (P. 760)

Notice that Baxter concentrates on the process by which individuals experience these scenes rather than upon the scenes themselves, which remain relatively indefinite. His primary concern is with stimulating the faith that makes such imaginings possible:

> Thus take thy heart into the Land of Promise; shew it the pleasant hills and fruitful valleys; Shew it the clusters of Grape which thou hast gathered; and by those convince it that it is a blessed Land, flowing with better then milk and honey; enter the gates of the holy City; walk through the streets of the new Jerusalem...that thou mayest tell it to thy soul. (P. 745)

Although Baxter encourages the use of the scenes, he is careful to avoid the kind of imaginative elaboration of actual historical scenes that characterizes much Catholic meditation,[52] instead suggesting by a sparing use of biblical detail what the Christian can anticipate in the future life. His mental pictures must be lively, the result of a conjunction of the imagination and the Word at a given moment in the life of the believer. To fix them by excessive detail, as by the strokes of a brush, would be to "draw down" the heart and prevent the kind of soaring that he sought to encourage.

Even when Baxter's meditation seems closest to Catholic practice, when he seeks to arouse a love of God by urging his readers to behold Christ crucified, to imagine his voice and look upon his wounds, he continues to focus upon problems of belief. His aim is not so much to stir the readers to empathize with Christ's sufferings, in the fashion of Catholic meditation, as to convince them of the fact of redemption; he repeats the question, "Dost thou not know him?" (p. 733). In Baxter one finds a particularly intense concern with applying the Word to the self. This concern prevented him from developing scenes so fully that they divert attention from the condition of the believer, and it led him to value meditation for its effect on daily life:

> The diligent keeping of your hearts on heaven, will preserve the vigor of all your graces, and put life into all your duties. Its the heavenly Christian, that is the lively Christian...the more frequently and clearly this end [heaven] is beheld, the more vigorous will all our motion be. (P. 618)

In this life vigorous motion, through imagining the rest to be won in the other; this is the Puritan formula that Baxter expresses so effectively.

Baxter's way of talking about the dynamic character of vision reveals how far he is from advocating a systematic progress up the mount of contemplation—either through the logical procedure advocated by Hall or through the exercise of memory, understanding, and will according to the Ignatian method:

> If thou canst get but the spirit of *Elias,* and in the chariot of Contemplation, canst soar aloft, till thou approachest neer to the quickning Spirit, thy soul and sacrifice [like Abel's] will gloriously flame, though the flesh and the World should cast upon them the water of all their opposing enmity.... Faith hath wings, and meditation is its chariot. Its office is to make absent things, as present. (P. 621)

Whatever rational procedures Baxter may urge to facilitate meditation, he places his greatest emphasis upon the necessity for a vital faith, and such a faith, through which one can make the unseen reality of heaven "as present," must be animated by the Spirit.

> Be a careful observer of the drawings of the Spirit, and fearful of quenching its workings; If ever thy soul get above this earth, and get acquainted with this living in heaven, the Spirit of God must be to thee as the Chariot to Elijah; yea, the very living principle by which thou must move and ascend. (P. 184)

Baxter speaks elsewhere of the need to watch for extraordinary revivings of the soul by God, as for favorable wind and tide (p. 705). The mystery for Baxter was not so much in the objects of contemplation as in the operations of the Spirit that make the imagination capable of soaring. One's ability to respond to these motions remains for him the secret of successful meditation, as of successful preaching. Yet Baxter denounces those who trust entirely to the Spirit and fail to make any efforts of their own. If the Christian must be alert to the "gales of the Spirit," he must also labor at heavenly-mindedness, hence the need for a work such as *The Saints Everlasting Rest*. God does not feed the saints as birds do their young, Baxter says as one point, but as he rewards the husbandman who plows and sows diligently with the fruits of the earth (p. 609).[53]

Baxter understood the possibilities of vision, and of any kind of communion with God, largely in terms of biblical models. He was drawn to Old Testament examples of converse with God: Abraham, Noah, Moses, David (whose songs prove that he was "neer the heart of God" [p. 631]), the prophets. Baxter begins his first attempt to describe the properties of the rest by wishing that his lips might be touched with fire, like Isaiah's. At another point he would imitate Paul, rapt to the third heaven in vision. Other visionary experiences described in the New Testament (those of Stephen, of the shepherds at the Nativity, of Peter at the transfiguration) serve Baxter in similar fashion as examples of the possibility of vision. Unlike Gerson and contemplatives like Bernard and Bonaventura, Baxter showed no interest in exploring the nature of the communion with God that vision makes possible, beyond demonstrating how one might transport himself to heaven in the imagination. When he talks about the ultimate union with God that the faithful can anticipate, he sticks close to biblical language. One should not think of a "Real Union" but of standing before the throne of God, of being "his child," "an heir of his Kingdom," "the Spouse of his Son" (p. 27). Although Baxter talks about the need to approach God with reverence, aware of divine majesty and the power of divine wrath, he presents meditation as a means of reaching a "familiar conceiving of the state of blessedness" (p. 761) that will take away the terrors of judgment. His conception of the end of meditation shows a characteristically Puritan concern with achieving familiarity with the divine. He would converse with God, walk with God, rather than enjoy some kind of rapture.

Baxter's mount of contemplation remains firmly rooted in the figurative landscape that he derived from the Bible. He thinks in terms of particular biblical mountains, including the celestial Zion, though he may use them virtually interchangeably as symbols of vision; all afford a prospect in which the earth shrinks to insignificance. Given this habit of conceiving spiritual progress in terms of the Exodus, the most appropriate place to associate with meditation was Mount Nebo, situated between the wilderness and Canaan:

> As *Moses* before he died, went up into Mount *Nebo*, to take a survey of
> the land of *Canaan;* so the Christian doth ascend this Mount of Contemplation, and take a survey by Faith of his Rest. (P. 846)

Baxter shows the Christian who surveys his promised rest from this imagined vantage point looking back as well, upon the struggles of the "believing, patient, despised Saints." This dual perspective expresses Baxter's Puritan sense of heaven and the world, Canaan and the wilderness, as irreconcilably opposed states of being and at the same time suggests a temporary resolution of the tension between them in the act of meditating. He also describes the mount of contemplation as an Ararat upon which the ark of the soul comes to rest.

The heavenly rest anticipated by the saints was one of the great themes of Puritan preaching and literary expression, and in his immense work Baxter offered the fullest exploration of the nature and importance of this rest. *The Saints Everlasting Rest* helped to condition the audience of *The Pilgrim's Progress* and that of *Paradise Lost* as well; both works ask the reader to respond to the prospect of "long wandered man" being brought "safe to eternal paradise of rest."[54] This rest was for Baxter the end that should govern all men's earthly motions. His sense of the attractiveness of the rest, and of the need to keep it in constant view, should be evident from the passages that I have quoted. In the simplest terms, the rest of the saints meant deliverance from a wearying struggle. Baxter's physical afflictions and his horror of the disorders amid which he found himself living made him peculiarly sensitive to the appeal of such a rest. In part 1 he enumerates the kinds of relief that heaven will offer; from temptation, from doubt, from the sense of divine displeasure, from all the suffering that the world can inflict. But Baxter never presents the rest itself as a passive state; he conceived it not as repose but as "a sweet and constant Action of all the Powers of the Soul and Body in [the] Fruition of God" (p. 28). He imagines himself as resting "in Knowing, Loving, Rejoycing, and Praising" (p. 791).

The "fruition" which the saints enjoy in heaven represents the full realization of the delights of which they have had a foretaste in this life. There they can feast on the abundance of Canaan that they formerly imagined in the act of meditation. Baxter describes this satisfaction more abstractly as feeding on the "sweetness" of God and also shows Christ offering the blessed the fruit of the tree of life and the hidden manna (of Rev. 2:17) and welcoming them to his table. He makes the experience "an everlasting Holy day of Pleasure" (p. 807) in which sensuous satisfaction becomes a way of expressing the intensified spiritual vitality of the soul nourished by the actual presence of God.

Baxter saw this fruition as an extremely joyful state based on a condition of loving and being loved by God. Joy and love are closely associated in Baxter's scheme of meditation. Love is first "acted" (by thinking on the love of Christ, as expressed by his passion and individual acts of mercy)—then joy can follow. In heaven they are inseparable, arising naturally from the "everlasting views of the face of the God of Truth" (p. 831), that the blessed enjoy. Such joyful love finds its natural expression in continuous praise of God. Baxter's celestial choir is a dynamic body that breaks out into shouts of joy; its obvious spiritual energies are perhaps the best expression of his sense of fruition as an active state reflecting the heightened alertness of the blessed. Baxter was an enthusiastic advocate of psalm singing as an act of worship:

> The Lords day is a day of joy and Thanksgiving, and the Praises of God are the highest and holyest employment upon Earth.[55]

He urges the readers of *The Saints Everlasting Rest* to "Be much in that Angelical work of Praise" because it is the "most heavenly work" and "likely to raise us to the most heavenly temper" (p. 680). Baxter himself was in the habit of singing a psalm upon retiring at night and another upon awakening; he even resorted to psalm singing in the middle of the night when he could not sleep.[56] He confessed in the preface to his *Poetical Fragments* that singing psalms in church was "the chief delightful Exercise of my Religion and my Life."[57]

The perfect harmony of the heavenly choir is the best emblem that could be found for the kind of fellowship that Baxter sought tirelessly in the earthly church and looked forward to in the heavenly. There are many indications in *The Saints Everlasting Rest* of his concern with the whole body of the faithful and not just the individual act of meditation. Baxter consistently thinks in terms of an elect, distinguished in this life by their capacity for "heavenly discourse" and destined to be separated from the unworthy at the time of judgment. And he gives numerous indications of his concern over the disorder in the church, inseparable from that in the state.

> Alas, poor England: how are thy bowels torn out! and the reformation and deliverance grown (as to man) impossible! because thy inhabitants, yea and Guides, run all into extreams! like a drunken man that reeleth from side to side, but cannot keep the middle way: nay they hate a man of peace that runs not out into their extreams. (P. 520)

This is the Baxter who was bitterly frustrated by his inability to make any headway among the sectarians of Cromwell's army and who was to find himself caught more than once in his subsequent career between conflicting religious movements. His advice to ministers to "study equally for Peace and Truth, as knowing that they dwell both together in the golden mean" (p. 524) was hopelessly unrealistic for the middle of the seventeenth century. But Baxter's disappointments only sharpened his desire for the peace of heaven where there would be no more "Anabaptist or Poedo baptist, Brownist, Separatist, Independent, Presbyterian, Episcopal" but one triumphant church gathered by Christ from the body of all the faithful:

> There will not be one for singing, and another against it; but even those that jarred in discord, shall all conjoyn in blessed concord, and make up one melodious Quire. (P. 120)

The Saints Everlasting Rest should continue to receive attention as the most impressive and influential work of Puritan meditation in the seventeenth century, but to classify the work by genre is only to begin to reckon with it. And even this classification must be qualified, given the fact that Baxter began his work as a sermon and continued to draw upon sermon devices and to speak with a preacher's voice. Baxter could prescribe a method for meditating and proceed to illustrate it, but his concerns were too urgent and all-encompassing for him to keep his subject within what a more careful writer such as Hall might have seen as a reasonable compass. *The Saints Everlasting Rest* should be regarded as an extraordinary personal statement of spiritual yearning and a mirror of the real disharmony and suffering of a country torn apart by religious and political conflict. Baxter felt the disorder more acutely than most and demonstrated an unusual intellectual and imaginative grasp of the implications of the promised rest. Despair over a people that run drunkenly to extremes and faith in the existence of a "melodious Quire" in which discords will be resolved and suffering transcended are the two poles of his discourse.

4. Gerrard Winstanley's Land of Righteousness

One of the strangest confrontations in a century marked by bizarre encounters took place on April 20, 1649, when Thomas Lord Fairfax, general of the Parliamentary armies, received Gerrard Winstanley and William Everard at Whitehall. The two men came in response to an investigation ordered by the Council of State, to explain why they and their followers had set about cultivating the common land at St. George's Hill in Surrey. They refused to remove their hats in the general's presence, "Because he was but their fellow-creature." Everard proceeded to explain that he was of the race of the Jews, claiming that the time when God would deliver his people from the tyranny imposed by William the Conqueror was at hand and that he had been led by a vision to dig the earth and receive its fruits.[1] Relying on God's promise to make the barren land fruitful, he and Winstanley sought to restore Creation to its original condition, in which all men enjoyed the fruits of the earth in common. Although Everard was reported to be the main speaker on this occasion, the ideas are those elaborated by Winstanley in a series of tracts proclaiming and defending the activities of the Diggers, as they came to be known.[2] Everard in fact dropped out in the early phase of the movement, and Winstanley became its effective leader until it disintegrated in the spring of 1650.

In a period in which Cromwell interrupted state business to interview prophetesses claiming to bring communications from God, the behavior of the Diggers would not have seemed unduly startling. Yet the kinds of claims that the Diggers made insured that they would arouse public alarm. In occupying common land on St. George's Hill and in nearby Cobham, to which they moved in the autumn of 1649, they infringed upon traditional rights of the lords of the manor in both places and appeared to threaten all landowners. Despite assurances that they would neither break down enclosures nor take up arms to defend themselves, the Diggers by their actions and public justifications challenged the concept of private property and the organization of labor upon which the agricultural economy of England was based.

Fairfax himself seems to have been only mildly concerned about the goings on in Surrey. He stopped by St. George's Hill to talk with the Diggers in late May and, in response to complaints and letters from Winstanley, appears to have restrained soldiers stationed in the area from harassing them. The local freeholders were considerably less tolerant, organizing periodic forays in which they destroyed crops and the makeshift dwellings that the Diggers had built themselves. Winstanley's "Bill of Account" of the sufferings of the Diggers cites numerous instances of violence, including severe beatings.[3] Harassment by the gentry took the form of legal action for trespass against Winstanley and several of his followers. Winstanley was not allowed to speak in his defense, or to introduce a written statement, because he refused to "fee" an attorney, an unthinkable act for someone who saw all lawyers as agents of an illegitimate and oppressive legal system. He had the satisfaction of knowing that the substantial fine levied by the court was uncollectible, although efforts by local authorities to collect it by seizing what possessions the Diggers did have caused considerable anguish.

With such forces arrayed against them, it is surprising that the Diggers lasted as long as they did. Winstanley's various appeals reveal the vision and the determined pacifism that sustained them until a final destructive raid in April of 1650 led by Parson Platt, lord of the manor of Cobham by marriage and Winstanley's chief antagonist, made it impossible to continue. Despite the obvious failure of the experiment, Winstanley claimed a moral and spiritual victory:

> The poor Diggers have got the Crown, and weare it, and the Priests and Gentry have lost their Crown: The poor have striven with them 12. moneths, with love and patience: The Gentlemen have answered them all the time with fury.[4]

Winstanley regularly condemned those who represented "kingly power"—by which he meant clergy, lawyers, and landowners generally as well as agents of the state—for choosing to fight with "the Sword of Iron, and covetousnesse" rather than "the Sword of the Spirit which is love" (329). He called the "poor oppressed people of England" to "be patient in your present bondage" (183), confident that the power of the Spirit was spreading daily. The digging itself is best understood not as a revolutionary act but as a sign, a symbolic witness to the impending age of the Spirit when the earth would again be a "common treasury."[5] Even after the digging was underway Winstanley saw the Spirit as counseling people to "lie quiet and wait for the breakings forth of the powerfull day of the Lord" (391).

Although the Diggers had no lasting impact on the society they sought to change,[6] their radicalism anticipated much in subsequent social thought and has generated considerable interest among students of history and politics. Ever since Winstanley's writings were rediscovered in the late nineteenth century, he has been regarded as a forerunner of communism and an acute and forceful social critic.[7] His preoccupation with class conflict and the injustices of a society based upon private property has made him seem to many twentieth-century readers remarkably farsighted. Those commentators most attracted by Winstanley's political radicalism have tended to emphasize his secularism, minimizing his millennial expectations and the biblical origins of much of his language and thought. My own concern is primarily with the aspect of Winstanley's work that has received least attention, the free adaptation of biblical themes and images that gives his visionary prose its uniqueness and force. The Bible gave Winstanley speech, as it did other relatively uneducated men and women of mid-seventeenth-century England. He was perhaps the most original and articulate of the host of self-proclaimed prophets who sprang up in the commonwealth period (the Quaker leader George Fox is another outstanding example). In him the Protestant principle of encouraging every man to read the Bible for himself produced some of its most surprising results.

In the brief period in which he published, 1648 to 1652, Winstanley moved from a densely biblical statement of his personal vision to the people of Lancaster (*The Mysterie of God Concerning the Whole Creation, Mankinde*) to a utopian design for reorganizing English society addressed to Cromwell (*The Law of Freedom in a Platform*). The latter shows a practical concern with the shape of the laws and institutions of society not apparent before the failure of the Diggers' efforts. In the ideal society that Winstanley envisioned, priests and lawyers would disappear and the authority of the state would serve primarily to ensure a fair and orderly distribution of the fruits of the earth. The sabbath would become a day for education, chiefly vocational and scientific, and for reading the law of the commonwealth. Formal religious instruction was to be avoided, because traditional divinity only succeeded in frightening the people or in consoling them with illusions. Winstanley's plan would in effect transfer the reverence normally reserved for Scripture to his simplified code of law, which he insisted would not need interpretation. Judges would merely "pronounce the bare letter of the Law" (554).

The society described in *The Law of Freedom in a Platform*, organized according to rational principles and dedicated to improving the welfare of the ordinary man in this world, reveals Winstanley at his most secular; yet a modern reader exposed to this work alone would be struck by the strong biblical coloration of much of the language and argument. Winstanley still quotes Scripture, if less freely than before, and holds up Israel as the model to be imitated.[8] His great hope is that the "Rule of right Government" may make the earth "one family of Mankind...as *Israel* was called *one house of Israel*, though it consisted of many Tribes, Nations and Family" (545). By Israel, Winstanley meant an idealized version of the society that existed in the period before the government of kings and their attendant scribes and Pharisees, precursors of the hated lawyers and clergy. For Winstanley the chief distinction of Israel, one that he mentions frequently in his works, was that it had no beggars. He saw the tribal organization of society as guaranteeing land and sustenance for everyone and regarded its laws—"few, short and pithy"—as providing a pattern for a revised legal code. Winstanley describes the governance of his ideal society only after beginning *The Law of Freedom* by laying a "Foundation" from "the Example of *Israels* Commonwealth, and Testimony of Gods Word" (525), having first appealed to Cromwell as the Moses who had cast out pharoah and could go on to eliminate the kingly power that lingered in the laws and institutions of England. The biblical impress on Winstanley's thought remains clearly visible, even after he has shifted his emphasis from the coming victory of the Spirit to plans for reforming existing institutions in the shorter run.[9]

One must of course understand how Winstanley reads the Bible to assess the extent of his indebtedness to it. It is apparent from any of his works that he treated the text with a kind of freedom that would have appalled Sibbes or Baxter. Winstanley's allegorizing imagination transmuted historical figures—Cain, Jacob and Esau, Abraham—into actors in a cosmic struggle between the forces of the flesh and those of the Spirit, between covetousness and love, that he saw as raging in the world and in the soul of man.[10] The Fall became for him a fall into the darkness of self-concern and Adam a symbol of "the wisdome and power of the flesh in every man" (158). Winstanley could show such indifference to the literal sense of Scripture because he believed, with many others in the middle of the seventeenth century, that the "word of life within" was more important than actual words. The Bible was to him a "report" of the Spirit's revelations to the prophets and the apostles, not a sacred text. He trusted the Spirit to reveal to him the truth embodied in the Scriptures, and this might have little to do with their apparent sense. Thus he could object that preachers had cheated the world "by telling us of a single man, called Adam, that killed us al by eating a single fruit, called an Apple" (203).

An insistence upon reading the Bible with the aid of the Spirit was a central strain of Protestant thought, as we have seen, but the Spirit was usually regarded as working in conjunction with the words of the text. Winstanley's attitude reflects a dramatic shift in the most radical Protestant thought toward relying primarily upon the Spirit.[11] Concern with the "leadings" of the Spirit can be found in the sect called the Family of Love (or Familists), founded by Henry Niclaes in the Netherlands and transported to England, and in the sermons of several influential preachers of the 1640s: John Everard (who popularized many of the ideas of Jakob Boehme), John Saltmarsh, and William Dell. The Quakers, emerging as a sect in the late forties and early fifties under the leadership of Fox and others, were to become the most determined advocates of the inner light. Radical believers in the possibility of direct revelations from the Spirit ("extraordinary" motions in the language of a critic such as Baxter, who argued that these had ceased with the apostles) were united by an extreme emphasis upon the "experimental" character of religion. They were unwilling to rely upon mere words, even when these were the words of Scripture.

Preachers such as Everard, Saltmarsh, and Dell—all Cambridge-trained divines who moved decidedly leftward in the 1640s—helped to create a climate of hostility to the strict Calvinism of more conservative Puritans with their rational theology, strong sense of church discipline, and systematic way of interpreting scripture. The radical preachers fostered a popular mysticism that found God in the natural world and encouraged a habit of reading Scripture allegorically which minimized the importance of the letter.[12] Everard spoke of the letter as the outward court of the tabernacle and urged readers to penetrate to the hidden manna of the sanctum sanctorum.[13] He argued against reading the Word as history, things done long ago without us "and not at present doing in us." Until the Word quickened the heart, it was "a Spring shut up, a Fountain sealed."[14]

The new emphasis on the Spirit led to strikingly unorthodox interpretations of Scripture in the light of individual experience and to a belief that the Spirit was the ultimate authority by which opinions and even the words of Scripture must be tried.[15] The Reformation principle of trial by the Word gave way, for men like Winstanley and Fox, to that of trial by each believer's experience of the Spirit: "It is the *Spirit* within man that tries all things: words cannot try all things" (101). The ministers that they attacked, Presbyterians and Independents and even Baptists, responded with accusations of denying the Scriptures. Fox's *Journal* records numerous confrontations in which he opposed a minister's interpretation of Scripture with his sense of the Spirit that informed the words as they were originally set down.

Winstanley felt that the Bible had become an instrument by which the clergy dominated the common people and insured their own well-being:

> The Scriptures of the Bible were written by the experimentall hand of the Shepherds, Husbandmen, Fishermen, and such inferiour men of the world; And the Universitie learned ones have got these mens writings; and flourishes their plaine language over with their darke interpretation, and glosses, as if it were too hard for ordinary men now to understand them; and thereby they deceive the simple, and makes a prey of the poore, and cosens them of the Earth, and of the tenth of their labors. (474–75)

Winstanley saw this "darke interpretation" as tearing the Gospel to pieces. Tyndale had wrested the Bible from the priests by translating it so that the plowman could read the Word of God for himself. Winstanley struggled with less success to free the Bible from the "inferences and constructions" of a new clerical caste: "Leave the pure Scriptures to shine in their own luster" (144). Instead of stressing the perspicuity of the Scriptures, as so many

Puritans did, he held up the elusive ideal of a marriage of the words of the text with the "word within:"

> And let us leave the pure teachings of the Father in every man, to conjoyn themselves with those Scriptures, and then there will be no jarring, but a sweet harmony of peace and love, betweene the experience of every man and those Scriptures. (144–45)

In *The New Law of Freedom* Winstanley sought to institutionalize a principle that he had articulated earlier with reference to Scripture: simply speak the words, without forcing meanings. It is a democratizing principle, based upon the impossible hope that all men could perceive the same truth shining forth from the words of the text, whether this was the Bible or the law that he imagined a wise Parliament as enacting. Winstanley spoke from a bitter recognition of the way priests on the one hand and lawyers and judges on the other had used language to tyrannize over the common people. His urge to simplify, to recover or somehow create (in the case of the law) a pure and unembellished text, reflects a deep distrust of language itself. The principle of speaking the words without allowing explanation allowed the freest play to each person's inward illumination. Even as Winstanley enumerated "particular" laws for his ideal commonwealth he appealed simultaneously to "the true ancient law of God," which he identified with "the inward power of right understanding...the true law that teaches people in action, as well as in words, to do as they would be done unto" (489).

The problem for Winstanley, as for Fox, was that words could too easily distort the truth or become instruments of deception. Winstanley speaks contemptuously of "hearsay-Preachers" who "preach the letter for the Spirit" without any "testimony of the light within themselves" (238), describing them as offering "words without life." One dramatic consequence of such a distrust of language can be seen in the silent worship of the Quakers. Edward Burroughs described this as waiting upon the Lord "in pure silence, from our own words, and all mens words" in order to feel the Word of God acting upon the heart.[16] Winstanley, though not concerned with the practice of worship, presents silence as a necessary stage in man's recovery of goodness: "For truly the time is come, that all flesh shal be made silent, and leave off multiplying of words without knowledge before the Lord" (224). He saw such silence as "the forerunner of pure language," pure because based solely upon experience.

Winstanley predicted that "verbal worship" would cease and that men would learn to worship God by "walking righteously in the Creation" (185). He rejected the forms as well as the language of organized worship, dismissing the ordinances as "new moulded" by the preachers. Although he described himself as having been "dipped," in an earlier period as a Baptist,

Winstanley came to believe that the only baptism that mattered was in the "water of life," which he understood to mean the Spirit (141). Worship "in spirit and in truth" meant for him a worship not confined by forms or by the doctrine and practice of Presbyterians, Independents, or any other church or sect:

> All of your particular Churches are like the inclosures of land which hedges in some to be heires of life, and hedges out others. (445–46)

Religious divisions were for Winstanley another manifestation of the possessiveness that he found everywhere in a fallen world. Particular differences were unimportant to him. What mattered was that churches of all kinds used their forms of worship and their control over numerous aspects of daily life to keep ordinary people in bondage. Their oppression was the most offensive of all because the other powers—rulers, lawyers, merchants —depended upon the clergy to "bewitch the people to conforme" (470). The role of the minister, whatever his church, was symbolized for Winstanley by his "covetous, proud black gowne" (475). A man must not take a wife, he complained,

> but the Priests must give her him. If he have a child, the Priest must give the name. If any die, the Priest must see it laid in the earth. If any man want knowledge or comfort, they teach him to go to the Priest for it. (187)

Winstanley was driven by a determination to win freedom from this kind of control as well as from economic exploitation. He saw the clergy as the chief enemy of the people and the key to perpetuating a social and economic order in which he and others like him were no better than slaves.

Winstanley objected with equal vigor to a "Divinity" that he regarded as destroying the possibility of true knowledge of God. His most fundamental criticism of the clergy is that they deceive the people by teaching them to seek God "at a distance," in a local heaven rather than within. Heaven and hell were to him fictions sustained by the priests in order to persuade men to accept their present condition. His preoccupation with a better life in this world meant that the traditional Augustinian opposition of heavenly and earthly cities does not figure in his writing. Winstanley did not deny that a local heaven could exist, just that anyone could be sure that it did on the basis of the evidence available, including Scripture. He insisted in a stubbornly commonsensical way that "men ought to speak no more than they know" (219). One of his heroes, not surprisingly, was "wise-hearted *Thomas*," who would believe nothing but what he saw.

Winstanley attacked the conceptualizations of the preachers as not deriving from experience and as limiting one's sense of God. With the Ranters and other radicals of the period he believed that the Father was to be found "in every place, and every creature" (114). Winstanley did not deny the existence of the historical Christ but emphasized the indwelling Spirit: "The Spirit in that humane body is the Saviour" (112). He understood the resurrection symbolically, as the spreading of that Spirit throughout mankind. Christ was for him "the universall power of Love...the power of Life, Light, and Truth, now rising up to fill the Earth, Mankinde with himselfe" (446). Winstanley tended to reduce all manifestations of divinity to Spirit. Father, Son, and Holy Ghost, he says at one point, are "three names given to one spirit" (131). He saw Old Testament types as pointing to the Spirit rather than to Christ: "The Spirit lay hid under those types and shadows, fighting against the Beast" (229). In Winstanley's loose theology there is no place for such traditional Protestant conceptions as redemption and justification, or indeed for attention to the historical role of Christ. His primary concern, akin to that of the Quakers, was with demonstrating the perfectibility of men transformed by the power of the Spirit.

For all the liberties that he took with the Bible, Winstanley nevertheless seriously regarded it as authorizing his unorthodox views. Like other radical Protestants, he could insist upon applying texts with strict literalness. If the Book of Acts described believers as having all things in common (4:32), then society should be reorganized to conform to this ideal:

> There shall be no buying nor selling, no fairs nor markets, but the whole earth shall be a common treasury for every man, for the earth is the Lords. And man kind thus drawn up to live and act in the Law of love, equity and onenesse, is but the great house wherein the Lord himself dwels, and every particular one a severall mansion: and as one spirit of righteousnesse is common to all, so the earth and the blessings of the earth shall be common to all; for now all is but the Lord, and the Lord is all in all. *Eph.* 4.5,6. (184)

Winstanley could just as readily take figurative descriptions of the restoration of Israel as literal justifications of his own blueprint for society. The peculiarities of his method of citing texts can be seen in a tract written as an earnest response to Parson Platt's facetious offer to join the Diggers if Winstanley could demonstrate from Scripture that the earth was meant to be a common treasury. Winstanley addressed his *Humble Request* to ministers of both universities and lawyers of "every Inns-a-Court," seeking to bring this learned audience around to his surprising view of the Bible as falling into three basic parts: one declaring "the righteous Law of Creation wherein God gives to all Mankind equall freedome," a second declaring the fall of man and his subsequent "unrighteous actings" under the power of darkness, and a third declaring the promised restoration of man to his "creation-righteousnesse" (423).

To support his unique reading of Scripture Winstanley mustered loose collocations of texts, typically combining references to Genesis with others to New Testament passages dealing with the workings of the Spirit:

> All the wars and divisions in Israels time, and since: and all buying and selling of Land, and the fruits of the earth, which is the art of cheating one another, is but the actings of Mankind in darknesse, under the power of the fall; for, both Kings, Rulers, and all people, have had their checks from God, for their unrighteous walking, or cruelty against *Abels* plain-hearted Spirit. And all the great combustions that hath been, and yet is, in the world, is but politick, covetous, murdering *Cain*; holding *Abel,* or the honest plaine dealing heart under him; or the son of bondage, perse-cuting the son of freedome. Gen. 23.4. Gal. 4.29. Jam. 4.1. Isa. 33.1. (425–26)

In his *Humble Request* as elsewhere Winstanley shows himself to be at-tracted by some of the most figurative language in the Bible: from Isaiah, Ezekiel, and especially Daniel and Revelation. He seizes upon Isaiah's prophecy that swords shall be beaten into plowshares and Ezekiel's that the desolate land shall be tilled, offering them as warrants for the enterprise of the Diggers. Any prophecy of the blossoming of Zion, or the coming of Christ's kingdom on earth, serves his special purpose. Winstanley saw no difficulty in using the metaphoric language of prophecy to justify his own efforts. By hoeing their grain on a hill in Surrey he and his followers were, to his mind, beating swords into plowshares; they embodied the spiritual truth expressed in Isaiah's words.

In a century in whch divines marshaled phalanxes of texts to settle the most minute questions of worship and church government, it is refreshing to find Winstanley citing Scripture in his freewheeling fashion to prove the right of the poor of England to plant common land. Yet he was clearly miscast as a controversialist. The role that came naturally to him was that of prophet. If he did not go about like Fox crying "Woe unto the bloody city of Lichfield," he cried woe often enough in his writing, sometimes to "the imaginary power that rules the world," sometimes to a more specific au-dience, as in his *Watch-Word to the City of London:*

> O thou city, thou Hypocriticall City! thou blindfold drowsie *England,* that sleps and snorts in the bed of covetousnesse, awake, awake, the Enemie is upon thy back, he is ready to scale the walls and enter Possession, and wilt thou not look out. (335–36)

Winstanley saw himself as offering reports of the revelations of the Spirit to him, "Declarations of the Lord through his servant" (204), and liked to assert that his writings were not indebted to books or to men. *Fire in the Bush* begins with the announcement, "This following declaration of the word of Life was a free gift to me from the Father himselfe" (445). He claims to have published it only after a voice commanded, "Goe send it to the Churches."

Winstanley makes his most striking claims for direct inspiration in connection with his digging. A voice came to him in a trance, he relates in *The New Law of Righteousness*, with the commands *"Worke together. Eat bread together"* (190) and *"Let Israel go free"* (199), repeated three times. The account of this vision is amplified in *The True Levellers Standard*, where *"Declare all this abroad"* is added to the initial command and another voice states *"Israel shall neither take Hire, nor give Hire"* (261). Winstanley gives the impression of writing always in response to divine impulses, and of having to write in order to quiet his spirit. He claims to have finished *The Law of Freedom* because the word, *"Thou shalt not bury thy talent in the earth,"* was "like fire in my bones ever and anon" (510).[17] Digging on St. George's Hill was another way of responding to the divine compulsion to publish the truth, a particularly appropriate way in view of his emphasis upon active as opposed to notional or verbal religion. As he puts it in concluding one of the tracts of this period: "I have Writ, I have Acted, I have Peace: and now I must wait to see the Spirit do his work in the hearts of others" (395).

To read Winstanley's description of the action he took in response to his inner voices one would think that nothing could be simpler or more obvious:

> The Work we are going about is this, To dig up *Georges-Hill* and the waste Ground thereabouts, and to Sow Corn, and to eat our bread together by the sweat of our brows. (257)

The blunt statement of fact seems incongruous in the midst of visionary prose announcing the appearance of "one house of Israel restored from Bondage"; yet Winstanley would have seen no incongruity. The Bible served him both as a source of images by which to develop his mythology of good and evil and as a warrant for specific action. Winstanley could become an actor in the drama that he projected in his writing because literal and metaphoric readings of Scripture ran together in his imagination.[18] With a persistent literal-mindedness, he singled out texts that would authorize the new Israel he sought to establish. At the same time he read the biblical history of Israel as a symbolic rendering of the continuing battle of flesh and spirit. Once loosed from its contextual moorings, a particular verse could serve virtually any purpose.

Winstanley's digging can be seen as one manifestation of the rampant millenarian expectations of the mid-seventeenth century, but the action has a peculiar simplicity and appropriateness. He did not try to inaugurate the reign of King Jesus with the Fifth Monarchists or pose as the Messiah, as the Quaker James Nayler did in allowing his followers to strew palms before him while leading him into Bristol on an ass. His action, and indeed his whole vision, sprang from a sense of the injustice of an economic system that exploited ordinary people who could, he thought, support themselves by planting common land. It was rooted in a conviction that the poor had been cheated again and again, most recently by a Parliament that had called upon them to give their blood and their money and then in victory had left the social order unchanged. Whatever theological significance Winstanley attempted to give his action, it seems a natural expression of opposition to those who, in his words, "bag and barn up the treasures of the earth" (196); there was in fact abundant precedent for this particular form of protest.[19]

Winstanley made the efforts of the Diggers memorable by publicizing them, in rough, vividly colloquial prose that gives his social criticism an unmistakable note of authenticity.[20] In his prefatory letter to Cromwell Winstanley described *The Law of Freedom* as being "like a poor man that comes cloathed to your door in a torn country garment" and urged him to recognize the beauty under his "clownish language." He wore his country garments proudly, in preference to aping the "unsetled" stylistic fashions of city and University writers; they were his guarantee of honesty. Winstanley would not have used "fine language" if he could, because he saw it as betraying a lack of true experience.

Winstanley had a gift for expressing the grievances of the people through arresting metaphors drawn from ordinary life. The hedges that came to divide the land with the growth of the enclosure movement provided him with a favorite image for the powers he saw as dividing and oppressing the people, including that of wealth: "Money must not any longer...be the great god, that hedges in some, and hedges out others" (270). He is particularly effective in describing the corruption of justice. England was to him a prison in which "the Lawyers are the Jaylors, and poor men are the prisoners" (361). In his tracts that seemingly impersonal agency, the law, becomes an antagonist that "frights and forces people to obey it by Prisons, Whips, and Gallows" (338). He uses a shrewd personification to call attention to its predatory habits:

> The Law is the Fox, poore men are the geesse; he pulls of their feathers, and feeds upon them. (468)

Winstanley slips easily into such vivid metaphors in a prose that carries the attack to the enemy with questions, taunts, and snatches of dialogue, arguing the case of the people in a plain and forceful language that anyone could understand. Yet his colloquialism blends with a visionary prose saturated in biblical idioms. His characterization of the law as a fox comes in the middle of a section of *Fire in the Bush* offering an extended allegory of the powers of the world as the four beasts that Daniel saw rising from the sea:

They devoure abundantly, and yet they rise out of the Sea, even from the body of deceived, covetous, darke, powered mankinde, in the night time of that world. (466)

The moral Winstanley points is that the creation will never be at peace until these powers are swallowed up by the sea, that is, by an enlightened mankind. The imagery of Daniel enabled him to raise his struggle against injustice and deception to the level of a cosmic drama in which evil would ultimately be reabsorbed by goodness. Abuses of the people appear as crimes against the universe, as in this characterization of the clergy, in his view the most "terrible and dreadful" of the beasts:

He makes a man a sinner for a word, and so he sweeps the Stars of Heaven downe with his tayle, he darkens Heaven and Earth, and defiles body and mind. (469)

Here Winstanley moves from a particular complaint—the clergy use language to tyrannize over the people—to a nightmarish image of evil based upon the dragon of Revelation.[21] The effect is to make the clergy appear a monstrous power destroying the original purity of man and nature.

It is Winstanley's visionary prose that shows the range and power of his imagination and invites comparisons with Blake. His characteristic vocabulary and the mythology that gave shape to his vision can be explained only by reference to his idiosyncratic reading of Scripture. Where the orthodox Puritan divine, instructed by Perkins, painstakingly collected parallel texts and tested his interpretations by the analogy of faith, Winstanley followed his intuitions of the Spirit in rendering what he saw as the truth behind the letter, not so much expounding Scripture as re-creating it by fashioning his own highly individual version of the Fall and redemption of man. Winstanley approached the Bible as a poet might, alive to the power of images and the symbolic force of names.

One implication of Winstanley's disregard for the possible historical and doctrinal significance of texts is that his terminology remains extremely fluid, evocative rather than precise. The various terms by which he identifies the opposing powers that dominate his world are virtually interchangeable. Adam, taken to symbolize the consequences of the Fall, becomes "the serpent, the Devil, the power of darknesse, the Beast, the Whore, the father of lies" (178). Winstanley frequently refers to the two powers as Jacob and Esau, taking Jacob as the persecuted younger brother and Esau as tyrannical force. He can assert that "*Jacob* is Christ, *the elect or chosen one*, or the *Almighty power and wisdome*, that first put forth his arm of strength in making man-kind" (179). Elsewhere he identifies Christ with David, and also with the archangel Michael, who appears periodically in his works as the antagonist of the Dragon. There was nothing unusual about associating Jacob or David with Christ, except that Winstanley did not see one as a type of the other. In fact, he blurs distinctions between the Old Testament and the New with what to a more sober reader may seem startling irresponsibility. Winstanley could let his imagination range freely over Scripture because the words of the text had no fixed meaning for him. All events became manifestations of the fundamental warfare of good and evil, and all names ways of referring to the action of either demonic or spiritual power.

Winstanley used abstract labels as well as names to describe the workings of the Spirit, calling it the "law of righteousness," the "universal power of love," and the "Spirit Reason" or simply "Reason." His justification of the term "Reason," which he substituted for God or the Spirit in several works, is revealing. He used "Reason" for "God," he explains, "because I have been held under darknesse by that word [God]" (105). Winstanley's original terminology was a way of freeing himself from the bondage of traditional understandings of God. Yet he made no exclusive claim for it, suggesting that each person find his own name for that "spirituall Power" that he feels and sees ruling in him. Winstanley defined "Reason" loosely as "that living power of light that is in all things" and the spiritual power "that guids all mens reasoning in right order, and to a right end" (105), which he understood to be that of knitting "every creature together into a oneness." This is obviously no ordinary conception of rationality, nor is it carefully delimited. Winstanley may not have been capable of more rigorous definition, but it is also true that he referred so variously to the spiritual power that he felt in himself because he did not think it could be contained by particular words. His refusal to be more precise should be seen as an extreme manifestation of the Puritan reluctance to bind the Spirit.

The Bible was for Winstanley a storehouse of terms by which to image the conflict of the Spirit with powers released by the Fall. Egypt was, of course, the "house of bondage," Canaan the "universal power of righteous Communitie" (199). Babylon may be substituted for Egypt, and Israel or Jerusalem for Canaan, but the nature of the contest remains the same. It is a struggle for ascendancy between the "Son of Bondage" and the "Son of Freedom," the "man of sin" and the "man of righteousness," both in society and in the individual. Winstanley saw the Fall as giving rise to a "subtil over-reaching imagination" that caused man to pursue his own well-being rather than take satisfaction in the original harmony of all creation. This selfish imagination begets covetousness, which in turn generates fear and the various arts by which men seek to dominate others. Winstanley pictures the original innocence of man as a state of "plain-heartedness" without envy or guile. The vice of "subtilty" came with the Fall, along with the aggressive impulses that result in all the manifestations of kingly power in society.

The heart of Winstanley's message to the people of England was that the Spirit would spread through the earth and come again to rule it. This theme dominates his first major work, titled in full *The New Law of Righteousness*

Budding Forth, to Restore the Whole Creation from Bondage of the Curse (1649). Winstanley was convinced that the Spirit would manifest itself in the common people. As he put it, addressing his "brethren" as "the Twelve Tribes of Israel that are Circumcised in Heart:"

> *Though dark clouds of inward bondage, and outward persecution have over-spread you; yet you are the firmament, in whom the Son of righteousnesse will rise up, and from you will declare himself to the whole Creation; for you are Sion whom no man regards, out of whom salvation shall come.* (149)

Winstanley repeatedly identifies the poor as "the seed of Abraham" and the people of Jacob. He asserts that power will rise up in mankind "to pull the Kingdom and outward government of the world" out of the hands of Esau. Such prophecies would seem to call for violent revolution, but Winstanley continued to reject violence as the way of the flesh. Unlike the peasant revolutionaries of the late middle ages inspired by Joachim of Fiore, he felt that in the age of the Spirit the kingdom of Christ would establish itself without the need for uprisings.[22]

Winstanley's confidence in the transforming power of the Spirit, strongest in *The New Law of Righteousness*, persists in one form or another throughout his work. In *The True Levellers Standard* Winstanley proclaimed that the "old World" was "running up like parchment in the fire" (252). In *Fire in the Bush*, not published until after the failure of the Diggers,[23] he could assert: "Rejoyce, your Redeemer is come, he rides upon the clouds.... This is the day of Sions glorie" (487–88). Even in *The New Law of Freedom*, a much more sober and practical work than anything that preceded it, Winstanley continued to look to the power of the Spirit, identifying it with the "righteous law" that informed his design for an ideal commonwealth: "In thee, O England, is the Law arising up to shine."[24] While he appealed to Cromwell as the instrument by which the commonwealth might be realized, confessing his own lack of power, he saw the power of the Spirit as a check on all rulers:

> The Spirit of the whole Creation (who is God) is about the Reformation of the World, and he will go forward in his work: For if he would not spare Kings...neither will he regard you, unless your ways be found more righteous than the Kings. (502)

The verses that serve as an epilogue to *The Law of Freedom* offer more insight into the frustrations that Winstanley must have experienced than anything that comes before. Here he confesses the painfulness of his knowledge of "the great deceit which in the World doth lie" (600) and asks: "O power where art thou, that must mend things amiss?" The very need to call upon the Spirit to "Come change the heart of Man" is a sign of strain. With so little evidence of the kind of radical change he anticipated, it must have taken a strenuous effort of will for Winstanley to sustain his vision of a new Israel as long as he did.

Winstanley's vision is most compelling when he writes out of a confidence that the power of the Spirit is irresistible. He pictures this power as sprouting, after a period of dormancy, and spreading like a "fruitfull vine" to fill the earth. It frequently appears as a fire burning the dross out of creation, as in the subtitle to *Fire in the Bush:* "The Spirit burning, not consuming, but purging Mankinde." Winstanley sometimes speaks of the "free running streams of the Spirit of life" (202), dammed up by imagination and the powers of the flesh; the universities, in his view, are "standing ponds of stinking waters" (238). Winstanley's habit of incorporating biblical images into his vision of a transformed England rather than seeking to decode them, as an expositor would have, shows a respect for their latent power. For him they remained living images, instinct with mystery. He saw himself as a prophet bringing the message that the fire of the Spirit was sweeping through the land. To explain his images more than he did would have been to dissipate their power in the kind of language that he scorned as mere words.

Winstanley's rendering of the Spirit as a dynamic force in the process of manifesting itself helps to explain why it was impossible for him to accept existing social institutions and forms of worship. They were inevitably imperfect and transitional. At one point he describes the "Father" as "driving this people through al the waies, and forms, and customs...and governments of the Beast, to weary them out in all" (230) until they abandon forms altogether and worship in spirit and truth. By an extraordinary imaginative leap he makes the devices by which men describe and order their world appear a chaos that must be transcended by a new act of creation:

> The Son of universal Love...moves upon the living waters of mankind, and makes him, who all the dark time past was a Chaos of confusion, lying under Types, Shadows, Ceremonies, Forms, Customes, Ordinances, and heaps of waste words...to worship in Spirit and Truth, and to bring forth fruit of Righteousness in action. (377)

What Winstanley imagines being created is a condition of absolute freedom, in which man can act and worship without regard to constraints of any kind. Such a position, carried to its extreme, does not allow for the emergence of new "forms" of any kind. Action must be spontaneous, completely unstructured, if it is to reflect the variable motions of the Spirit.

The elusive phrase "in Spirit and Truth" (echoing John 4:23, 24) gave Winstanley's readers little to grasp, however appealing it may have seemed. They could respond more readily to his vision of an earth restored to all the people. This offered not only the hope of breaking the power of the local gentry over common land but the larger prospect of recovering their "creation-right" to the benefits of the earth, which once more would become a land without hedges. In his view of Eden Winstanley stressed the original dominion of man over the earth. Because man "lived in his Maker the Spirit," "the whole Creation lived in man" (155), in the sense that man embodied the same Spirit that informed the natural world and thus lived at peace with all its creatures. The Fall brought disharmony between man and creation and also a division of mankind into two classes: "teachers and rulers" on the one hand and "Servants and Slaves" on the other. Digging on St. George's Hill symbolized for Winstanley escape from servitude and the beginnings of a recovery of harmony with the Spirit. Significantly, he did not reject the idea of labor but sought to dignify it, proclaiming that he and his followers aimed "to eate our Bread together by righteous labour, and sweat of our browes" (260). Winstanley ignored the fact that Genesis explains the necessity for sweating as part of the curse placed on Adam by God. For him it was "unrighteous" labor, labor for hire, that marked man's fallen condition.

The natural world dominates Winstanley's vision because he could believe in no other. He begins *Fire in the Bush* by asserting that the "whole Creation," the elements and all they compose, is "the cloathing of God" (451). In *The New Law of Righteousness* he had described the "great world" with its variety of creatures as "no other but Christ spread forth in the Creation...for he is the maker, preserver and restoring Spirit" (164–65). A sense of the immanence of God in nature was clearly abroad when Winstanley began writing. Everard, for example, saw God as a "beam of divinity" present in every creature.[25] In their readiness to see God literally everywhere the Ranters reduced the idea to absurdity. Jacob Bauthumley found God not only in "man and beast, fish and fowl, and every green thing" but in his pipe and stool.[26] If God appeared in themselves and everything around them, then any kind of behavior was holy, the Ranters concluded, and quickly made themselves notorious by their ostentatious swearing, drinking, and sexual promiscuity.

Winstanley vigorously defended the Diggers against charges of ranting. He saw the "Ranting Power" as a "devouring Beast" that was tearing people to pieces by reducing them to confusion. The error of the Ranters, in his view, was in placing all their trust in a "Kingdome that lies in objects; as in the outward enjoyment of meat, drinke, pleasures, and women" (399). They might talk of the Spirit but in fact acted directly contrary to Winstanley's understanding of it. The distinction is important if one is to appreciate Winstanley's sense of how and to what ends one should seek God in nature.

By the time he wrote *The Law of Freedom* Winstanley could advocate active study of the natural world, in order to attain what he calls "the practical knowledge of God:"

> To know the secrets of nature, is to know the works of God: And to know the works of God within the Creation, is to know God himself, for God dwels in every visible work or body. (565)

If God was to be found in the created world rather than in a remote heaven, what could be more natural than to seek to understand this world, especially if such "practical" knowledge would improve the condition of the ordinary man? Winstanley's theology could readily accommodate a Baconian sense of the utility of unlocking the "secrets of nature." Yet it is misleading to read such a statement simply as a glorification of science, as Christopher Hill does, and to conclude that Winstanley arrived at a "kind of materialist pantheism:"[27]

> If God is everywhere, if matter is God, then there can be no difference between the sacred and the secular: pantheism leads to secularism.[28]

Such a formulation ignores the role of the Spirit in Winstanley's thinking about the natural world. God was not simply matter for him. Winstanley at his most pragmatic saw the Spirit as an external force awakening the desire to study nature and leading to a right understanding of how to make use of its secrets. The first step to true knowledge for him was always feeling the Spirit as a "power within." In opposing traditional religion, Winstanley was arguing against the habit of equating "spiritual" with "heavenly" and chiding the pious to enjoy the things of the earth honestly, since they obviously cared about them, instead of branding them "carnal." His concern was with teaching men to look for evidences of God where they might expect to find them, in the creation of which they were a part. To study the natural world without recognizing the Spirit that informed it was "to seeke for a Kingdome without that lies in objects" (496), the failing he censures at the end of *Fire in the Bush* and numerous other places. This failing was the true materialism, or, in Winstanley's terminology, bondage to the covetous power.

Winstanley's educational program, much of which would have pleased a Baconian reformer like Hartlib, should be seen in the context of his persistent millenarian expectations. He assumed that those who learned "to speak a pure language" (564) by reading the law of nature as God had written it would naturally abandon the economic and social systems under which they had formerly existed. They would live at peace with the earth instead of trying to possess it. The most remarkable thing about *The Law of Freedom* is the way practical designs for studying nature and educating youth in trades coexist with a vision of society transformed through the influence of the Spirit. Winstanley still insists that "the old Heaven, and the old Earth" (531) of kingly power must pass away and predicts the fall of "that great City Babylon, that mighty City Divinity" (570). The army of his commonwealth, unlike the actual Parliamentary army which overthrew the king without changing the structure of society, will make way "for the spirit of Peace and Freedom to come in, to rule and inherit the Earth" (576). *The Law of Freedom* differs from Winstanley's previous works in its hope that a reconstructed government will act as the agency of social change, "the Restorer of ancient Peace and Freedom" (533), but the underlying myth remains the same. The earth will be restored to its original condition, in which peace pervaded creation, and bondage—to external or internal powers—did not exist.

Winstanley frequently described the regeneration worked by the Spirit by means of images drawn from the natural world. A poetic fragment included in *The Law of Freedom*—beginning "The Winter's past, the Springtime now appears" (533)—recalls a fuller and more lyrical rendering of the springtime of the soul in *The New Law of Righteousness:*

> The windows of heaven are opening, and the light of the Son of Righ-tousnes, sends forth of himself delightful beams, and sweet discoveries of truth that wil quite put out the covetous traditional bleareyes...the warm Sun wil thaw the frost, and make the sap to bud out of every tender plant, that hath been hid within, and lain like dead trees all the dark cloudy daies of the Beast that are past.... Now the tender grasse wil cover the earth, the Spirit wil cover al places *with the abundance of fruit.* (207)

Given Winstanley's extraordinary feeling for the sacredness of the earth itself, it is not surprising to find him associating the coming of an age of the Spirit with the miraculous greening of the land. The renewal of the earth was for him more than a metaphoric way of describing a spiritual condi-tion. Winstanley confidently expected that the purifying action of the Spirit would cleanse the earth of the corruption introduced by the Fall[29] and restore its original fertility:

> There shall be no barrennesse in the earth or cattle, *for they shall bring forth fruit abundantly.* Unseasonable storms of weather shall cease, for all the curse shall be removed from all, and every creature shall rejoyce in Righteousnesse one in another throughout the whole Creation. (186)

Winstanley often conflates literal and metaphoric senses of landscape, as in the following adaptation of the message of the voice crying in the wilderness to Isaiah (Isa. 40:3-5):

> He is now coming to raign, and the Isles and Nations of the earth shall all come in unto him.... He will throw down the mountaines of the flesh, fill up the low valleys of the spirit, he will make rough wayes smooth, and crooked wayes strait, he will make the earth fruitfull, and the winds

and the weather seasonable; he will throw all the powers of the earth at your feet, and himself will be your governour and teacher, and your habitations on earth shall be in peace. (152–53)

The imagery of Isaiah, which follows upon the command of the voice to "make straight in the desert a highway for our God," becomes for Winstanley a means of evoking the power of the Spirit to transform the soul, the earth itself, and human society. He moves between inner and outer worlds with no apparent sense of discontinuity.

Winstanley's metaphoric use of Eden in *Fire in the Bush* to represent the state of the soul has the effect of breaking down the distinction between man and the natural world. They appear as different aspects of one creation:

For as the great Earth, and the inferiour creatures therein are as the Commons, Forrests, and delights of God in the out Coasts of the Creation: Even so Mankind, The living Earth is the very Garden of *Eden*, wherein that spirit of Love, did walke, and delight himselfe principally, as being the Head and Lord of all the rest. (451)

Winstanley pictures the warfare of Michael and the dragon as raging not in some external heaven but in the soul, understood as Eden.[30] In this allegorized Eden the original four rivers become five, representing the senses: "And these five water springs do refresh and preserve the whole creation, both of the out-coasts and of the garden" (452). Here Winstanley makes the purity of the natural world seem to depend upon man's uncorrupted perception. It is his innocent vision that makes creation whole, uniting him with nature.

When the "selfish imaginary power" arises within man, in Winstanley's version of the Fall, he is "driven out of the Garden, that is, out of himselfe, he enjoyes not himselfe, he knows not himselfe" (452). Banished into a condition of living upon external objects, man restlessly pursues power, wealth, and pleasure until he comes to a moment of recognition: "and you see your selfe naked and are ashamed" (452). Winstanley regarded universal love, symbolized by the tree of life, as the restorative power that would draw man "up into himselfe againe" and enable him to live "a life above objects...in the enjoyment of Christ, the righteous spirit within himselfe" (453). The key to this condition of recovered innocence is a renewed vision in which the senses become "pure rivers of the water of life" and bring "all into oneness." Then the whole creation will "laugh in righteousnesse." As he puts it elsewhere, when man has the Spirit within, "the Creation is his clothing." The metaphor implies that a restored mankind can dwell in nature, as God does. Winstanley's ideal is a pervasive harmony in which man is united with God (seen as walking and delighting in "his garden, mankind"), with other men, and with the natural world. He offered his readers not an abstract paradise within but a rich inner landscape nourished by the rivers of the senses, predicting that all mankind would become a garden in which God would walk, in the "coole of the day" (Gen. 3:8) when "the heate of opposition betweene flesh and spirit begins to decline" (460). Only in such a state could man find peace and satisfaction, in Winstanley's view:

> All bondage within is gone, sighing and sorrowing is done away; my heart now indeed is a Land of Righteousnesse, full of life, light, and fruit of peace and truth. (454)

Winstanley also describes this state as one in which man enjoys God's kingdom and the Word "within himselfe" (453), but his most characteristic and telling images are those in which he identifies mankind with the earth. By picturing unfallen man as "The living Earth" and the heart of the restored man as a "Land of Righteousness" he insists upon the fundamental unity of a creation infused with the Spirit.

Restoring the unity of creation was Winstanley's deepest and most persistent concern. His ideal of mankind as a community freely sharing the fruits of the earth reflects his confidence that an all-embracing "unitie of the Spirit" could be recovered. In *The New Law of Righteousness* he prophesies the Spirit will draw all things "back again into himself" (162); he will "gather the scattered of Israel together...out of all forms and customes of the Beast, to worship the Father in spirit and truth, being made to be all of one heart and one minde" (163). In *Fire in the Bush* Winstanley looks back to a time "when whole mankinde walked in singlenesse and simplicity each to other" (489) before falling into the division that was symbolized most vividly for him by the parceling out of the earth. Simplicity was inevitably joined with "singleness" for him, hence his concern with simplifying language and simplifying law. What may look like strikingly progressive social theory, anticipating some of the central concerns of Marxism, can better be understood as a profound nostalgia for an idealized life of perfect simplicity and "plain-heartedness." For Winstanley such simplicity antedated the complexities of the Norman law perpetuated by kings and the lawyers who served them as well as the comparable complexities of the doctrine and practice of the clergy and of an economic system upheld by merchants and landowners.

Although the visionary gleam is almost gone from *The Law of Freedom*, Winstanley's concern with unity and simplicity is still apparent in his last work. The design offered there was a means, more concrete than anything he had advanced before but sufficiently at odds with institutional realities to be ignored, to his unchanging goal of seeing all become "of one heart, and one mind" through the spreading power of the Spirit. He saw the "true ancient law of God" underlying any particular laws adopted by his commonwealth as uniting Jew and Gentile into "one brotherhood" and "making Christ's garment whole againe" (589) by setting the earth free. As we have seen, the verses that follow this last work offer a glimpse of Winstanley's disillusionment with men who fail to respond to the Spirit. These conclude, significantly, with a call to death to release him to join the elements:

Come take this body, and scatter it in the Four,
That I may dwell in One, and rest in peace once more. (600)

This is a final, surprising variation on a theme that runs through Winstanley's work. His mysticism culminates in an appeal to death, as the one means left him of participating in the unity of creation.

Winstanley's vision obviously failed to transform England, and it appears to have deserted him after the period of intense activity in which he did all his writing. Yet this vision remains compelling, for the originality and force of the prose in which it is expressed as well as for the radicalism of Winstanley's proposals for reform. Winstanley had a talent for transmuting spiritual conflict and social injustice into an apocalyptic drama unfolding simultaneously in the natural world and the soul of man. His fantastic reading of the Bible was possible only for someone who combined a sense of prophetic vocation with an intense awareness of the grievances of the poor. Such a person was peculiarly well suited to appreciate the explosive force of the Word. Freed from the concern with doctrine and exegetical procedure that bound orthodox Puritans, he could view the Bible as a source of images by which to describe the eruptions of Spirit that he felt in himself and his surroundings. The irony of Winstanley's situation was that so few people were able to view the substantial world in which they lived as "a parchment running up in the fire." It would prove easier to see it as Bunyan's Vanity Fair, a seductive environment to be traversed on the way to the New Jerusalem.

5. Milton and the Spirit of Truth

John Milton entered the ecclesiastical controversy that erupted in England in the early 1640s with all the conviction of someone who found himself called by God to take part in a holy war. He did not fall into a trance and hear voices, like Winstanley, nor did he identify with Jeremiah to the extent of feeling the word of God as a fire in his bones. Milton invoked Jeremiah by way of analogy, chiefly to justify the vehemence of his writing. Yet he clearly thought of himself as assuming a prophetic role, out of a divine compulsion to speak the truth as he understood it:

> But when God commands to take the trumpet and blow a dolorous or a jarring blast, it lies not in mans will what he shall say, or what he shall conceal.[1]

This sense of mission and the style it engendered distinguish Milton's antiprelatical tracts from the other writings that addressed the question of the proper form of church government, including those of the moderate Presbyterians whose cause he embraced, the five ministers who adopted the pseudonym Smectymnuus.[2] While these were capable of writing vigorous prose, their two pamphlets are considerably more subdued than Milton's and more taken up with details of the controversy over the origins of the liturgy and of episcopal government. Only Milton could soar to a vision of zeal triumphant, as in his account of "the invincible warriour Zeale" arming himself in "compleat diamond" and ascending his "fiery chariot" to bruise the stiff necks of the prelates under "flaming wheels" (1:900).

What Milton saw as zeal in a sacred cause Bishop Joseph Hall, his prime antagonist, dismissed as "spleen." A modern reader may feel inclined to sympathize with the response by an anonymous supporter of Hall to Milton's attack on Hall and prelacy in *Animadversions:*

> Such language you should scarce hear from the mouths of canting beggars, at an heathen altar; much lesse was it looked for in a treatise of controversial theologie.[3]

Even allowing for the rhetorical tactics of the time—Hall himself was called down for the abusiveness of his style by the Smectymnuans—Milton's invective must have seemed shockingly violent. In the view of his opponents Milton broke the rules of civilized discourse. One wonders, however, whether Milton would have agreed that what he had produced was "a treatise of controversial theologie." He thought of himself as assuming a role considerably larger than that of a mere controversialist and wrote out of a sense of decorum quite different from Hall's.

Critics have explained and perhaps even justified the style in which Milton wrote against the establishment of the Anglican church and, subsequently, against critics of the Commonwealth.[4] Milton was capable of using the satirist's plea of moral righteousness and of bringing the satirist's weapons to bear on his enemies. He could find precedent for his use of invective in classical rhetorical theory. He found the most important justification for the vehement expression of indignation in the Bible, however, chiefly in the example of Christ and that of the Old Testament prophets. Luther, whom Milton described as writing so "vehemently" against Rome that he offended his friends by "the fierceness of his spirit" (1:492), provided an example closer to home.[5] My concern here is not primarily with style, however, but with an underlying reason for Milton's stance in these tracts—and one that has received relatively little critical attention—his sense of the Bible as a force transforming England. I am not primarily interested in biblical proofs for specific doctrinal points (e.g., that bishops and presbyters are the same thing). Milton's arguments for the "one right discipline" of presbyterian church government are less significant, finally, than the complex of attitudes toward the Bible that emerges in these tracts. Although these attitudes are modified in Milton's subsequent prose and poetry, important continuities can be found, especially having to do with a sense of the dynamic operation of the Holy Spirit.

In arguing for the supreme authority of Scripture in doctrinal matters, as he does in Of Prelaticall Episcopacy and elsewhere,[6] Milton was enunciating a basic principle of Protestantism. Defenders of episcopacy appealed to Scripture as predictably as did their challengers. Yet, as the earlier battle over presbyterianism between Hooker and Cartwright demonstrates, people might disagree in fundamental ways about the sufficiency of Scripture, its scope, its perspicuity, and its power to change men's lives. Anglican apologists, following the lead of Hooker, sought to limit the authority and force of Scripture, whereas Puritan reformers tended to see themselves as champions of irresistible biblical truths. One of the most remarkable aspects of Milton's argument in the antiprelatical tracts is the way he appropriates the Bible for his side, reducing the conflict to a simple contest between Scripture and tradition:

> But let them chaunt while they will of prerogatives, we shall tell them of Scripture; of custom, we of Scripture; of Acts and Statutes, stil of Scripture, til the quick and pearcing word enter to the dividing of their soules, & the mighty weaknes of the Gospel throw down the weak mightines of mans reasoning. (1.827)

Arguments from antiquity and custom simply cannot stand against the power of the revealed Word, in this view. The sword of the Spirit will pierce souls and expose the error of practices based upon "mans reasoning." All Milton need do is "tell" of Scripture. In practice, this telling becomes more a matter of invoking the "inward power and purity of the Gospel" (1:766) than of pointing to specific texts.

In his early prose Milton insists vigorously upon the "clearnesse" of Scripture, which he typically identifies with truth:

> The very essence of Truth is plainnesse, and brightnes; the darknes and crookednesse is our own.... If we will but purge with sovrain eyesalve that intellectual ray which *God* hath planted in us, then we would beleeve the Scriptures protesting their own plainnes, and perspicuity, calling to them to be instructed, not only the *wise*, and *learned*, but the *simple*, the *poor*, the *babes*, foretelling an extraordinary effusion of *Gods* Spirit upon every age, and sexe, attributing to all men, and requiring from them the ability of searching, trying, examining all things, and by the Spirit discerning that which is good. (1:566)

This emphasis upon the ability of anyone to understand Scripture, with the aid of the Holy Spirit, goes back at least to Tyndale. Its corollary for Milton, as for Tyndale, was a belief that the church fathers had complicated and thereby obscured biblical truth.[7] Milton represents his Anglican opponents as spiritual heirs of the fathers, unable to confront the dazzling truth of Scripture directly, and caricatures them as taking refuge in "that wild, and overgrowne Covert of antiquity" (1:648). Shying from "the plain field of the Scripture," they search out "the dark, the bushie, the tangled Forrest, they would imbosk" (1:569). Such imagery serves Milton's polemic by implying that his antagonists argue exclusively from tradition and by reducing this tradition to an uncontrollable growth that serves only to shut out the sun of the gospel. The implication is that one must cut away the thickets of commentary and precedent in order to get at the simple, originally accessible, truth of Scripture.

For Milton plainness was inseparable from purity, "the purity of Scripture which is the only rule of Reformation" (1:912). The prelates had not only fled the truth of Scripture; they had debased it. In some of the harshest language to be found in the early tracts Milton describes the "undeflour'd and unblemishable simplicity of the Gospell" as prostituted by the church's commercializing of spiritual discipline: "Contrition, humiliation, confession the very sighs of a repentant spirit are sold there [in ecclesiastical courts] by the penny" (1:849). Denunciation of the venality of the church, English or Roman, was scarcely new, but Milton's personification of the Gospel, or rather a "resemblance" of the Gospel fashioned by the "sorcery" of the prelates, as "[giving] up her body to a mercenary whoredome," is distinctive. For him the degradation of the Gospel becomes a version of the Fall. It is as though the prelates have transformed Una into Duessa.

It was almost as bad in Milton's view to disguise the purity of the Gospel as to corrupt it. Elsewhere he turns his attack on the church's practice of clothing spiritual truth with ceremony, to make it seem more "decent:"

> Tell me ye Priests wherfore this gold, wherfore these roabs and surplices over the Gospel? is our religion guilty of the first trespasse, and hath need of cloathing to cover her nakednesse?... Believe it, wondrous Doctors, all corporeal resemblances of inward holinesse & beauty are now past; he that will cloath the Gospel now, intimates plainly, that the Gospel is naked, uncomely. (1:828)

In this sophisticated variant of Puritan praise of the naked truth, Milton makes the prelates appear to recoil in shame from the Gospel in its pure form, undistorted by the accretions of tradition. Their rites, identified throughout the tracts with the carnality of Mosaic ceremonial law, become a sign of the church's fallen state. Milton's denunciation of what he saw as clothing the Gospel forms part of a general attack on Anglican "decency" in worship.[8] For him beauty and holiness could only be "inward."

A powerful nostalgia for the church in its primitive state underlies Milton's representations of the purity of Scripture. In his efforts to recall his countrymen to this obscured ideal he appealed not so much to particular texts as to a conception of the Gospel as simple and accessible:

> If the religion be pure, spirituall, simple, and lowly, as the Gospel most truly is, such must the face of the ministery be. (1:766)

Milton's task was to bring his readers to learn to respond to the pure Word of God, free from what he saw as the contaminations of ecclesiastical tradition. This entailed discrediting the customary view of truth as the daughter of time in order to rescue that truth from the deformations of history. Milton speaks contemptuously of the habit of

> searching among the verminous, and polluted rags dropt overworn from the toyling shoulders of Time, with these deformedly to quilt, and interlace the intire, the spotlesse, and undecaying robe of Truth, the daughter not of Time, but of Heaven. (1:639)

Milton's quest for the "recovery of lost truth" was among other things a quest for a renewed perception of the Gospel in its pristine state. He sought to convince his readers that such scriptural truth was not only spotless but undecaying, the embodiment of a perfection that outshines any merely human truths.

Milton says little in the antiprelatical tracts about the actual process of interpreting the Bible, other than that men are called to search and try Scripture with the aid of the Spirit.[9] One of the most striking things about these tracts is his overwhelming confidence in the power of Scripture to impress its truth upon the understanding. In a series of arresting images he offers his own version of the doctrine of Scripture as *autopistos*. Like Whitaker, and Calvin, Milton was extremely sensitive to the energy of the Word. He saw it, with many others, not only as a sword dividing the soul ("the quick and pearcing word") but as the sun of truth banishing the powers of darkness from a whole society. One of the most lyrical passages in *Of Reformation* describes the Reformation, with its recovery of the Bible from "the dusty corners where prophane Falshood and Neglect had throwne it," as a miraculous dawn striking through "the black and settled Night of *Ignorance* and *Antichristian Tyranny*" (1:524). In *Animadversions* it is a "morning beam" that melts away the "fleshy reasonings" by which antiquity and custom are sustained (1:705).

In the antiprelatical tracts Milton attacked a particular kind of reasoning, not reason itself.[10] He saw what he calls "fleshy reasoning," or simply "mans reasoning," as contaminated by a willingness to accept the results of historical process rather than confront Scripture directly. Such reasoning was unacceptable because it was "carnal," employed in justifying man's traditions rather than in understanding God's dictates, but also because it was collective. In *Animadversions* Milton opposes the individual exercise of reason to the wisdom of church councils:

> I shall be bold to say that reason is the gift of God in one man, as well as in a thousand....
> What if reason now illustrated by the word of God, shall be able to produce a better prevention then these Councells have left us against heresie, ignorance or want of care in the Ministry. (1:684–85)

Milton here shows reason "illustrated" by the Word itself. Previously he had described the necessity of purging "that intellectual ray which *God* hath planted in us" (1:566). Milton assumed that to "search the scriptures" entailed using one's "regenerate" reason, aided by the Spirit, yet he gave less attention in the antiprelatical tracts to the proper uses of reason than to its abuses. He was engaged in a work of demolition, and his primary intellectual weapon was the idea of the pure, simple, and powerful Word of God, accessible to every individual.

Rather than talk about how to read Scripture in the antiprelatical tracts, Milton stressed its inherent power to make its truth felt. After chiding his opponents for fleeing the truth of the Word, he exhorts ministers to confront them with it:

> Wherfore should they not urge only the Gospel, and hold it ever in their faces like a mirror of Diamond, til it dazle, and pierce their misty ey balls? (1:569–70)

This way of imaging the miraculous power of goodness suggests the world of romance. One is reminded of that moment in the first book of *The Faerie Queene* (1.8.19) when the "blazing brightnesse" of Arthur's diamond shield, suddenly unveiled, dazes the giant Orgoglio.[11] Milton at one point identifies the prelates with the "huge dragon of Egypt" slain by St. George and urges the princes and knights of England to imitate "that old champion" and "make it their Knightly adventure to pursue & vanquish this mighty saile wing'd monster that menaces to swallow up the Land" (1:857). In this characterization theological controversy becomes a simple combat of good and evil and Milton, by implication, the premier Christian knight. A subsequent comparison of prelacy with the python that guarded the shrine at Delphi, which Milton imagines as spreading contagion "til like that fenborn serpent she be shot to death with the darts of the sun, the pure and powerful beams of Gods word" (1:858), shifts the focus to the force of Scripture. The Word itself, by virtue of the divine light that it expresses, here acts as the scourge of error.

This Spenserian mode was only one means that Milton found for rendering the combat that so engaged him. He could invoke the prophets, or mount the chariot of zeal, or, in a striking use of biblical imagery, identify the horseman of Revelation 6:2 as the "Angell of the Gospell".

> The Gospell being the hidden might of Christ...hath ever a victorious power joyn'd with it, like him in the Revelation that went forth on the white Horse with his bow and crown conquering, and to conquer. (1:850)

All Milton's images of the power of Scripture serve to embody the paradox, central to the argument of the early tracts, that the "strength of fleshly pride and wisdom" cannot stand against the "pure simplicity of saving truth" (1:827). The zeal that so offended Bishop Hall sprang from a conviction that the strength of the established church was only apparent. Milton saw antiquity, the church's support, as a *"livelesse Colossus,"* a "carved Gyant" that menaces children. With the weapon of Scripture, he asserts,

> wee shall not doubt to batter, and throw down your Nebuchadnezzars Image and crumble it like the chaffe of the Summer threshing floores. (1:700)

Milton was confident that Scripture would prevail because he regarded it as dynamic, full of "the hidden might of Christ." He saw tradition, by contrast, as static, lifeless, an idol to be smashed.

Scripture was dynamic because the "renovating and re-ingendring Spirit of God" acted through it. In the antiprelatical tracts Milton was particularly concerned with the operation of the Holy Spirit, through Scripture and otherwise. He saw the early English reformers as receiving "the sudden assault of his reforming Spirit warring against humane Principles, and carnall sense" (1:704) and proclaimed fresh assaults of the Spirit in his own time. This sense of active and continuous intervention by God, through the agency of the Spirit, explains Milton's extravagant expectations for the perfecting of the reformation in England, and also his extreme hostility to traditions that prescribed the form of worship and church government. If the renovating work of the Spirit was indeed continuous, those who imposed a set liturgy upon ministers were guilty of the tyranny of "impropriating the Spirit of God to themselves" (1:682). Prayer, as the gift of the Spirit, should be spontaneous. As Milton vehemently puts it in the opening pages of his *Of Reformation*, one must not "draw downe" the discourse of God and the soul into a "bodily forme;" this is to "bring the inward acts of the *Spirit* to the outward, and customary ey-Service of the body" (1:520).[12] In *Eikonoklastes* he denounced the liturgy as imprisoning and confining "by force, into a Pinfold of sett words, those two most unimprisonable things, our Prayers [and] that Divine spirit of utterance that moves them" (3:505). The complaint reminds one of Cartwright's objection that Whitgift pinned the Word in a narrow room.

Milton saw the power of Scripture as the means by which men would be liberated from strictly prescribed forms of worship, which he understood as manifestations of the "bondage of the Law" (1:763). He believed that the truth he and others were deriving from Scripture, "publickly taught," would "unyoke & set free the minds and spirits of a Nation...from the thraldom of sin and superstition" (1:853). The concern that was to grow into a carefully articulated doctrine of Christian liberty found expression in the earliest tracts chiefly in images of carnal power destroyed by spiritual truth. At this point Milton was more interested in proclaiming the character of this truth—its simplicity, its purity, its dynamism—than in defining it.

Given Milton's strong sense of Scripture as a vital, liberating force, it is surprising to find him substituting one highly structured form of church government for another. Of course he could not know that Presbyterianism, "the only true Church-government" that could be derived from Scripture, would in practice appear to him rigid and retrogressive and prompt the bitter accusation: "*New Presbyter* is but *Old Priest* writ Large."[13] This system was championed by the divines whose cause he took up, and it offered a less hierarchical form of governance than that of the established church, one under which individual congregations appeared to have considerable freedom. Moreover, presbyterian discipline seemed to him appropriately militant. According to this model, as Milton imagined it, local and regional bodies enjoy a harmonious relationship with the general assembly, "as those smaller squares in battell unite in one great cube, the main phalanx, an emblem of truth and stedfastnesse (1:789).[14] Yet his deepest attraction seems to have been to a more broadly conceived ideal of discipline that had relatively little to do with the details of presbyterian governance.

Milton saw the "Doctrine, and Discipline of the Gospel" as "two grave & holy nurses" (1:639) whose teaching produced a kind of church government appealing in its orderliness. He found the pattern for the order he sought in the church "here below" in heaven, where the "golden survaying reed" of discipline "marks out and measures every quarter and circuit of new Jerusalem" (1:752). It was inconceivable to him that God would leave the church "to the perpetuall stumble of conjecture and disturbance in this our darke voyage without the card and compasse of Discipline" (1:753). The task that Milton set himself in *The Reason of Church Government* was to demonstrate the nature of this discipline. He took for granted the right of the church "to demand from us in Gods behalfe a service entirely reasonable" (1:748); the question was whether the "manner" and "order" of this government should be presbyterian or episcopal.

Milton found the best figurative expression of the spiritual order that attracted him in the elaborate instructions for rebuilding the temple set forth in Ezekiel. He read these typologically, as evidence that God intended to regulate man's spiritual life by a "prescribed discipline." This he found fleshed out in the epistles of Paul to Timothy and Titus,

> where the spirituall eye may discerne more goodly and gracefully erected then all the magnificence of Temple or Tabernacle, such a heavenly structure of evangelick discipline so diffusive of knowledge and charity to the prosperous increase and growth of the Church, that it cannot be wonder'd if that elegant and artfull symmetry of the promised new temple in *Ezechiel,* and all those sumptuous things under the Law were made to signifie the inward beauty and splendor of the Christian Church thus govern'd. (1:758)

Discipline is the key to the order that Milton celebrates here; through it the ideal form of the church could be realized, "in all her glorious lineaments and proportions."

The church was also for Milton, as for the makers of the Geneva Bible, a living temple of believers developing under the influence of the Spirit. In *Of Reformation* he demonstrates how the practices of the episcopal establishment have impeded "the edifying of Christs holy *Church,*" "the flourishing and growing up of Christs mysticall body" (1:613). In *The Reason of Church Government* he denounces the physical churches consecrated and embellished by the prelates as "Idolish temples" (1:851). Their furnishings betray the success of episcopacy in pillaging the estates of the people. The true Christian is for him "Gods living temple," while the priests are custodians of "dead judaisms" (1:843). The preface to the Geneva Bible had opposed the living God to the "dumme and dead idoles" of a backsliding church and urged Elizabeth to rebuild the spiritual temple.

These two visions of the church, as a "heavenly structure of evangelick discipline" and as an evolving community of believers, coexist in the anti-prelatical tracts. Yet there are latent tensions between these ideals, and between the underlying assumptions that the Gospel could be both a dynamic force and the authority for a particular form of church government, which became manifest as presbyterian discipline took visible form in England. What had appeared to Milton initially as "an emblem of truth and steadfastnesse" turned out in practice to be static and confining. Milton found numerous reasons for denouncing the presbyterian leaders, among them their appetite for spoils and their refusal to support the execution of Charles, but perhaps the most fundamental was that they restricted the spiritual liberty of the people. Their design for order in the church became an excuse for what he branded a "censorious and supercilious lording over conscience." The new hierarchy proved as rigid as the old:

> Dare ye for this adjure the Civil Sword
> To force our Consciences that Christ set free,
> And ride us with a classic Hierarchy
> Taught ye by mere *A. S.* and *Rotherford?*[15]

While Milton's vision of an ordered church in *The Reason of Church Government* goes beyond a strictly presbyterian sense of discipline, the kind of order that he described there eventually became less important to him than the ideal of a "living" fellowship of believers free to choose their own forms of worship. At bottom, his attack on the "New Forcers of Conscience" reflects an antipathy to set forms of all kinds that was to produce the extreme defense of the liberty of the spirit that Milton offered in his late tracts, *Of Civil Power* and *The Likeliest Means to Remove Hirelings from the Church.*

As I have suggested, Milton in his earliest controversial writings was more concerned with celebrating the attributes of Scripture, from its "plaine and homespun verity" to its "purity and power," than with developing the kind of painstaking argument from texts that characterizes the two Smectymnuan tracts. When he set out to justify his liberal conception of divorce, however, he had to focus sharply upon texts, particularly the pronouncement of Christ that seemed to limit the grounds for divorce to adultery (Matt. 5:31–32) and the broader decree of Moses (Deut. 24:1) that much more nearly suited his purposes. The need for close scrutiny prompted a shift of emphasis to the way the Bible was to be read. Instead of simply pointing to Scripture, Milton called for renewed study, and he stressed the qualifications of his lay interpreters. They are no longer the "poor" and "simple" but men whose learning suits them for combat with "Scholasticks and Canonists:"

> Let the statutes of God be turn'd over, be scann'd a new, and consider'd; not altogether by the narrow intellectuals of quotationists and common placers, but (as was the ancient right of Counsels) by men of what liberall profession soever, of eminent spirit and breeding joyn'd with a diffuse and various knowledge of divine and human things. (2:230)

In his writings on divorce and more amply in his *Christian Doctrine* Milton advocated principles of interpretation that can be found in Perkins and other influential commentators, including knowledge of the original languages of Scripture, examination of the context of a passage, comparison of similar texts, and recourse to the analogy of faith.[16] In the divorce tracts Milton appeals also to the "light of reason" (2:242), no longer the vulnerable "reasoning" that he had associated with arguments from tradition in his attacks on prelacy but a commendable "free reasoning" by which one may discern the agreement of Scripture with the "good of man." Ernest Sirluck has demonstrated how Milton in the process of writing on divorce worked out the principle of testing interpretation against the secondary law of nature, as this is understood by the light of reason.[17] The fundamental principle from which his interpretation of texts bearing on divorce derives, however, is one found in Augustine's *Christian Doctrine* that Milton called the "rule of charity." On the title page of the first edition of the *Doctrine and Discipline of Divorce* Milton describes himself as restoring divorce "From the bondage of Canon Law, and other mistakes, to Christian Freedom, guided by the Rule of Charity." This principle is the "key" that unlocks Christ's words on divorce. It was unthinkable to Milton that Christ would bind man irrevocably in marriage to an incompatible spouse. The rule of charity invalidated a narrow conception of divorce as permissible only on the grounds of adultery, as it did a legalistic interpretation of the Sabbath:

> It is not the formal duty of worship, or the sitting still, that keeps the holy rest of Sabbath; but whosoever doth most according to charity, whether hee work, or work not. (2:750)

The "reason" that Milton invokes in the divorce tracts, and the sense of the "good of man" to which it guides him, must be understood as consonant with "the all-interpreting voice of Charity" (2:309). In responding to criticism in *Colasterion* Milton noted that in saying love is "the fulfilling of every commandment" he "cited no particular Scripture, but spake a general sense, which might be collected from many places" (2:750). From this "general sense," really the common doctrine that charity is the end of all Scripture, he fashioned an extraordinarily flexible hermeneutical principle,[18] which allowed him to take the same broad view of marriage that he did of the sabbath:

> Hee who doth that which most accords with charity, first to himself, next to whom hee next ows it, whether in mariage or divorce, hee breaks the Ordinance of mariage least. (2:750)

Milton may talk about the law of nature, but his arguments spring from an individualistic sense of the spirit of the text. While his learning and his familiarity with standard methods of interpretation enabled him to mount sophisticated attacks upon particular misinterpretations, he was basically criticizing an attitude toward Scripture, with the aid of the most general principle that he could find. The error of his opponents was "resting in the meere element of the Text" rather than "consulting with charitie, the interpreter and guide of our faith" (2:236). Milton's prose is animated by a refusal to see Christ's words "congeal'd into a stony rigor" (2:231). He would not be bound by unduly literal readings of Scripture any more than by externally imposed forms of worship.

Milton had nothing but scorn for those unable to see beyond the letter of the text: the "crabbed textuists" with whom Christ argued, the canon lawyers with their "letter-bound servility," and anyone else who preferred the "dead letter" to the "living Spirit." By opposing the "divine and softning breath of charity" to "the stubborn letter" (2:604), he made it clear that to interpret by the rule of charity is to interpret according to the guidance of the Spirit.[19] At times his justification of this rule recalls the appeals of more radical Protestants to the Spirit as arbiter of the sense of Scripture:

> For no other cause did Christ assure us that whatsoever things wee binde, or slacken on earth, are so in heaven, but to signifie that the christian arbitrement of charity is supreme decider of all controversie, and supreme resolver of all Scripture; not as the Pope determines for his owne tyrany, but as the Church ought to determine for its own true liberty. (2:637)

The difference between Winstanley's "Spirit" and Milton's "charity" has to do with the place Milton assigns to reason. Its liberating role cannot be understood, however, without reference to Milton's sense of the action of the Spirit. He would have felt the "quickning power of the *Spirit*" informing his interpretation and enabling him to resist the sort of literalism that would "bind so cruelly a good and gracious ordinance of God" (2:282) to a single, restrictive meaning. The position of the canon law on divorce represented a deathly stasis because it denied the dynamic operation of the Spirit in the text.[20]

Milton's concern with the opposition of spirit and letter in the writings on divorce, a natural outgrowth of his preoccupation with the broader opposition of spiritual and carnal in the earlier tracts, is the most important

evidence of the continuity in his thinking about Scripture but not the only
evidence. The prefatory epistle to the *Doctrine and Discipline* sounds many
notes heard previously. Custom again appears as the villain, now accompanied by Error, the latter introduced with a Spenserian allusion to its
serpentine nature. Milton recognizes the difficulty of disentangling truth
from historical process with a scornful reference to Time as "the Midwife
rather than the mother of Truth" but nonetheless insists upon the possibility
of knowing truth in its original purity: "For Truth is as impossible to be
soil'd by any outward touch, as the Sun beam" (2:225). He still sees himself
as engaged in a process of recovering a lost understanding of Scripture, here
by restoring "the misattended words of Christ to the sincerity of their true
sense from manifold contradictions" (2:355).

One different note is Milton's praise of the "majesty" of the Law, which
provided the textual basis for his position on divorce. Milton justified this
new interest in the Law (the Gospel had appeared as the great source of light
in the antiprelatical tracts) by arguing that the moral law expressed by
Moses continues to operate for Christians.[21] To maintain this posture he
had to see Christ as making the Law clear by removing "the Pharisaick mists
rais'd between the law and the peoples eyes" (2:301), rather than changing
its apparent sense. He extended his efforts to reclaim the true meaning of
Scripture by picturing the Law as "perspicuous," "just," "incorruptible,"
"the pure and sacred Law of God;" we are told of its "sad and awful
majesty." It was primarily in the Old Testament that Milton found the sense
of divine power and dignity that he characterized as "majesty."[22]

Where the divorce tracts show Milton laboring to derive truth from
Scripture by wrestling with individual texts, *Areopagitica* reveals a broader
and more tentative kind of search for truth. The battleground has shifted
from Scripture to the tracts flowing from the presses of contemporary
London, and truth itself has come to seem much more elusive than it did in
the antiprelatical tracts. Milton now insists upon the progressive character
of revelation and thus of efforts to know the truth.[23] God deals out his beam
"by degrees, so as our earthly eyes may best sustain it" (2:566). The human
condition is "to be still searching what we know not, by what we know, still
closing up truth to truth as we find it" (2:551). Milton's concern with the
nature of this search in *Areopagitica*, and with the role of reason in "closing
up truth to truth," resulted naturally from the waning of his earlier expectations that the kingdom of God on earth was "shortly expected."[24] The
struggle of truth and error proved to be more complex than it had seemed
when he first mounted the chariot of zeal, and he found himself having to
deal with the process by which men found the truth in order to justify the
intellectual ferment that he took to be the essence of reformation.

Milton could denounce licensing because he believed in man's rational
ability to separate truth from error. The wars of truth offered an oppor-

tunity for "the triall of vertue, and the exercise of truth" (2:528). This "exercise" came to seem essential to the discovery of truth. The grappling of truth and falsehood that Milton pictures in *Areopagitica* was something to relish. We are a step beyond the combat of the antiprelatical tracts, in which the Gospel simply overwhelms the forces of tradition. Milton is no less confident in the ultimate victory of truth, but he has come to think in terms of the continuing warfare of the Christian soldier rather than the inevitable triumph of the knight who brandishes his diamond shield.

Milton's phrase, "the exercise of truth," recalls Sibbes's references to the exercise of the soul and points to an essential characteristic of the reason described in *Areopagitica*, its energetic action. Sibbes had said that the Spirit "doth awake the soul, and keep it in a holy exercise, by stirring up the grace of faith to its proper function" (1:199). He was talking about the soul's continuous efforts to purify itself, under the stimulus of the Spirit, which he saw as the heart of the process of sanctification. Milton came to think about the activity of reason, engaged in the continuous discovery of truth, in comparable ways. Exercise seemed necessary to both Sibbes and Milton because they saw fallen man as having to struggle constantly toward the ideals that they upheld, a secure faith on the one hand and the ability to apprehend and act upon truth on the other. They resemble each other in seeing the Spirit as intimately involved in the spiritual and intellectual dynamism that they regarded as the proper response to trial.

In *Areopagitica* Milton transferred to reason, more generally to the English people seen as exercising reason in the pursuit of truth, much of the energy that in the antiprelatical tracts he had associated with the Spirit, acting through the "quick and pearcing word." Instead of celebrating the "morning beam of Reformation," Milton focuses on the dynamic activity of the people themselves, awakening and soaring to purge their sight at the source of truth:

> Methinks I see in my mind a noble and puissant Nation rousing herself like a strong man after sleep, and shaking her invincible locks: Methinks I see her as an Eagle muing her mighty youth, and kindling her undazl'd eyes at the full midday beam; purging and unscaling her long abused sight at the fountain it self of heav'nly radiance. (2:557–58)

Milton's sense of the resurgent energy of his people permeates *Areopagitica*. They muse and search by their "studious lamps," they gather the scattered pieces of truth, they rebuild the temple, they do battle with error.

The ultimate source of this dynamism is still the Spirit, now seen as manifesting itself primarily through the search itself. People were writing furiously because God was shaking the kingdom "with strong and healthful commotions to a generall reforming" (2:566). Milton's sense of the presence of the Spirit was strong enough at this point for him to find a "concurrence of signs" in the activity around him and to feel that the time had come when "Moses the great prophet" could rejoice in heaven to see that "all the Lords people are become Prophets" (2:556). He believed in the possibility of prophetic utterance. A sentence of "a ventrous [venturous] edge" that might draw the attention of the licenser, Milton speculates at one point, could well be "the dictat of a divine Spirit" (2:534).[25] For the most part, however, the truth that Milton describes in *Areopagitica* should be seen as emerging from the interaction of reason and the Spirit, understood to be working together.

Milton's attraction to prophecy and his sense of an "approaching Reformation" did not, of course, lead him to endorse a particular version of the truth in *Areopagitica*. On the contrary, he took the appearance of conflicting versions as a sign of spiritual vitality. When he returned to the image of the temple, Milton stressed the "schisms" and "dissections" involved in the process of building the house of God rather than the splendor of the structure itself. He did not abandon his belief in the "gracefull symmetry" of the whole but ceased to associate this symmetry with presbyterian discipline. It would emerge in time. Such confidence is scarcely warranted by the image, which threatens to fly apart (how can one expect that stones cut so differently will fit together?), yet Milton had to believe in the "unity of the Spirit" to sustain his faith in the progress of reformation.

Milton could accept and even rejoice in the fact of controversy because he took this as evidence that truth had not stagnated. Those who supported licensing were in effect decreeing that "the cruse of truth must run no more oyle" (2:541):

> Truth is compar'd in Scripture to a streaming fountain; if her waters flow not in a perpetuall progression, they sick'n into a muddy pool of conformity and tradition. (2.543)

Milton had spoken of the "streams" of truth and the "fountains" of the Gospel in the antiprelatical tracts, even while defending the apparently settled truth of Presbyterianism. In his concern with a "living" Word and a "living" church Milton mounted a much more vigorous and comprehensive attack on the regulation of worship than did his Smectymnuan allies, but it took the threat of licensing and the new pressures for conformity issuing from the Westminster Assembly to bring him to the recognition of the variousness of truth that he articulated in *Areopagitica*. His inversion of the Proteus myth puts it best: "Do not bind her when she sleeps, for then she speaks not true" (2:563). Milton's acceptance of the protean nature of truth ("she may have more shapes than one") may appear to contradict the position of the early tracts but in fact should be seen as a logical extension of his belief in the dynamism of the Word. What Milton came to realize, in the tumult of the 1640s, was that this truth was neither as simple nor as readily apprehended as he had initially assumed. When Milton personified truth in

Areopagitica, he tended to invest it with the dynamism that he attributed to the Spirit and to reason. The terms ("truth," "Spirit," "reason") are not truly separable because they represent different ways of getting at the nature of the same process.

In talking about Milton's sense of the Spirit—whether seen as manifesting its power through Scripture, as informing the reading of Scripture, or as animating the search for truth—I have of course been talking about his concern with the liberty enjoyed by Christians, a subject much discussed by students of Milton. Those critics who have done the most to elucidate Milton's concept of Christian liberty (primarily A. S. P. Woodhouse, Arthur Barker, and Douglas Bush) have stressed its relationship to right reason. For them Milton is above all a Christian humanist, whose writing is remarkable for its success in joining the spheres of nature and grace. Milton's interest in the exercise of reason by the regenerate is plainly visible in *Areopagitica. Paradise Lost* amply illustrates his conviction that man is free to act morally only when reason exercises its proper rule over the passions. One consequence of the Fall, Michael tells Adam, is that "true Liberty / Is lost, which always with right Reason dwells" (*PL*, 12.83–84). Through regeneration the "extensive darkening of that right reason" (6:395) that results from the spiritual death of the Fall can be counteracted, at least in part.

The most important theoretical support for Milton's confidence in reason as a basis for moral action can be found in *Christian Doctrine,* particularly in one frequently quoted description of man's recovery of his original understanding of the law of nature:

> The unwritten law is the law of nature given to the first man. A kind of gleam or glimmering of it still remains in the hearts of all mankind. In the regenerate this is daily brought nearer to a renewal of its original perfection by the operation of the Holy Spirit. (6:516)

Milton distinguishes between the teaching of Scripture, "under the promised guidance of the Spirit of truth," and that of a law "written in the hearts of believers" (6:534), the "internal scripture of the Holy Spirit" (6:587). The predominant critical emphasis has been upon the intelligibility of this law written on the heart. Woodhouse describes it as "conceived as ethical and rational in character, and identified with the law of nature," Barker as "the renewing of the original moral law of nature."[26] The activity of reason, seen as capable of knowing an internal law of morality, becomes the key to Christian liberty.

Milton's comment on the gradual renewal of the law of nature in man invites a view of the Holy Spirit as a kind of purgative of the intellect. Barker speaks of "eternal principles," or the "perfect law" that is the basis of Christian liberty, being "rendered clear" in men's hearts by the Spirit. He argues, in connection with the divorce tracts and *Areopagitica*, that "the beam which God dispenses is 'that intellectual ray,' and its product is the activity of 'free reasoning.'"[27] Woodhouse claims that for Milton "the gift of the Spirit means essentially the clearing of the intellectual faculties and the progressive restoration of the intuitive perception of the law of nature which was obscured but not obliterated by the Fall."[28] Such comments describe very well the way Milton saw the Spirit as renewing the intellect of fallen man; yet they neglect other aspects of the operation of the Spirit and can lead to an overemphasis upon Milton's affinities with Hooker and seventeenth-century exponents of a rational Christianity. It is not enough to say that the divine light is "that intellectual ray." Milton saw the operation of the Spirit as more complex and mysterious than this formulation would imply. He called attention to other gifts of the Spirit, including prophecy and prayer ("as he left our affections to be guided by his sanctifying spirit, so did he likewise our words to put into us without our premeditation" [3:506]), and understood the liberty that it made possible as depending upon the love as well as the knowledge of God. The affective dimension of his Christianity deserves more attention.

One cannot appreciate fully how the inner law functions by thinking of it solely as a moral law ascertainable by right reason. Milton describes it variously, among other things as the "Law of Faith" written in the heart by the Spirit "working through love" (*PL*, 12.488–89). In his discussions of Christian liberty in *Christian Doctrine* he speaks of the purpose of the Mosaic law as "attained in that love of God and our neighbor which is born of faith, through the spirit" (6:532). In that work, as in the divorce tracts, Milton appeals to charity as arbiter. One can satisfy the substance of the Mosaic law (with regard to the sabbath or to marriage, for example) by attending to "the requirements of charity." One should interpret the precepts of Christ in the sermon on the mount "in a way that is in keeping with the spirit of charity" (6:533). Milton's massive quoting of New Testament texts reinforces his fundamental point that enjoying Christian liberty means being able to "serve God in charity through the guidance of the Spirit of Truth" (6:537). He describes charity as "arising from a sense of divine love which is poured into the hearts of the regenerate through the Spirit" (6:479). This charity, which he also describes as "holiness of life," is one of two results of the new life in Christ enjoyed by the faithful. The other is an ability to understand spiritual affairs through an enlightened intellect or, as one of Milton's supporting texts (1 Cor. 2:10) puts it, a capacity to discern spiritually things "of the Spirit of God" which appear foolish to the natural man. Such spiritual knowledge and charity should be regarded as interdependent. Neither is conceivable in the absence of the other.[29]

It is impossible to say exactly how the "Spirit of Truth" leads man to truth[30] because the process, as Milton describes it, retains an irreducible element of mystery. The Holy Spirit daily renews the unwritten law of nature given Adam (6:516), and also awakens a "spirit of charity," after first engendering the saving faith that makes a new spiritual life possible. One can acknowledge the dependence of reason upon regeneration and the existence of faith without taking sufficient account of Milton's sense of the need for that faith to remain lively and to be accompanied by charity, "the soul / Of all the rest" (PL, 12.584–85) of the virtues.[31] Although Milton was not so concerned as Sibbes with "experimental" religion and the drama of the Christian's progress in sanctification, he did see the action of the Spirit as continuous and as involving the affections (guided by the "sanctifying spirit") as well as reason. One should think of the law written on the heart by the Spirit as becoming known by a process that involves the whole man and, as I have argued, one should think of this process as dynamic. As Milton's understanding of the uses of reason evolved, along with his sense of how the truth of Scripture made itself known, he continued to find new ways to make the point that the interaction of man and the Spirit must not be inhibited. He attacked any practice that he saw as binding the Spirit, including prescriptions for worship, literalistic interpretation, and efforts to regulate the truth. This does not mean that Milton saw the Spirit as a force acting contrary to reason—not, at least, to "intuitive" reason directed to holy ends.[32] Rather, its "leadings" revealed how man should use his reason to perceive the truth of God and act in conformity to it.[33]

Nineteenth-century readers of Milton's *Christian Doctrine* exclaimed over his Quakerism.[34] Such reactions may be extreme, but they testify to real affinities with radical Protestant thinking, now beginning to receive more critical attention.[35] While one would not confuse Milton's sense of an inner light with George Fox's, given Milton's heavy reliance upon Scripture and his commitment to the proper use of reason, one should not see them as diametrically opposed.[36] Milton and Hooker would have agreed that reason was guided by the Spirit (Hooker imagines reason as the "hand" by which the Spirit leads man).[37] They differ sharply, however, in the scope that they allow to the Spirit. Hooker consistently challenged claims to inspiration, decrying them as leading to the "utter confusion" of the church.[38] He would have recoiled from Milton's assertion that in reading Scripture the supreme authority is "the authority of the Spirit, which is internal, and the individual possession of each man" (6:587). Such a principle meant, ultimately, that no one had a right to impose doctrine upon another or to reject any reading of Scripture advanced by an apparent believer. Hooker, always moving toward the "plainer ground" of reason, looked for "some judicial and definitive sentence"[39] and regularly found it in the pronouncements of the established church, which he insisted that everyone accept. Milton's sense of the dynamic operation of the Spirit in the lives of individual

Christians prevented him from accepting the kind of consensus of rational men that was such a powerful ideal for Hooker. He asserts that "it is not the visible church but the hearts of believers which, since Christ's ascension, have continually constituted the *pillar* and *ground of truth*" (6:589). Like the "rule" of charity, the inner "law" of Christians allows for strongly subjective versions of the truth. If the hearts of believers constitute the ground of truth, and if "all things are eventually to be referred to the Spirit and the unwritten word" (6:590), the inner law cannot be verified except by the conscience of the individual Christian. Milton's own evolving understanding of the truth of the Spirit led him to the ultimate iconoclasm of rejecting all forms of worship and governance established by visible churches.

The law written on the heart was for Milton preeminently the "law of liberty," a "law of the Spirit and of freedom" seen as replacing the Mosaic "law of slavery." Milton came to reject the Mosaic law absolutely, even in its moral aspect, because to accept it would have checked the individual's capacity to act from the "spirit of charity." It is in the late prose and poetry that one finds Milton's most vehement objections to restraints that would inhibit the dynamism of the Spirit's action. The fundamental charge that he brings against the magistrates in *Of Civil Power* is that "they force the Holy Ghost."[40] His arguments against such power proceed from the assumption that the individual conscience, guided by the Spirit, must be the judge of religious truth.[41] The ideal that follows is the freedom of worship comprehended in the biblical phrase "in spirit and in truth." Thus Milton rejects the "forcible imposition of those circumstances, place and time in the worship of God."[42] The corollary of the precept that he cites from Corinthians, "where the Spirit of the Lord is, there is liberty" (2 Cor. 3:17), is of course that the Spirit cannot be present where liberty is denied. The logic of this position would seem to dictate absolute toleration, but Milton, in denying Catholics the liberty he was willing to claim for Protestant sects, stopped short of Roger Williams.[43]

In *Of Civil Power* and *The Likeliest Means* Milton came closest to the position of the radical Protestants. Although he did not denounce "steeple houses" with the followers of Fox, he vigorously championed what he called "apostolical and primitive meetings" of believers and argued that they could take place anywhere; "he who disdained not to be laid in a manger, disdains not to be preached in a barn."[44] He seriously advocated the apostolic ideal of itinerant ministers supported by alms. Milton saw himself as returning to "true fundamental principles of the gospel" in opposing any kind of system for maintaining the clergy. In his sonnet to Cromwell he had denounced the committee of Independents seeking to regulate the ministry as "hireling wolves" who were "Threat'ning to bind our souls with secular chains." His heroes were the Waldensians, "Ev'n them who kept thy truth so pure of old,"[45] whom he praises in *The Likeliest Means* for learning trades so that they might support themselves in their ministry.

In his attacks on the idea that ministers had to be educated in the university (God may choose the "meanest artificer" to preach) and his sense of the social injustice of tithing (the "seising of pots and pans from the poor") Milton sounds at times like a more learned Winstanley. He most nearly resembles the radical writers of the forties in his uncompromising opposition to the forms of organized worship. The sources of whatever similarities there are is a common regard for the dynamism of the Spirit. Milton could have agreed with Saltmarsh that "God does not *fix* himself upon any one *form* or outward dispensation."[46] While Milton's sense of the operation of the Spirit and of the liberty of the individual Christian to follow its guidance was far more clearly defined than Winstanley's,[47] he would have shared the latter's reluctance to see anyone dam the "free running streams of the spirit of life."

Many of the attitudes that I have been tracing in Milton's prose come together in the passionate attack on the corrupt clergy that occurs near the end of *Paradise Lost*:

> Wolves shall succeed for teachers, grievous Wolves,
> Who all the sacred mysteries of Heav'n
> To thir own vile advantages shall turn
> Of lucre and ambition, and the truth
> With superstitions and traditions taint,
> Left only in those written Records pure,
> Though not but by the Spirit understood.
>
> (12.508–14)

The prediction that they will "taint" the truth recalls the emphasis of the earliest tracts upon the purity of Scripture and the denunciations of the church for prostituting scriptural truth. The venality of a wolfish clergy is of course one of Milton's most persistent themes, going back to Peter's resonant denunciation in *Lycidas*. The real thrust of Milton's attack, however, is directed against those who appropriate to themselves "the Spirit of God." They are guilty of what to Milton was the supreme violation of forcing "spiritual laws" on the conscience by "carnal power:"

> What will they then
> But force the Spirit of Grace itself, and bind
> Her consort Liberty; what, but unbuild
> His living Temples, built by Faith to stand,
> Thir own Faith not another's: for on Earth
> Who against Faith and Conscience can be heard
> Infallible?
>
> (12.524–30)

For Milton, to force the Spirit was necessarily to bind liberty, because he saw liberty as dependent upon the ability to respond to the Spirit's dynamism. Northrop Frye puts it well: "Liberty for Milton is a release of energy through revelation."[48] The effect of Milton's repeated emphasis upon the action of the Spirit—whatever he calls it (the "Spirit of Truth," the "Spirit of Grace," the "spirit of charity") and however he describes the law written on the heart (the "law of nature," the "law of liberty," the "Law of Faith / Working through love")—is to force one to recognize the need for continuing revelation. The reason by which man acts upon the inner law should be seen as energized by this revelation.

To force the Spirit meant also, in Milton's experience, to "unbuild" the living temple of the believer in the name of enforced dogma and controlled worship. Significantly, he focuses in *Paradise Lost* upon the individual, the "upright heart and pure" (1.18) that the Spirit prefers before all material temples. The prospect of collectively rebuilding the temple, understood to represent the common faith of Christians, has receded. Rather, Milton holds out the ideal of persevering in the worship "of Spirit and Truth," in the face of persecution and the example of the majority who settle for "outward rites and specious forms" (12.534). This deliberately general ideal is consonant with the promise that God will send a "Comforter" to men "to guide them in all truth" (12.490). All truth, as if to say any truth that the Spirit may reveal, in whatever time or place.

In Milton's gloomy account of the lot of the faithful, the "written records pure" promised Adam's descendants figure less prominently than the direct influence of the Spirit, especially in the form of the "Law of Faith" written in the heart. We have come a long way from the exultation over the recovery of the "pure and powerful" Word that so strongly colors the antiprelatical tracts. Milton concentrated in the latter part of *Paradise Lost* on the state of the Christian in a hostile environment, guided in truth and armed with spiritual armor by a protective Spirit. His early expectation that the beams of the Gospel would defeat a materialistic and tradition-bound religion is largely replaced by a quieter confidence that the Christian will be able to learn what he needs to know to live in the world. Such knowledge will depend in part upon learning to read Scripture, and Milton by having Michael trace for Adam the movement from law to grace, "From shadowy Types to Truth, from Flesh to Spirit" (12.303), instructs the reader in this activity. The meaning of Scripture does not appear so plainly evident as it did in the early prose. Milton's emphasis at the end of *Paradise Lost* is upon the need for guidance ("though not but by the Spirit understood").

In *Paradise Regained* Christ describes the "Spirit of Truth" as being sent to dwell "In pious hearts, an inward oracle / To all truth requisite for men to know" (1.463–64). Instead of looking for assaults of the reforming Spirit, Milton now appears content to think of a more modest and constant presence, an "inward oracle" that guides and comforts. This emphasis upon the indwelling Spirit suggests another change in Milton's sense of how one apprehends the truth. It had seemed at first that man had only to look upon the blazing light of the Gospel, then (in *Areopagitica*) that he had to search energetically;[49] now it appears that the chief virtue is learning to listen to inward promptings from God.[50]

If *Paradise Lost* registers Milton's disillusionment with the course of reformation in England, it also offers a compelling view of the Word in its primal form by picturing the Son going forth, "Girt with Omnipotence," to accomplish the work of creation. The scope of epic allowed Milton to render the action of the "Omnific Word" in stilling the wild seas of Chaos and circumscribing the universe. Through his account of the creation he could take his readers beyond the words of the familiar text to confront the power of the creating Word, the Logos. We see heaven open,

> To let forth
> The King of Glory in his powerful Word
> And Spirit coming to create new Worlds.
> (7.208–9)

The archangel Uriel's eyewitness report effectively summarizes the action of the Word:

> Confusion heard his voice, and wild uproar
> Stood rul'd, stood vast infinitude confin'd;
> Till at his second bidding darkness fled,
> Light shone, and order from disorder spring.
> (3.710–13)

By showing order emerging from unruly matter at the divine command Milton animated the text and at the same time gave the most impressive evidence he could have of the power of the Word that speaks through it. This power seems all the more remarkable because of the dynamism of the response that it produces: light springs from the deep, the mountains "upheave" their backs, the lion paws his way up out of the earth and breaks free.

In *Paradise Lost* Milton moved beyond his early concern with the power inherent in Scripture, a power to dazzle the blear-eyed and smash the idols of a decadent church, to attempt to represent the ultimate source of all power. Instead of invoking the "Angel of the Gospell," he shows the Son triumphant in the "Chariot of Paternal Deity, / Flashing thick flames, Wheel within Wheel, undrawn, / Itself instinct with Spirit" (6.751–52). Like the chariot of zeal that Milton in his prophetic mood imagined himself riding over the prelates, this even more formidable machine represents an irresistible force, with its "burning Wheels" and eyes glaring lightning.[51]

Having abandoned his hope for a definitive victory over error and moral corruption in human society, Milton concentrated upon a form in which he could indulge his sense of the immeasurable power of God to conquer evil. Consolation for the failure of reformation in England lay in taking long views, such as that of the Son sealing up the jaws of hell:

> Then Heav'n and Earth renew'd shall be made pure
> To sanctity that shall receive no stain.
>
> (10.638–39)

This sanctity beyond the possibility of stain is the ultimate purity of the righteous who will inhabit the new heaven and earth.[52] From an apocalyptic perspective Milton can look beyond the struggle to recover the purity of Scripture to attaining the state of unblemished sanctity imaged by it.

Paradise Regained can be regarded as a final effort to dramatize the nature of biblical truth and the problems of understanding it.[53] The poem reveals the growing insight with which Christ perceives the meaning of Scripture and the combination of blindness and perversity with which Satan repeatedly fails to acknowledge it. We see Christ progress from the early reading in the Law that aroused his patriotic desire to throw off the "Roman yoke," to a more pointed "searching" of the Law and the prophets for clues to the career of the Messiah, to the insight into prophetic language that enables him to speak of his kingdom as a stone or tree, to the sense of identity that enables him to speak the scriptural words ("Tempt not the Lord thy God" [4.561]) that signal the defeat of Satan. Although Christ's sense of his future course is clarified by his dialectic with Satan, as he answers bad reasons with good, his grasp of the meaning of Scripture appears to be largely intuitive. To understand what it will mean to sit on David's throne he must comprehend and accept the concept of God's time and the indefiniteness of scriptural metaphor. One cannot say exactly how he arrives at his mature understanding of the written record, only that it depends in some measure upon faith: "For what concerns my knowledge God reveals" (1.293). The agent of revelation is the Spirit that descended "in likeness of a dove" at his baptism and "by some strong motion" led him into the wilderness: "Who brought me hither / Will bring me hence, no other Guide I seek" (1.335–36).[54]

Satan illustrates the perils of discursive reasoning, endlessly complicating Christ's situation with his talk of means for achieving an earthly kingdom. He wanders in mazes of his own construction, unable or unwilling to recognize the essential simplicity of the biblical message:

> All things are best fulfill'd in their due time,
> And time there is for all things, Truth hath said.
>
> (3.183–84)

Satan is defeated by such statements because he thinks only in terms of specific and immediate solutions. He is too doggedly pragmatic to appreciate the possibility of a future that does not make a readily comprehensible kind of sense. The truth that Christ embraces is paradoxically simple and mysterious at the same time:

> Know therefore when my season comes to sit
> On *David's* Throne, it shall be like a tree
> Spreading and overshadowing all the Earth.
> (4.146–48)

Such language, drawn from Daniel (4:11), reaches beyond the categories of ordinary experience; it calls for a willingness to believe in a kingdom whose nature and scope can be expressed only in figurative terms.

Paradise Regained is concerned not only with the right understanding of Scripture but with the unique role of Christ as both embodiment and prophet of truth. Christ is spiritually nourished by the Word, as it provides him means to withstand Satan's arguments; yet in another sense he becomes the Word. His accomplishment is to realize his identity as the "living Oracle" sent to teach God's "final will." There are signs that he has begun to carry out this mission before encountering Satan, among them the response of the disciples: "we have heard / His words, his wisdom full of grace and truth" (1.33–34). But it is not until the end of the poem, in the affirmation of divinity with which he responds to Satan's final temptation, that Christ appears fully sure of his nature and power.

Paradise Regained is among other things Milton's most subtle and complex statement about the power of the Word. In the early tracts Milton found it sufficient to assert the power of scriptural truth to destroy error. The Bible appeared a newly found weapon that would smash the "Nebuchadnezzars Image" of formal religion. *Paradise Regained* corrects these expectations about the imminence of true reformation by offering a different version of how the power of the Word manifests itself. Like *Paradise Lost*, it views the kingdom of Christ in apocalyptic perspective; this will be a stone dashing to pieces "All Monarchies besides" in some indeterminate future time. Moreover, *Paradise Regained* suggests that Milton could understand and illustrate the paradox of the "mighty weakness" of the Gospel in ways that were beyond him in the early days of the wars of truth. In this most fundamental version of the combat between truth and error an ability to wait for illumination from the "fountain of light" becomes the way to victory. Such waiting recalls the essentially Quaker emphasis, seen in Winstanley, upon waiting for leadings from the Spirit. Milton's waiting is not so passive as that of the Quakers, however, depending as it does upon a patience realized through resistance to temptation. This patience—"the exercise / Of saints, the trial of thir fortitude," as Milton calls it in *Samson*

Agonistes (1287–88)—enables Christ to withstand Satan's assaults as a rock the "surging waves." Milton allows Satan to unveil his panoramas of worldly luxury, power, and civility to demonstrate their irrelevance to Christ's mission and, by implication, to the Christian's understanding of how to live.

In his arguments with Satan Christ draws upon the power that Milton regarded as inherent in scriptural truth, but he does not fully possess or embody that power until the end of the poem. This final development is anticipated by Milton's description of the dawn that follows the night of storms and "Furies" patiently endured by Christ:

> Who with her radiant finger still'd the roar
> Of Thunder, chas'd the clouds, and laid the winds,
> And grisly Specters which the Fiend has rais'd.
> (4.428–30)

The image recalls an earlier assertion that divorce "like a divine touch in one moment heals all; and *like the word of God* [italics mine], in one instant hushes outrageous tempests into a sudden stilnesse and peacefull calm" (2.333), as well as the description of the creating Word in *Paradise Lost*. The single beam of light is the dramatic equivalent of the "beams of God's Word" that Milton had seen as destroying the serpent of prelacy, yet it offers a striking contrast to the violence of that image and others in the early prose that Milton used to represent the divine force acting through Scripture. It brilliantly expresses the concept of strength in apparent weakness, suggesting a power in the gentle and natural coming of the dawn that goes beyond anything to be found in the kind of reasoned argument that Christ has offered up to this point.

Milton's personification of the dawn is so effective partly because it mirrors the "mighty weakness" of Christ himself, who sits "unappall'd in calm and sinless peace" through the night and yet when Satan forces their struggle to a climax asserts his power calmly and decisively. When Christ responds to Satan from the pinnacle of the temple, he takes the name of God and miraculously stands, thereby justifying his claim to be regarded as the oracle of truth and removing the possibility for Satan to understand his nature in anything but a "single sense."[55] He speaks for the first time with the full "authority" that he recognizes as "derived from heaven" (1.289) and that the angels warn Satan he must learn to fear:

> Hereafter learn with awe
> To dread the Son of God: hee all unarm'd
> Shall chase thee with the terror of his voice
> From thy Demoniac holds.
> (4.626–29)

This is the power of the living Word in the person of Christ. It can "command" Satan and his legions "down into the deep" at any time. Yet *Paradise Regained,* like *Paradise Lost,* expresses Milton's mature recognition that for the time being man must endure the world's abuses of truth and trust to the guidance of the Spirit, the "inward oracle."

6. John Bunyan and the Experience of the Word

John Bunyan approached the Bible as only a relatively uneducated person of the seventeenth century could, with an acute sense of the power of the Word to terrify or comfort one who wrestled with it. The story of his artistic development is one of learning to understand and control this power. Bunyan was a man of many talents, including an ability to render the ordinary life of his times in a pungently realistic fashion, but perhaps the most important of these was his gift for exploiting the dramatic potential of biblical metaphors and events in such a way as to give shape and meaning to the spiritual life of the people for whom he wrote. *Grace Abounding to the Chief of Sinners, The Pilgrim's Progress,* and *The Holy War* offer the most important evidence of Bunyan's experience of Scripture and his genius for making imaginative use of it.[1] The obvious place to begin is with *Grace Abounding,* Bunyan's record of his own early efforts to reckon with the force of biblical texts.

Grace Abounding reveals a fundamentally Calvinist understanding of the stages of spiritual life that would have been familiar to Bunyan's readers from other sectarian autobiographies as well as from sermons and works of practical divinity. The worldly unconcern of the young man yields to a conviction of sin, followed by a vain effort to live a morally righteous life in conformity with the law. Genuine faith becomes possible only when he recognizes the impossibility of satisfying the law and, finally convinced by the message of the Gospel, believes himself to be justified by the righteousness of Christ, though even then he remains vulnerable to temptation. In its broad outlines the pattern was thoroughly conventional. Like other exemplary Christians who set down their experiences, Bunyan ended his narrative with an account of his ministry. His point of view, established in the preface and maintained throughout, is that of the fatherly pastor recounting his spiritual history for the edification of his flock. At some points—when he magnifies his early sins or numbers the providences by which he was saved from death—Bunyan seems particularly influenced by the expectations of the genre in which he wrote. Yet to say that *Grace Abounding* belongs to a tradition of Calvinist spiritual autobiography is to say nothing about the extraordinary intensity of Bunyan's spiritual struggle, or about the fact that the drama of conversion claims a disproportionate amount of attention in his narrative.[2]

We still read *Grace Abounding* because Bunyan was able to convey a strongly individual experience in language that compels by its concreteness and its colloquial immediacy. It would be a mistake to claim too much for any particular tradition or to try to explain its power by appealing to sources, but it is important to recognize Bunyan's spiritual kinship with Luther, whose commentary on Galatians came to his attention at a critical period in his religious development.[3] Bunyan's account of his discovery of the book suggests that its impact was considerable:

> I found my condition in his experience so largely and profoundly handled, as if his Book had been written out of my heart.[4] (129, p. 41)

The Bible excepted, Luther's commentary was the book "most fit for a wounded Conscience" in Bunyan's view. The introduction to the Elizabethan translation that Bunyan knew pictures Luther the monk reading Paul and being tormented by Satan, "with fierie darts, with doubts and objections, with false terrors and subtile assaults."[5] According to this account Luther spent three days and nights on his bed wrestling with a verse from the third chapter of Romans. It is not hard to imagine Bunyan finding an image of his own condition in Luther's, even shaping his account of his fears and doubts with words of Luther in mind. Luther described his reactions to scriptural passages declaring God's judgments of sinners under the law in terms that suggest Bunyan's ("yea it [the law] accuseth me, terrifieth me, and driveth me to desperation")[6] and diagnosed the spiritual malady of the man tempted not by lust or covetousness but "assailed with more vehement and grievous motions, as with bitterness and anguish of spirit, blasphemy, distrust and desperation."[7]

In *Grace Abounding* Bunyan dramatized a state of hypersensitivity to the threats of the law, and the contrasting promises of the Gospel, that Luther would have understood. At one point Bunyan pictures himself as "lying and trembling under the mighty hand of God, continually torn and rent by the thunderings of his Justice" (247, p. 77) and as a consequence turning over "every leaf" of his Bible to discover his fate. Augustine's spiritual awakening in a garden in Milan, however wrenching emotionally that may have been, appears straightforward and decisive by comparison. When the voice called "Tolle, lege" ("Take up and read"),[8] he opened his Bible to a text on concupiscence that pinpointed his condition and started him on his future course. But Bunyan's voices are often contradictory. His torment is that of an unlearned man who must search the Scripture with the conviction that any one verse can save or damn him. Luther, the doctor of theology, would not have felt the impact of disembodied texts so directly and physically as Bunyan did, but his sense of the force of Scripture and of the conflict of wrath and grace in the individual who reads it in the hope of salvation seems to have conditioned Bunyan's understanding of his experience in important ways.

Much of the drama of *Grace Abounding* arises from Bunyan's prolonged struggle to arrive at a secure conviction of his election. The characteristic pattern of the central part of the work is that of alternating states of comfort and despair, prompted by the momentary ascendancy of particular texts in Bunyan's consciousness. The reader learns to recognize that periods of hopefulness are exceedingly fragile, since a threatening text may "seize upon" Bunyan's soul at any time. Bunyan's experiences could be taken as an illustration of the kind of warfare of texts that Luther had outlined. Some of the most vivid passages in Luther's commentary show the grip of the law upon the imagination:

> But when in the very conflict we should use the Gospel, which is the word of grace consolation and life, there doth the law, the word of wrath, heaviness and death prevent the Gospell and beginneth to rage, and the terrors which it raiseth up in the conscience, are no lesse then was that horrible shew in the mount *Sinay*. So that even one place of the Scripture containing some threatening of the law, overwhelmeth and drowneth all consolations besides, and so shaketh all our inward powers, that it maketh us to forget justification, grace, Christ, the Gospell and all together.[9]

The law has an essential role to play at an early stage in the Christian's experience; he must feel the power of divine wrath if he is to overcome what Luther calls "the opinion of righteousness."[10] But when the law rages, neutralizing the promises of the Gospel by arousing excessive fear, Satan is at work—in Luther's view and in Bunyan's.

Bunyan tends to personalize this conflict, imagining Satan pulling at his clothes or whispering in his ear and God as casting Luther's book into his hand. He even sees himself as having a tug of war with Satan over the meaning of a verse in John, striving with him for the "good word of Christ" (215, pp. 67–68). Verses themselves become alarmingly real in Bunyan's experience. These "imprison" and "pinch" him or, when they console, offer "hints" and "touches" of grace and sometimes a "sweet glance." Bunyan's instinct for discovering figurative language that will express his sufferings is apparent from the way in which he elaborates metaphors suggested by Luther. He feels as brass fetters on his legs the sense of being confined by the law that Luther communicates. Where Luther speaks of Satan as stirring up "stormes and tempests" to hinder the course of the Gospel,[11] Bunyan in describing periods of despair conveys the experience of being tossed helplessly in a storm like a "broken Vessel" driven by the winds (186, p. 58).[12] Luther describes "the great and horrible rorings of the law, of sin, of death, of the devil, and hell;"[13] Bunyan imagines his "tumultuous thoughts" as "masterless hellhounds" roaring and bellowing within him (174, p. 53).

Luther does not offer anything exactly comparable to the internal drama generated by Bunyan's obsessive concern with his own sins, but his accounts of the terrors of the law and its raging in the world suggested ways in which this drama might be rendered. And in its repeated assertions of the power of the Gospel to calm the soul the commentary on Galatians offered the kind of consolation for a "wounded Conscience" that Bunyan sought. The cry *"Abba, Father"* will surmount all the roaring, Luther insists.[14] The Gospel comforts and quickens; it offers sentences that may be used as a sword against the devil. But to believe in the truth of the Gospel and feel the force of its promises, according to Luther, one must first abandon any idea of achieving righteousness without divine help. Only the conviction that Christ has purchased an "everlasting righteousness" for sinners will save.[15] This is the point at which Bunyan has arrived at the end of his period of doubt when he hears the words, "Thy righteousness is in Heaven," and can see Christ sitting at the right hand of God (229, p. 72).[16]

In their differing ways Luther and Bunyan both demonstrate the force with which individual verses, even single words of Scripture, act upon the soul to arouse fear and joy. Both are concerned with the problem of how to experience the saving power of the Word. Yet Luther's work proceeds systematically through Galatians, however charged his exegesis may be by his sense of spiritual struggle, where Bunyan's offers what appears to be a chaos of conflicting attitudes. Texts "dart" into his mind from widely separated parts of the Bible, causing sharp and unpredictable reversals of mood. In the long central portion of *Grace Abounding* devoted to the drama of conversion there may seem to be little clear sense of progression. Nevertheless, one can discover a kind of development in Bunyan's perception of Scripture and his confidence in the promises of grace.

In his erratic progress Bunyan learns to look upon the Bible with "new eyes" when he discovers the epistles of Paul (46, p. 17), then subsequently finds himself shutting the Word out in his unbelief, as though setting his shoulder to a door (81, p. 76). Fragmentary perceptions of the possibility of grace, hints and glances, suggest an increasing sensitivity. Bunyan's encounter with Gifford, minister of the Bedford church, marks his first major advance. Under Gifford's tutelage he learns to pray that God might set him down "by his own Spirit in the reality of the Word" (117, p. 37) and is rewarded by the experience of being "led from truth to truth by God" (119, p. 37) in such a way that he sees the Gospel whole for the first time and feels its comforting presence:

> He did...lead me into his words, yea...he did open them unto me, make them shine before me, and cause them to dwell with me and comfort me over and over. (126, p. 39)

One is struck by Bunyan's sense of being led "into" the Gospel by God, as into a new world of experience. This remarkable intimacy with the Word does not last. When Bunyan becomes convinced that he has committed the unpardonable sin against the Holy Ghost by yielding to the compulsion to "sell Christ," he finds himself assailed by a text from Hebrews that describes the rejection of Esau for selling his birthright. His belief in the truth of the Scriptures only increases his vulnerability and drives him to the despairing thought that the Word has "shut him out" (186, p. 58).

In his moods of estrangement from the Word Bunyan describes his encounters with hostile texts as being like running upon pikes, or being held off by a spear, or a flaming sword in the hand of God. Bunyan can escape the text that condemns Esau only when he feels that it is defeated by a stronger text, "Mercy rejoyceth against Judgment" (213, p. 67). Then he can rest in the belief that "the Word of the Law and Wrath must give place to the Word of Life and Grace" (214, p. 67) and can "venture to come nigh unto those most fearful and terrible Scriptures" (222, p. 70) and consider their implications calmly for the first time, as though freed from their spell. He can go on to examine the dreadful text from Hebrews rationally and discover that it need not apply to him at all.[17] For much of the central portion of Grace Abounding Bunyan seems helpless before the forces that are released by his belief in the reality of Scripture. Stability comes when he is sufficiently assured of the relationship of law and grace and of the redeeming righteousness of Christ to see himself "in Heaven and Earth at once; in heaven by my Christ, by my head, by my Righteousness and Life, though on Earth by my Body or Person" (233, p. 73). In this state Scriptures "spangle" in his eyes and he can praise God, confident of having a secure place in the World opened up to him by the Gospel.

At times in Grace Abounding Bunyan shows the talent for representing spiritual experience in visual terms that he was to exercise so successfully in The Pilgrim's Progress. Two visions stand out, the frequently noted one in which he sees the poor people of Bedfordshire "set on the Sunny side of some high Mountain" (53, p. 19) separated from him by a wall, and a parallel one in which he sees himself trembling at the gate of Joshua's "City of Refuge," pursued by the avenger of blood, waiting for the Elders of the city (the apostles, in Bunyan's imagination) to judge him. Both scenes reflect his strong fears of exclusion from salvation and serve to confirm the existence of a spiritual realm in which salvation is possible. In the first instance Bunyan imagines himself forcing his way through a gap in the wall to join the fellowship of the godly in the sunshine of divine favor, as if breaking through into "the reality of the Word" by a terrific act of will. In the second he eventually decides that he has the right to enter the city, though the scene remains one of the most powerful images of spiritual isolation in Grace Abounding. These visions are more vivid than the physical circumstances of Bunyan's life in Bedfordshire. As Edward Dowden aptly put it, "the dominant characteristic of Grace Abounding is its intense realization of things unseen."[18] Most of the detail of everyday life is burned away by the intensity of Bunyan's concern with his spiritual state. Those scenes that he does record, like the commonplace one of crows in the plowed fields, take on an unnatural clarity because of his sense of the intrusion of the divine.

Although in reading *Grace Abounding* we continue to be reminded of Bunyan's existence in Bedfordshire, as when he feels that the very stones of the street would banish him from the world he inhabits (187, pp. 58–59), the unseen world of his spiritual life becomes increasingly real. Bunyan not only feels warring texts as physical presences, he sees Christ looking down at him from heaven. When he is "led into" the Gospel, he experiences it visually: "Me thought it was as if I had seen him [Christ] born, as if I had seen him grow up, as if I had seen him walk thorow this world, from the Cradle to the Cross" (120, p. 38). At one point he feels that he has "evidence" of his salvation from heaven, "with many golden Seals thereon, all hanging in my sight" (128, p. 40). Bunyan must see the evidence of his salvation, whether as a legal document or as the vision of "the blessed things of heaven" that he reports at the end of his account of his temptations. Such a capacity for seeing the world evoked by the Gospel is for him a final demonstration of its reality.

Although Bunyan's glimpses of the unseen world (in *Grace Abounding*) are fitful, and his sense of spiritual progress often dissolves into confusion, the final account of his ministry shows him secure in his understanding of the Word and seeking to apply its power to others. As a minister he labors "to find out such a Word as might, if God would bless it, lay hold of and awaken the Conscience" (272, p. 84). Bunyan's narrative makes it clear that he remained alive to the terrors of the law and still subject to old temptations. At this point, however, he appears to be in control of his experience and able to make the Word efficacious.

The preface of *Grace Abounding* displays an imaginative grasp of the reality of the Word and a capacity to read his own experience in its terms toward which Bunyan shows himself struggling in the narrative itself. He moves naturally into a figurative mode suggested by the Bible, picturing himself as looking after his people *"as before from the top of* Shenir *and* Hermon, *so now from* the Lions Den [Bedford gaol] *and from the Mountains of the Leopards (Song* 4:8)*."* He is a Daniel, a Samson, a David showing that his former fears and doubts *"are as the head of* Goliah *in my hand,"* a Moses exhorting his people to "go in to possess the land." This is not simply the vernacular of the times, as it might be spoken by any mechanic preacher. Bunyan shows an extraordinary ability to appropriate biblical language and events, especially from the Old Testament, and convert them to his uses. To view his own experience from this perspective was to understand it and to claim for it a kind of validity that could only be established for Bunyan by the Word:

Yea, it was for this reason I lay so long at Sinai (Deut. 4:10, 11), *to see the fire, and the cloud, and the darkness,* that I might fear the Lord all the days of my life upon earth, and tell of his wondrous works to my children, *Psal.* 78:3,4,5. (P. 2)

It seems unlikely that Bunyan is referring to this biblical vein when he speaks of rejecting a higher style in *Grace Abounding* in order to "be plain and simple, and lay down the thing as it was." As the conclusion of the first part of *The Pilgrim's Progress* and much of *The Holy War* demonstrate, he could rise to a grander, more rhetorically elaborate style when he chose. What the preface to *Grace Abounding* reveals is that Bunyan had already learned to find analogues for his experience and that of any ordinary Christian in scattered biblical texts with little regard for historical context. Shifting from the world of the Bible to that of Bedfordshire presented no difficulties. Bunyan could readily cite the example of Paul recalling his first visitation of grace and that of the Israelites thinking back to their experience at the Red Sea in exhorting his readers to remember *"the Close, the Milkhouse, the Stable, the Barn, and the like, where God did visit your Soul."* He conflates Old and New Testaments and moves easily from their language to that of his everyday experience.

Bunyan's condition at the end of the period described in *Grace Abounding* is one in which, in the language of his early tract *A Few Sighs from Hell* (1658), he has found "his soul and Scripture...to embrace each other, and a sweet correspondency and agreement between them."[19] The preface to his autobiography demonstrates an imaginative control of scriptural material that looks ahead to the much larger achievement of *The Pilgrim's Progress.* Bunyan's sense of the evocative power of the biblical language is apparent even from his early commentary on the last two chapters of Revelation, *The Holy City* (1665). This work suggests that the effort to expound "shadowish and figurative expressions" of a text need not cripple the imagination. For all of his efforts to discover types and allegorize descriptive details—gates, jewels, even the measurements of the city—Bunyan effectively conveys a sense of the glory of the saints, sometimes breaking into lyrical celebration:

Never was fair weather after foul—nor warm weather after could—nor a sweet and bountiful spring after a heavy, and nipping, and terrible winter, so comfortable, sweet, desirable, and welcome to the poor birds and beasts of the field, as this day will be to the church of God. Darkness! it was the plague of Egypt: it is an empty, forlorn, desolate, solitary, and discomforting state; wherefore light, even the illuminating grace of God, especially in the measure that it shall be communicated unto us at this day, it must needs be precious.[20]

He goes on to contrast the darkness with the "warm and spangling beams" of divine grace and to invoke the language of the Song of Songs to describe this new springtime of the church. Bunyan repeatedly draws upon the great eschatological passages of the Old Testament prophets, especially Isaiah, to identify the lot of the saints with the promised restoration of the scattered sons of Israel. In pulling together such passages and commenting upon them, with the end of arousing desire and wonder in his readers, Bunyan practiced a very loose kind of typological reading that could as well be called meditation. He was not so much finding particular typological equivalences—although he does this at times—as responding to the power of Old Testament description to represent spiritual satisfactions in sensuous terms. Bunyan's freedom in the handling of individual texts in *The Holy City* appears in his readiness to paraphrase or to adapt passages to his subject, as by taking a verse from Psalms (Ps. 20:5) as a warrant for imagining the victorious saints setting up banners on towers of the wall around the New Jerusalem.[21]

Bunyan saw in the description of the New Jerusalem compelling evidence of the triumph of the Word. When the Gospel breaks out in its primitive glory with the fall of Antichrist, it will convert multitudes, including the Jews:

> Now will all the doctrines of the gospel spangle and sparkle; out of every text will the ministers of God make to issue exceedingly most precious and heavenly fire; for these stones are indeed the stones of fire.[22]

Bunyan appropriated these "stones of fire" from Ezekiel's vision of the holy mountain of God (Ezek. 28:16), making them into a symbol of the power of the Word to transform the world in the last days. He found an even more important symbol of the operation of the Word in the golden reed by which the city was to be measured, the antitype of which Ezekiel's line of flax (Ezek. 40:3) is the type. The measuring of the gates suggested to him "an opening of the excellencies of Christ...even by the full sway, power, majesty, and clearness of the Word;"[23] the measuring of the wall shows "that all things now are according to the rule of the Word."[24] He imagines the church's disordered parts brought into "exact form and order"[25] by this realization of the rule of the New Testament. In its triumphant state the church will believe in what he calls the doctrine of the twelve apostles (signified by the twelve gates of the city) rather than a popish, and a Quaker, and a Presbyterian doctrine, "thus distinguished, and thus confounding and destroying."[26] Bunyan plainly shared in the millenarian interests of the times, but it is significant that he did not reduce Revelation to a calendar of the events of the last days.[27] His interest in *The Holy City* was in celebrating the joys of universal fellowship that he felt would be made possible by conformity to the "pure and unspotted Word of God."

In his preface to *The Holy City* Bunyan invokes Christ's miracle of feeding the multitude with a few loaves and fishes to explain how the work grew out of his efforts to expound a text from Revelation to his companions in Bedford gaol:

> We all did eat, and were well refreshed; and behold also, that while I was in the distributing of it, it so increased in my hand, that of the fragments that we left, after we had well dined, I gathered up this basketful.[28]

One may be pardoned for doubting that there were enough fragments left to fill the almost sixty double-columned pages that the work occupies in Offor's edition, but Bunyan's figure is interesting for the sense it conveys of a miraculous exfoliation of his text. A similar feeling underlies the passage in the prefatory verses to *The Pilgrim's Progress* in which Bunyan describes his ideas as multiplying like sparks from coals after he "Fell suddenly into an allegory." In both instances Bunyan finds a figurative way of suggesting that his writing develops spontaneously and mysteriously, as though hesitating to claim any credit for his own imaginative powers.

In expounding Revelation Bunyan could let his imagination play over Old Testament texts and could develop a vision of the future blessedness of the saints without feeling any need to apologize for this activity. Both the Apology to *The Pilgrim's Progress* and the verse Conclusion are remarkable for Bunyan's preoccupation with justifying his figurative method to skeptical Puritan readers, whom he imagines objecting, "Metaphors make us blind." Bunyan defends his form of pointing to the substance it contains, as in the comparison of his work with a cabinet offered in the Apology ("*My dark and cloudy words they do but hold / The Truth as Cabinets inclose the Gold*"),[29] but he does not thereby imply that the form is an inadequate means of expressing his message. I would argue, with U. Milo Kaufmann, that Bunyan was in truth uncomfortable with the Puritan habit of reducing biblical metaphor to doctrine.[30] The very fact that Bunyan protests so much in attempting to justify his method reveals the depth of his commitment to "similitude" as a means of expressing God's truth. Some of his formulations actually tend to undermine the conventional distinction between kernel and husk. In the Conclusion, for example, he suggests that the reader might not be able to "extract" his gold from the ore in which it is wrapped and chides: "*None throws away the Apple for the Core*" (p. 164).

Bunyan's most significant appeals are to scriptural authority, and underlying these appeals is a conviction about the metaphoric nature of much biblical truth. Bunyan saw that the prophets "*used much by Metaphors / To set forth Truth*" (p. 5) because God's truth could best be comprehended figuratively. He never suggests a separation between the "*Types, Shadows, and Metaphors*" of the Bible and the truth that they express. For Bunyan the light of the Gospel "springs" from its "Dark Figures." He felt that by employing a similarly "dark" method he could make truth "*cast forth its rayes as light as day*" (p. 6). Such language does not suggest a concern with doctrine and uses (though Bunyan was of course concerned with showing his readers how to conform their lives to God's truth) but with conveying the kind of joyful illumination that he found in Scripture. He would make *"The Blind...delightful things to see"* (p. 7).

To appreciate the nature of Bunyan's commitment to the metaphor of the "way" of Christ in *The Pilgrim's Progress* one must recognize that he used this metaphor in two basic senses, both of which are important. His genius for exploiting the dramatic potential of biblical metaphor is perhaps most apparent from his success at holding in suspension these two senses of his central figure. The way is the path of all Christians through the wilderness of the world, the way "From This World To That Which Is To Come," and simultaneously the inner way of faith of the individual believer. Without a strong conviction about where the way leads the pilgrim would never set out at all; yet he cannot arrive at the promised end unless he understands *how* to walk.

Bunyan talks about the second sense of his metaphor, what it means to walk in the way of faith, in *The Holy City*. He explains that "it is usual in the Holy Scripture to call the transformation of the sinner from Satan to God a holy way, and also to admonish him that is so transformed to walk in that way, saying, Walk in the faith, love, spirit, and newness of life, and walk in the truth, ways, statutes, and judgments of God."[31] Here and in *The Pilgrim's Progress* Bunyan draws upon the Old Testament sense of walking in the "way of the righteous" (Psalm 1:6), in the "truth" of God, as well as upon the New Testament sense of walking "in the Spirit" (Gal. 5:16) and "in newness of life" (Rom. 6:4), but of course the New Testament meaning is primary. Faith must be attested by a genuine "newness of life."

This sense of the way as determined by the faith of the individual pilgrim coexists with the other sense of the way as a common journey of all the faithful from the City of Destruction to the New Jerusalem. The design of *The Pilgrim's Progress*, and much of its force, depends upon the figurative reading of the experience of the Israelites that Bunyan and countless other Puritans learned from Hebrews.[32] *The Heavenly Footman* shows more explicitly than its successor, *The Pilgrim's Progress*, the centrality of the figure of the journey to Bunyan's understanding of the Christian life: "Because the way is long (I speak metaphorically) and there is many a dirty step, many a high hill, much work to do, a wicked heart, world, and devil, to overcome; I say, there are many steps to be taken by those that intend to be saved, by running or walking, in the steps of that faith of our father Abraham. Out of Egypt thou must go through the Red Sea; thou must run a long and tedious journey, through the vast howling wilderness, before thou come to the land of promise."[33] Bunyan saw that he did not speak any less truly for speaking "metaphorically." The metaphor, which he saw as embodying God's promise that his saints would succeed in making their way through the wilderness to the "land of promise," is the key to his conception of *The Pilgrim's Progress* and to the appeal of the work for his Puritan readers. His "dream" could succeed because the habit of thinking of the world metaphorically, as a wilderness to be journeyed through, was ingrained in his readers, and because they could identify readily with someone who could show them what it meant to follow "in the steps of that faith of our father Abraham."[34] The ground of their faith was a belief in the possibility of progress from this world to the next, and Bunyan's work offered them the hope that an ordinary believer, not without weaknesses, might attain the New Jerusalem.

The encounter of Christian and Hopeful with the shepherds of the Delectable Mountains provides a revealing illustration of Bunyan's ability to combine the two basic senses of the metaphor of the way. This episode offers one of the best examples in *The Pilgrim's Progress* of the subjectivity of the individual way of faith:

Chr. *Is this the way to the Coelestial City?*
Shep. You are just in your way.
Chr. *How far is it thither?*
Shep. Too far for any, but those that *shall* get thither indeed.
Chr. *Is the way safe, or dangerous?*
Shep. Safe for those for whom it is to be safe, *but transgressors shall fall therein.* (p. 119)

The deliberate ambiguity forces one to recognize that the nature of the way —its length and the specific dangers to be encountered—depends upon the faith of the individual pilgrim. The shepherds can assess the spiritual health of the wayfarers at the moment ("You are just in your way"), but this spiritual condition is dynamic and precarious. To give definite answers to the pilgrims' questions would be to ignore the uncertainty with which faith must live. In *The Heavenly Footman* Bunyan says, "as the way is long, so the time in which they are to get to the end of it is very uncertain; the time present is the only time."[35] Christian's faith exists only in this "time present," because faith must be renewed continuously.

Alice's encounter with the Cheshire Cat reads as though Carroll might have conceived it as a parody of Bunyan's meeting with the shepherds:

"Would you tell me, please, which way I ought to go from here?
"That depends a good deal on where you want to get to," said the Cat.
"I don't much care where—" said Alice.
"Then it doesn't matter which way you go," said the Cat.
"—so long as I get somewhere," Alice added as an explanation.
"Oh, you're sure to do that," said the Cat, "if you only walk long enough."[36]

The Cheshire Cat's responses appear nonsensical only because he does not give Alice the kind of certainty she wants. His logic is impeccable, and it serves as an amusing way of pointing up her confusion. One way is as good as another unless she decides the "ought." She is bound to get "somewhere" if she walks "long enough," but whether she thinks she is "somewhere" will depend upon her expectations. The response of the shepherds to Christian's inquiries has the similar effect of turning the questions back on the questioner, though they can offer no assurances that Christian will get anywhere at all, because they are talking about a metaphorical way that depends upon a faith that may collapse at any moment. Carroll's logical cat would find them incomprehensible, and probably silly.

Yet Bunyan's shepherds are also talking about the one true way that leads to the New Jerusalem (and not just "somewhere"), and the Delectable Mountains mark a station along the way, as the Interpreter's House and House Beautiful mark earlier stations. Christian's actions describe a progression through stages of spiritual life.[37] This progression is clearer in some places than in others—notably near the beginning and the end of the journey—but its outlines would have been familiar to readers acquainted with Puritan spiritual autobiography. Together Christian's experiences constitute a "Calvinist soul-history" (to use Sharrock's term)[38] proceeding from an initial conviction of sin that lands him in the Slough of Despond to the instruction in Scripture that he receives in the Interpreter's House (where he is exposed to scenes designed to "prick him forward" in the way), and through the various trials of the major part of the journey until he finally arrives at the assurance of God's mercy represented by Beulah.

Leonard Trinterud has remarked that Bunyan wove into the traditional pattern of the pilgrimage of the soul "the whole of the covenant theology's conception of the various stages by which man was regenerated (the *ordo salutis*)."[39] These stages were commonly understood to be effectual calling, justification, sanctification, and glorification, all contingent upon the prior election of the soul by God.[40] They imply faith, repentance, and perseverance in spiritual warfare on the part of the Christian. Where the central drama of *Grace Abounding* turns on the question of justification, most of *The Pilgrim's Progress*—from the loss of Christian's burden to his arrival in the New Jerusalem—has to do with the process of sanctification, by which the Christian moves with the aid of the Holy Spirit toward an ideal of holiness. Bunyan at one point speaks of salvation as preserving Christians by delivering them "from all the hazards that we run betwixt our state of Justification, and our state of Glorification."[41] The long period of sanctification was clearly a time of trial, but it was also expected to be a time of growth in righteousness.[42]

One should not attach too much significance to the order of the temptations that Christian encounters; yet there is some point to the sequence. The more violent, and dramatic, assaults on Christian's faith come early—the most violent, that of Apollyon, soon after he has put on the Pauline armor of the soldier of Christ. The transition from the Valley of Humiliation to the Valley of the Shadow of Death makes sense in terms of Christian's experience; he has just faced the prospect of annihilation in the battle with Apollyon. After escaping the fiends of the Valley of the Shadow, Christian must face the hostile society of Vanity Fair (after an interlude occupied by conversation with Faithful and Talkative). Again the threat is overt and violent, although violence in Vanity Fair is more insidious and contemptible for being sanctioned by social forms. Later Christian encounters more subtle kinds of temptations, involving fraud or deceptive appearances (Demas, By-Path Meadow, Flatterer, the seductive appeal of the Enchanted Ground for the pilgrim nearing the end of his journey).

The Doubting Castle episode proves that Christian can lose the way at a relatively late point in the journey through overconfidence, not that he has failed to grow in faith and understanding. The very intensity of his despair suggests bitter chagrin at having erred so foolishly after having come through so many trials. In Doubting Castle, Hopeful appeals to Christian's past victories over Apollyon and the terrors of the Valley of the Shadow ("remembrest thou not how valiant thou has been heretofore" [p. 116]), but valor will not help him in this very different kind of dilemma. In the first instance he had saved himself by continuing to fight, in the second by continuing to walk. In Doubting Castle Christian is baffled and dismayed by the fact that it seems impossible either to defeat the enemy or to get his key. The brilliance of the episode lies in the fact that Bunyan makes escape seemingly so difficult yet paradoxically so easy; Christian has only to remember that Scripture has provided him with his own key, a solution that comes to him as a result of prayer.

Christian again lapses into doubt at the River of Death, this time a paralyzing "darkness and horror" that causes him to forget temporarily the "sweet refreshments" he had met with in the way and the assurance they had given him of reaching the "Land that flows with Milk and Honey" (p. 157). Bunyan's emphasis upon the "sorrows of death" does not subvert Christian's progress; it merely indicates his acute sense of the dangers of this final obstacle, even for those who have persevered in the way of holiness. Reaching the plane of assurance represented by Beulah does not relieve one of the necessity of making the crossing.

Christian continues to be vulnerable to doubt throughout his pilgrimage because Bunyan believed that faith could never be completely secure in this world. But his doubts are prompted by very different kinds of trials, appropriate to different stages of the journey, and in each case we are reminded of what has gone before. Christiana's journey presents a clearer, less interrupted sense of progress, of course, because her way is so much easier. Giant Despair falls before Great-heart, the last of a succession of giants to suffer such a fate. Christiana receives so much support from her guides and the companies of Christians she encounters that she scarcely has the opportunity to doubt her salvation. After leaving the Delectable Mountains she sings: *"Behold, how fitly are the Stages set! / For their Relief, that Pilgrims are become"* (p. 289).

My point is simply that one can and should talk about stages in the journey that correspond to mileposts in the development of spiritual vitality. Christiana follows the same way that Christian does, though her temptations differ in degree from his, because Bunyan believed that patterns could be found in Puritan spiritual life. Kaufmann has suggested that Christian "helps to define the road to be walked" and prepares the way for his wife and family; by markers and victories "he transforms the way he covers" without, however, changing its outlines.[43] One could take Kaufmann's argument a step further and say that by elaborating the metaphor of the way, Bunyan ordered and explained the potentially chaotic events of spiritual life for his readers. In describing the Valley of the Shadow of Death and showing Christian passing through it he localized the terrors of death and suggested that they could be overcome.

To understand the nature of Christian's spiritual progress one must look more closely at the stages of his journey, particularly at his experience in such places as the Delectable Mountains and the land of Beulah. Those episodes that mark Christian's growing awareness of divine favor serve to establish the truth embodied in the biblical metaphor of the journey and hence to convince the reader that the goal for which Christian strives is real. Bunyan's narrative works by establishing the credibility of an entire world of spiritual experience, based upon the Word and opposed to the actual world, the world of his readers' everyday experience, in which Christian first appears. But Christian, and the reader, can enter this spiritual country only by recognizing the absoluteness of the claim made by the Word and by stripping themselves of the assumptions that govern life in the secular world. One must first understand the form that this process of disengagement takes in Bunyan's narrative.

Christian's sudden recognition that the world he inhabits belongs to the City of Destruction—that he is subject to judgment and must, according to the roll that Evangelist gives him, "Fly from the wrath to come"—propels him into what Bunyan in the Apology calls "our Gospel-day," a time defined by the Word. In this "Gospel-day," according to a verse from Corinthians that Bunyan quotes in *Come and Welcome to Jesus Christ:* "Now is the acceptable time, behold now is the day of salvation" (2 Cor. 6:2). In the perpetual "time present" of faith it is always "now," and Bunyan's Christian acts out of a sense of urgency that is incomprehensible to anyone who does not recognize the same biblical imperative. Obstinate speaks for the community when he dismisses him as "brain-sick."

Christian's dramatic flight from his family—with his fingers in his ears and crying, "Life, Life, Eternal Life"—appears ludicrous from any perspective other than the biblical one that Bunyan labored to establish. Mark Twain had Huck Finn encounter Bunyan at one point in his journey, when he investigates the books in the Grangerfords' library: "One was *Pilgrim's Progress,* about a man that left his family, it didn't say why. I read considerable in it now and then. The statements was interesting but tough."[44] Huck is an ideal vehicle for Twain's irony. To one schooled in the hard business of survival in the world, Christian's way of faith makes no sense at all. Bunyan knew that his message was "tough," and he chose to emphasize its difficulty so that there could be no mistake about the kind of renunciation that following the way demands. That is, Bunyan knew that biblical truth was "dark" not only because it is often metaphoric but because it is at bottom paradoxical, riddling (he exhorts Christiana to expound her "riddles" in the prefatory verses to part 2 of *The Pilgrim's Progress*).

The Gospel demands that one lose his life in order to save it (Mark 8:35) and further that one hate his family in order to follow Christ (Luke 14:26). If one chooses the way of Christ, one will necessarily appear foolish in the eyes of the world. The Pauline opposition between the spirit and the flesh, which provided the basis for Augustine's conception of rival cities of God and man, lies behind Bunyan's sense of a way that inevitably brings the pilgrim into conflict with the world (one must go "out of the World" to avoid Vanity Fair) and yet leads him beyond it. Bunyan's narrative insists that the claims of the way and those of the world are mutually exclusive. The pilgrim must set his course *"against Wind and Tide"* (p. 100), as Christian increasingly realizes. Faithful relates that he has learned to ignore the "hectoring spirits of the world" because he recognizes that "what God says, is best, though all the men in the world are against it" (p. 73).

Bunyan's account of his own trial dramatizes as clearly as anything in *The Pilgrim's Progress* the unavoidable conflict between the claims of the world and those of the Word. When the magistrate demanded that Bunyan show how it could be lawful to preach, confident that the law against unlicensed preaching left no room for doubt on the subject, Bunyan responded by quoting Peter: "As every man hath received the gift, so let him minister the same."[45] They might as well have spoken two different languages, so fundamentally opposed were their ways of ordering their lives. Bunyan went to jail, for a period that stretched to twelve years, because he could no more stop preaching than he could renounce the Word. To be a "servant in the Gospel," as Bunyan signed himself, meant to act upon it.

The Vanity Fair episode constitutes the most important statement of the warfare between spirit and flesh in *The Pilgrim's Progress*. By reducing secular society to a fair, Bunyan could imply that the collective opinion and power of "all the men in the world" are devoted to upholding the economic (and class) system upon which their material well-being is founded. In Bunyan's severe view even family relationships have a commercial aspect (his catalog of merchandise includes "Wives, Husbands, Children"), and the end of all human activity, limited by the perspective of the world, is vanity. At his trial Faithful charges that Christianity and the values of the town are *"Diametrically opposite."* Bunyan heightened the contrast by exaggerating the strangeness of the pilgrims, showing them to be peculiar in dress, in speech, and in their complete indifference to the wares pressed upon them; to the townspeople they are "fools," "Bedlams," "Outlandishmen." As strangers and pilgrims on the earth, seeking a better country, Christian and Faithful simply have no interest in the town; they *"buy"* the truth, which is to be found only in the Word. Although the justice of the burghers is a cruel farce, they act upon the correct assumption that Faithful's attitude threatens the very basis of their existence. The whole episode illustrates the necessity of choosing between two modes of life that are irreconcilable, between "carnal sense" and "things to come," to use the distinction made for Christian by Interpreter.

All the assumptions about the end of human activity that underlie Vanity Fair, and the indulgence of "fleshly appetite" that they allow, can be comprehended in the term "carnal sense" (or a comparable one, "carnal temper," which Evangelist applies to Worldly Wiseman). One can see a similar repudiation of carnality in Christian's rejection of the appeal of Worldly Wiseman, whose patronizing line finally depends upon the assumption that Christian will be attracted by the prospect of a comfortable, secure existence in the Village of Morality. He offers an ordered society based on a respect for law and class distinctions (to accept his gentlemanly authority and that of Legality would be for Christian to admit that he is one of the *"weak"* who meddle with *"things too high for them"*).

Vanity Fair strongly suggests actual fair towns of Bunyan's day, and, with the Village of Morality and the City from which Christian sets out, it embodies the material attractions of the real world which Christian must put behind him if he is to attain his goal. These places must be distinguished from landscapes that reflect Christian's inner struggles. Although the Village of Morality and the Slough of Despond can both be located along the "way" that Christian travels, they reflect different orders of experience. The same can be said of the Valley of Humiliation and Vanity Fair. The latter presents the sort of external challenge that the warfaring Christian continually meets in society and can resist successfully if he only remembers the scriptural language, typically riddling, that enables him to see his life in a heavenly rather than an earthly perspective. To pass through the Valley of Humiliation and other landscapes that dramatize the crises of his inner life Christian must depend upon the action of grace to reveal how the Word will save him. These landscapes appear more perilous because of his uncertainty.

Bunyan's spiritual landscapes have a fluidity that recalls the shifting terrain of *The Faerie Queene*. They are often surreal, more like what one might expect in a dream than the actual landscapes one might encounter in Bedfordshire or anywhere else.[46] The experience of the pilgrim (either Formal or Hypocrisy) who follows the way of Destruction "into a wide field full of dark Mountains, where he stumbled and fell, and rose no more" (p. 42) suggests the abrupt transitions of dreams. One cannot really explain these strange "dark Mountains," even by appealing to Bunyan's source in Jeremiah, except to say that the episode provides a commentary on the nature of spiritual blindness. Dangers rise up unpredictably, and one cannot cope with them by native wit.

The spiritual world that Christian enters in setting out for the New Jerusalem resembles the country he knows yet surprises him in strange ways. The Slough of Despond was obviously inspired by the conditions of Bedfordshire roads (and has been taken as an instance of Bunyan's realism), yet this Slough quickly assumes alarming proportions. Pliable cries out *"where are you now?"* (p. 14) as Christian begins to sink and flees, unable to tolerate a hazard that refuses to conform to the limits of his experience. Pliable is the epitome of the practical man, the sort who has to know exactly where he is going and how, and he cannot follow Christian into the treacherous spiritual landscape that he has entered. Christian himself quickly learns that he is helpless without the Word in this world; only by recognizing the *"steps"* it provides, with the aid of Help, can he get through the Slough.

The Valley of Humiliation, the Valley of the Shadow of Death, the Delectable Mountains, and the other landscapes that Christian must traverse define a world that is open only to those who believe in the Word sufficiently to seek the goal that he does. These landscapes do not exist for Pliable, who refuses to enter the spiritual country to which they belong, or for Atheist, who cannot find it. The topography of this country is determined largely by Bunyan's experience of Scripture, and the key to Christian's progress through it is his understanding of the power of the Word.

Christian's near disaster in his struggles with Apollyon suggests that this understanding does not come easily. The education in the Gospel that he has received from Evangelist, Interpreter, and the inhabitants of House Beautiful prepares him to resist Apollyon's arguments successfully.[47] Yet his failure in the physical combat that follows suggests that Christian is deficient in faith and needs the intervention of the Spirit—whose help Bunyan felt all Christians required, if they were to understand the implications of Scripture or even to pray successfully—to be able to manage his sword ("the sword of the Spirit, which is the Word of God" [Eph. 6:17]). The verse that

Bunyan chose to signal Christian's new grasp of the power of the Word is particularly suggestive: *"Rejoyce not against me, O mine Enemy! when I fall, I shall arise."* It points to the paradoxical nature of biblical truth (a difficult lesson for Christian to learn) and thus to his own providential recovery, and also, typologically, to Christ's resurrection and his ultimate victory over Satan (Bunyan would have regarded the verse from Micah as foreshadowing these truths).

Christian's encounter with Apollyon has meaning only for one who grants the fundamental truth of Scripture (Atheist would not conceive of evil in this way). The indefiniteness of the landscape in which Christian meets him can be explained by his spiritual condition and his sense of Scripture at this point. In his guilt and fear Christian imagines the power of the demonic forces that oppose God to be greater than it is. It is startling to discover in reading part 2 that the Valley of Humiliation is "fat Ground;" Great-heart tells Christiana, "Behold, how green this Valley is, also how beautiful *with Lilies"* (p. 237). At a comparable stage in his journey Christian lacks the steady spiritual vision that Christiana demonstrates here; he can see only Apollyon coming "over the field" and then straddling the way. Thus preoccupied with the monstrous appearance of evil, he cannot experience the foretaste of Canaan that his more tranquil, and humble, wife does.

Christian defeats Apollyon by discovering how to use the power over evil inherent in the Word. He conquers the darkness and terrors of the Valley of the Shadow of Death by learning to rely upon the illumination of the Word, which enables him to keep to the path. Bunyan associated the darkness and the confusion of this second valley with a loss of the sense of God's presence. Like Milton's hell, it offers a desolate, sterile landscape (*"A Wilderness, a Land of desarts, and of Pits, a Land of drought, and of the shadow of death"*), and in this "very solitary place" Christian experiences a terrifying feeling of aloneness. In one of the passages that inspired the episode Job in his helplessness sees himself as going to the "land of gloom and deep darkness, the land of chaos, where light is as darkness" (Job 10:22). Bunyan saw that the terror of this "deep darkness" lay in a loss of the confidence and the sense of order that assurance of the comfort of the Spirit affords. Yet Christian's dilemma is finally simpler than Job's, for he can get through the darkness through prayer and a reassertion of faith (*"I will walk in the strength of the Lord God"*). His ability to believe in the light of the Gospel, unlike the man in the Iron Cage of Despair who has "sinned against the light of the Word" and so grieved the Spirit that "he is gone" (p. 34), causes the light and the Spirit to return. Again the passages that Bunyan quotes point to the paradoxical nature of biblical truth: "He hath turned the shadow of death into the morning" (Amos 5:8); "He discovereth deep things out of darkness, and bringeth out to light the shadow of death"

(Job 12:22). As in the previous episode Christian's experience adds a new dimension to his understanding, and the reader's, of the power of God to bring forth good out of apparent evil.

In retrospect one can see that Bunyan's use of passages from Job to establish Christian's "dark and dismal state" implies his release from that state, for other passages from the book describe the way God enables one to conquer the darkness. One can find a similar implication in Bunyan's use of Jeremiah at the very beginning of the episode. The lines that he draws upon come from God's reproach of the Israelites for forgetting their prior deliverance: "Neither said they, Where is the Lord that brought us up out of the land of Egypt, that led us through the wilderness, through a land of deserts and pits, through a land of drought, and of the shadow of death, through a land that no man passed through, and where no man dwelt? And I brought you into a plentiful country, to eat the fruit thereof and the goodness thereof." (Jer. 2:6–7). Christian is not deterred by the two men who warn him of the dangers of the Valley ("Children of them that brought up an evil report of the good Land," that is, the spies of Numbers 13), because they in fact confirm that "this is [the] way to the desired Heaven" (Bunyan cites Jeremiah 2:6 again at this point). In other words, Christian can go forward because the valley makes sense to him in terms of the larger pattern of the journey; he understands that the "plentiful country" lies beyond it. Although Christian's confidence is eclipsed temporarily once he is in the valley, Bunyan's readers would have taken the references to the Exodus as an earnest of his, and their, ultimate deliverance. And they would have seen the whole episode—showing Christian's progress through the wilderness, and from darkness to light—as a miniature version of the larger journey.

Thus far I have dwelt on the ways in which Christian, having entered the "Gospel-day," uses the Word as a means to spiritual survival. It is just as important to consider how the Word sustains him by offering consolation, in the form of anticipations of the rewards of the "land of promise." The growth of Christian's capacity to perceive the delights of Canaan is the surest index to his spiritual progress. Bunyan characteristically pictures these delights in terms of Old Testament imagery of fertility, of "fatness" (usually drawn from the Psalms, Isaiah, and the Song of Solomon). He shows Christian experiencing a foretaste of these delights as early as his stay in House Beautiful. In that hostel, built "for the relief and security of Pilgrims" (p. 46), Christian is seated at a table "furnished with fat things, and with Wine that was well refined" (p. 52) and subsequently shown the Delectable Mountains that lie ahead in his journey: "Behold at a great distance he saw a most pleasant Mountainous Country, beautified with Woods, Vineyards, Fruits of all sorts; Flowers also, with Springs and Fountains, very delectable to behold. Then he asked the name of the Country, they said it was *Immanuels Land:* and it is as Common, said they, as this *Hill* is to, and for all the Pilgrims. And when thou comest there, from thence, thou mayest see to the Gate of the Coelestial City, as the Shepherds that live there will make appear" (p. 55).

Although the senses must be repudiated when one is trying to resist the temptations of this world (hence Christian stops his ears with his fingers and looks to heaven when in Vanity Fair), they do have a proper use: in experiencing, or anticipating, the delights of the world to come. In *The Pilgrim's Progress* Bunyan could express metaphorically, in terms of Christian's sensuous awareness, those heavenly delights that Puritan writers and preachers exhorted the faithful to work at imagining.[48] One can trace a progressive awakening of Christian's senses—in the House Beautiful, beside the River of Life, on the Delectable Mountains, and in Beulah—that corresponds to his increasing awareness that he enjoys the favor of God and the growing satisfaction that he derives from this awareness.

The Delectable Mountains constitute a spiritual height attained only by the stalwart ("For but few of them that begin to come hither, do shew their face on these Mountains," say the shepherds [p. 120]); from this height Christian and Hopeful anticipate pleasures to be realized more fully in Beulah. The "Gardens, and Orchards, the Vineyards, and Fountains of water" serve as tangible proof of God's marvelous bounty. When Christian reaches Beulah, the gate of the New Jerusalem is "within sight" and he is able to solace himself with the delights of the place: flowers, singing birds, "abundance" of corn and wine, and, not least, the presence of "shining Ones." Christiana and her company stay up all night listening to the bells and trumpets, so "refreshing" is the place. Their chambers are perfumed, and their bodies anointed, with spices that rival those to be found in Milton's Eden. They are able to experience such sensuous pleasure, paradoxically, because they have achieved the "fullness of the Spirit" that Matthew looks forward to earlier in part 2.

In the first stages of his journey Christian moves through an inhospitable terrain, where he must take refuge in a way station such as House Beautiful and where evidences of divine favor are fleeting and mysterious (for example, the hand that appears with leaves from the Tree of Life to heal Christian's wounds when he is in the Valley of Humiliation). By the time Christian and Hopeful have reached the River of Life the landscape itself sustains them; it is an oasis where they may *"lie down safely"* and enjoy the lifegiving fruit and water of the place. The Delectable Mountains suggest a large region (Immanuel's land) that embodies the promise of salvation, Beulah a whole "country." Bunyan's great talent for expressing the marvelous in simple terms makes these places convincing for the reader. The pilgrims seem to come upon them quite naturally. When Christian and Hopeful arrive at the Delectable Mountains, they lean upon their staves, as might any "weary Pilgrims," and ask their improbable question (*"Whose delectable Mountains are these?''*) with a disarming straightforwardness.

The relationship between Bunyan's pilgrims and these sustaining land-scapes can be described as reciprocal. The sequence of numinous landscapes offers increasing evidence of divine grace and simultaneously an increased faith in "the reality of the things of the world to come"[49] that grace makes possible. Beulah is there for Christian, finally, because he wants and believes it to exist. In his allegorizing commentary on Revelation 22:1, *The Water of Life*, Bunyan interprets the "pure river of water of life" that flows from the celestial throne as "the Spirit of grace, the Spirit and grace of God."[50] He goes on to say: "All men...though elect, though purchased by the blood of Christ, are dead, and must be dead, until the Spirit of life from God and his throne shall enter into them; until they shall drink it in by vehement thirst, as the parched ground drinks in the rain."[51] In addition to the River of Life the springs and fountains that Christian encounters in his journey, beginning with the spring at the foot of the hill Difficulty, embody the "Spirit of grace." As Christian drinks these waters, and eats the fruit of the Tree of Life and of the vineyards of Beulah and the Delectable Mountains, he may be said to grow in spiritual strength and vitality. The process that Bunyan dramatizes would be described in the language of Calvinist theology as "vivification," the "quickening of the spirit" that marks the new life of the Christian.[52]

Bunyan relied increasingly on Scripture in describing the landscapes at the end of Christian's journey, skillfully fusing the Old Testament and the New. The Delectable Mountains do not correspond exactly to anything in the Bible. Bunyan placed the shepherds who witnessed the Nativity (as described in Luke) in a landscape that is closer to the Old Testament than to anything else, thereby offering a symbolic confirmation of Isaiah's prophecy about the coming of Immanuel and exploiting, as he does repeatedly, the suggestiveness of the vineyards and fountains of Canaan. Old and New Testaments also blend in Bunyan's account of the River of Life; it is David's River of God as well as the river of Revelation, and the lush meadow surrounding it recalls Old Testament description. Bunyan's most significant effort to fuse Old and New Testament visions of blessedness comes at the end of *The Pilgrim's Progress*, in the juxtaposition of Beulah and the New Jerusalem. The two episodes give Christian's journey a double climax. The delights of Beulah suggest the high level of spiritual satisfaction that can be attained by the faithful in this life, but Christian must cross the river (a spiritual Jordan) to reach the true promised land. The Old Testament vision must be completed by that of the New.

The prominence that Bunyan gave Beulah illustrates better than anything else in *The Pilgrim's Progress* his strong attraction to Old Testament accounts of the fruitfulness and rest to be found in Canaan[53] and his ability to see in the saving history of the Israelites the special destiny of the saints in his own time. Bunyan confirms Christian's election in the terms Isaiah used to prophesy the salvation of the *"daughter of* Zion;" he is, like Israel, *"redeemed of the Lord, sought out."* Beulah is the antithesis of the Valley of the Shadow of Death for Bunyan, a place where one can rejoice upon entering a new relationship with God, expressed metaphorically as that of bride and bridegroom, and can rest in the assurance of Isaiah's promises: "Thou shalt no more be termed Forsaken; neither shall thy land any more be termed Desolate" (Isa. 62:4). Bunyan would have seen the land as mirroring Christian's righteousness as well as his sense of election; one implies the other. In reaching this point Christian has himself become fruitful, bearing "the fruits of the Spirit, the fruits of righteousness."[54]

Bunyan's Beulah takes on some of the characteristics of the heaven it borders (the sun shines perpetually, "shining Ones" come and go) and serves as a preparation for the transition to the New Jerusalem. The pilgrims learn to bear what Bunyan, in the language of the Song of Songs, calls the "sickness" of love for the divine and, since they are not yet ready to experience the glory of the New Jerusalem directly, gaze at the city through an *"Instrument"* designed to protect them from its dazzling brightness. The fact that Christian no longer needs to worry about relaxing his vigilance (Beulah is beyond the Valley of the Shadow and Doubting Castle, Bunyan says) or about keeping to the way (he can wander into the orchards, vineyards, and gardens whose gates open onto the "Highway" because they belong to the King) suggests that his faith is as certain as it can be. This new certainty is anticipated in Christian's definite response to Hopeful's query ("I would know where we are") as they near the end of the Enchanted Ground: *"We have not now above two Miles further to go thereon"* (p. 151).

In the New Jerusalem the pilgrims will be beyond the need for faith. As Stand-fast puts it in part 2: "I have formerly lived by Hear-say, and Faith, but now I go where I shall live by sight, and shall be with him, in whose Company I delight my self" (p. 311). Bunyan's narrative no longer depends upon the riddling or metaphoric expression of divine truth but uses the descriptive language of Revelation to establish the reality of the heavenly country that Christian had set out to find: "There, said they, is the Mount *Sion,* the heavenly *Jerusalem,* the innumerable company of Angels, and the Spirits of Just Men made perfect" (p. 159). "Now just as the Gates were opened to let in the men, I looked after them; and behold, the City shone like the Sun, the Streets also were paved with Gold, and in them walked many men, with Crowns on their heads, Palms in their hands, and golden Harps to sing praises withal!" (p. 162). Bunyan has carefully prepared the reader for the imaginative leap to the New Jerusalem by foreshadowing the divine reality in the landscapes that lead up to it, but he must interpret a landscape such as Beulah typologically, as an expression of the promise and the fruits of the salvation of individual Christians. In the New Jerusalem he will see God not by the metaphoric light of the Word but in fact: "In that place you must wear Crowns of Gold and enjoy the perpetual sight and Visions of the *Holy One, for there you shall see him as he is...*There your eyes shall be delighted with seeing, and your ears with hearing, the pleasant voice of the mighty One" (p. 159). The Gospel day will give way to the eternal day made possible by the glory of God.

For all his emphasis on the splendor of the New Jerusalem Bunyan tried to accommodate its glories to his readers' understandings. His angels are simply "shining Ones," and they offer the pilgrims what Bunyan describes in *The Heavenly Footman,* in the process of reassuring readers who think heaven too grand for them, as a "hearty good welcome," helping them up the hill and explaining what they will encounter inside the city. These guides describe an approachable God with whom the pilgrims will be able to "walk and talk" familiarly and ride out in an "equipage" worthy of the occasion. As Christian and Hopeful approach the gate of the city in the friendly company of the angelic trumpeters they hear bells ringing, as they might on a Sunday in Bedfordshire. One could call such a heaven comfortable.

Yet Bunyan shows his pilgrims, "transfigured" by their heavenly garments, entering into a state of bliss and rest that surpasses anything they could have known in the world and justifies all the trials they have endured there. The holy joy that they experience can be attained only in the presence of God, in the act of praising him. We last see Christian and Hopeful as they blend into the festive chorus of angels and saints singing: "Holy, Holy, Holy, is the Lord" (p. 162). One cannot overemphasize the importance of this final episode to the structure of *The Pilgrim's Progress* and the experience of its contemporary readers. The emotional intensity of Bunyan's narrative, as it rises to a series of peaks leading up to the moment of Christian's and Hopeful's reception into the New Jerusalem, registers in unmistakable fashion his own estimation of how far his pilgrims have progressed.

Bunyan's rendering of the glory of heaven, and of the preliminary delights of Beulah, is one of the great triumphs of the Puritan imagination and the ultimate justification of his use of the metaphor of the journey. The climactic episodes of *The Pilgrim's Progress* bring the reader all the way from the "carnal" world in which the narrative began up to the contemplation of a transcendent world whose reality is validated by the Word. In the terms of Bunyan's narrative one can gain entrance to heaven only by learning to understand the visible world of ordinary experience in the metaphoric terms established by the Word: as an alien, and ultimately insubstantial country through which God's people must journey until they attain the ultimate satisfaction of communion with God. To accept this mode of thought is to see in the Exodus a pattern explaining and assuring the deliverance of the faithful of all times.

It may seem anticlimactic to turn to *The Holy War* after *The Pilgrim's*

Progress, but it is in Bunyan's attempt at writing an epic that one finds his most ambitious and inventive use of biblical materials. Although *The Holy War* has never received the critical acclaim or attention that *Grace Abounding* and *The Pilgrim's Progress* have and seems unlikely to overtake these works in popularity,[55] it deserves to be studied more thoroughly than it has been. In *The Holy War* Bunyan was able to achieve new kinds of dramatic effects by projecting the struggles of the soul upon a larger screen, at the same time giving a concrete shape to the millennial expectations of the saints and commenting indirectly upon the persecution of nonconformists in Bedfordshire.[56] The epic mode enabled him for the first time to render the warfare of Christ and Satan on the scale he thought it demanded, and the task called forth a versatility that he had not needed in his earlier works. Tillyard saw *The Holy War* as the work with the best claim to be called England's Puritan epic and cautioned against using *The Pilgrim's Progress* as a norm by which to judge it.[57] The warning bears repeating. If we can avoid the assumption that spiritual warfare was somehow an inferior subject, and one unsuited to Bunyan's talents, we are more likely to recognize, with Tillyard, that Bunyan's epic represents a significant "deepening" of his art.

In his prefatory verses to *The Holy War* Bunyan sets the truth of his narrative against accounts of feigned historical events, "vain stories." For him this truth was attested by the "best of records," Scripture, and by the experience of Christians (*"What here I say, some men do know so well, / They can with tears and joy the story tell"*). But his chief means of validating his history of Mansoul was to make the extraordinary assertion that he witnessed everything himself:

> *Let no men then count me a Fable-maker,*
> *Nor make my name or credit a partaker*
> *Of their derision: what is here in view*
> *Of mine own knowledg, I dare say is true.*
> *I saw the* Princes *armed men come down*
> *By troops, by thousands, to beseige the Town.*
> *I saw the* Captains, *heard the* Trumpets *sound.*[58]

The running commentary that follows—punctuated by such phrases as "I saw," "I heard," "I was there"—has the effect of confirming the authority of the narrator, an authority based ultimately upon experiential knowledge of spiritual struggle. In presenting his most elaborate allegory Bunyan sought a dramatic way of proving that he was not a mere "Fable-maker."

Bunyan's bold device of posing as an eyewitness can be seen as an extension of his efforts in *Grace Abounding* and *The Pilgrim's Progress* to establish the reality of spiritual experience engendered by the Word. In *The Holy War* Bunyan, confident of his own powers of invention, appears more determined than ever to make the unseen world visible. In elaborating the familiar metaphor of Christian life as a perpetual warfare he used biblical texts more freely than before to create a dramatic form that would speak to the experience of his readers. Bunyan realized that his allegory would require some explanation, hence the advice that the key to his "riddle" is to be found in the margin, but the confident march of his verses sweeps aside any possible objection to his narrative as mere feigning.

Scripture figures most simply and obviously in *The Holy War* as an instrument of warfare employed by the forces of Emmanuel. Boanerges and the other captains ("Ministers of the Word") lead an army of forty thousand that Bunyan at one point labels the "words of God." Bunyan describes the speeches of these captains as beating against Eargate, the focal point of the battle. He identifies the battering rams of the attackers with "the sentence and power of the word" (p. 232) and derives the apparatus of war—including trumpets, standards, and mounts for besieging the city—from Scripture. Emmanuel mounts the final assault on Mansoul, after persuasion has failed, with the resolution to "try by the power of my sword." In the second phase of the war, when the reclaimed inhabitants of Mansoul are struggling to keep from slipping back into the power of Diabolus, the battle cry of the captains is *"The Sword of the Prince Emmanuel, and the Shield of Captain Credence"* (p. 401). Taken out of their dramatic contexts these examples may only suggest that Bunyan takes every opportunity that an allegorical narrative provides to insist upon the power of Scripture. The cumulative effect of these devices, however, is to develop in emphatic and often subtle ways the fundamental Protestant lesson that faith depends upon hearing the Word.

How one hears and responds to, or fails to respond to, the Word was a complex enough question to provide Bunyan with material for considerable allegorizing drama. The initial fall of Mansoul represents an almost total loss of consciousness of the Word. Recorder, the figure who represents conscience, preserves the memory of the law and with his thundering voice, "the voice of God in him" (201), shakes the town, but Diabolus destroys what he can find of the records of the law and discredits Recorder. He then manages to keep from the city the good news of the covenant that Emmanuel undertakes to rescue Mansoul. Bunyan's most ingenious treatment of the conspiracy to keep the Word out is his Diabolonian parody of the traditional armor of the Christian soldier. The breastplate of righteousness described in Ephesians (Eph. 6:13–17) becomes a breastplate of iron, derived from the scales of the locusts of Revelation 9:9, or a hard heart. The sword of the Spirit becomes a "Tongue that is set on fire of Hell" (p. 216) to speak against Shaddai and Emmanuel, the shield of faith a shield of unbelief. The episode underscores Diabolus's fears of the truth represented by threats of judgment and promises of mercy. He must convince the inhabitants of Mansoul of their self-sufficiency as well as bind them to him by oaths to uphold the civil order that he has established.

Bunyan makes the demands of the Law terrifying and absolute. In a series of speeches that progressively intensify the threats of what will happen if Mansoul does not submit, the four captains of Emmanuel—Boanerges, Conviction, Judgment, and Execution—deliver the message of the Law in an idiom that is based in large measure upon Scripture, sometimes incorporating whole verses, but one that responds to the dramatic demands of the situation. Execution, the last to speak, steps out of the parable of the barren fig tree to brandish a literal axe: "Wilt thou turn? or shall I smite? If I fetch my blow, *Mansoul*, down you go" (p. 228). The response, fittingly delivered by Incredulity, is a contemptuous dismissal of the authority of the attackers; they are made to seem vagabonds who run around trying to force their way in where they can. From a practical point of view such a response is perfectly appropriate. As Incredulity later says to the townspeople, "to give up your selves to an unlimited power, is the greatest folly in the world" (239).

As in *The Pilgrim's Progress* Bunyan found dramatic ways of showing the unreasonableness of the claims of the Word when viewed from a worldly perspective. In *The Holy War* these claims threaten the apparent liberty and security of people who characterize their attackers, in accents that sound suspiciously royalist, as "the men that turn the World upside down...the destroyers of our peace" (p. 222). From this point of view the efforts of Diabolus to negotiate peace, culminating in the offer of such modest conditions as being allowed to visit the town occasionally *"for old acquaintance sake"* (p. 260), appear eminently reasonable. Bunyan's strategy was to attack the kind of worldly-mindedness for which Diabolus serves as a model by showing Emmanuel refusing all proposals for compromise. Any suggestions that Diabolus makes can only be "ensnaring Propositions" because, as Emmanuel charges, "nothing is done by thee but to deceive" (p. 266). The only way to deal with Diabolus is to root out his influence:

> Yea, I will pull down this Town, and build it again, and it shall be as though it had not been, and it shall then be the glory of the whole Universe. (P. 267)

The Holy War looks ahead to the renovation of the corrupted world promised in Revelation and at the same time points to the regeneration of the individual Christian. At times the allegory extends to contemporary events, and it may at times embrace the history of God's dealings with the church, but the two levels most obviously included in the prophecy are primary.[59] The dual focus of *The Holy War*—on the apocalyptic struggle of Christ and Satan in the world and the continual struggle of the Christian to withstand evil—makes for some difficulties. In his decisive conquest of

Mansoul Emmanuel seems to be playing the role of the militant Christ of Revelation. The new modeling of the town, and the accessibility of Emmanuel, feasting the inhabitants and welcoming their visits, suggests the glorification of the saints in heaven. Yet the plot of *The Holy War* demands that we see this period of harmony and joy as offering only a foretaste of the final victory of the saints. The town remains in a state of warfare with Diabolus and falls under the influence of Carnal Security all too easily: "And the glory of *Mansoul* was laid in the dust" (p. 387).

The Pilgrim's Progress asks that the reader understand the metaphor of the way in two senses, *The Holy War* that he see the warfare of Christ and Satan as taking place on two different levels simultaneously. Bunyan had to pose such riddles for his readers if he was to represent their condition as Christians in an imperfect world where the way and the battle could be lost and still convince them that they would at last reach the goal and share in Christ's triumph over evil. It is easier to accept the precariousness of the way than the necessity for battles to be fought over again. After the first splendid victory of Emmanuel a second battle is bound to appear anticlimactic and a third, with a hastily recruited army of Doubters and Bloodmen, even more so. Diabolus himself becomes a cruder and less interesting kind of villain when cast in the role of attacker concocting hellish plots and then ravaging the town when he gets back into it.

The form of *The Holy War* would be more satisfying if Bunyan had stopped with Emmanuel's conquest of Mansoul, but then he could not have dealt with important aspects of his readers' experience. The second war serves to dramatize the necessity for watchfulness in a world in which Diabolus remains at large and dangerous, and it introduces an effective symbol, the Diabolonian "Hell-drum." Bunyan may well have got the idea for this from Luther's commentary, with its emphasis on the roaring of Satan in the world.[60] The townspeople meet this threat with the slings that were previously identified with the force of the Word: "For as there is nothing to the town of *Mansoul* so terrible as the roaring of *Diabolus's* Drum, so there is nothing to *Diabolus* so terrible as the well playing of Emmanuels slings" (p. 373). The roaring of the drum corresponds to the speeches of the captains in the first war, but where these were a necessary application of the law as part of Shaddai's design to redeem Mansoul, the drum is simply an instrument of terror and confusion. Its roaring is mere noise, intended to overwhelm the senses of the hearers.

Bunyan took some large artistic risks in making Christ so prominent an actor in the drama of *The Holy War*. It is hard to imagine Emmanuel achieving a reversible victory, or offering consolation of the sort that one might expect in heaven, only to withdraw it later. Yet if the plot of *The Holy War* strains credibility at times, Bunyan's characterization of Emmanuel remains one of the great successes of the work. In *The Pilgrim's*

Progress Bunyan had represented Christ largely in emblematic terms: as the way, the narrow gate, the cross at which Christian's burden drops from him. The conception of a warrior Christ, embodying the truth and the irresistible might of the Word, allowed him to give his imagination freer play than that of Christ on the cross. His Emmanuel can be a familiar and approachable figure, an embodiment of divine mercy as well as of divine power. The hazards of portraying the relationship of God and man in dramatic terms can be seen in Bunyan's treatment of the Holy Spirit. As the "Lord high *Secretary*," who instructs the people of Mansoul in matters of doctrine, and when they are on sufficiently good terms with him helps them draft petitions to Emmanuel, the Holy Spirit becomes too human a figure to retain much if any sense of divinity. Emmanuel, on the other hand, remains majestic, even when he is most accessible.

This majesty is most apparent in Emmanuel's triumphal entries into Mansoul, welcomed with garlands and shouts of rejoicing. In these scenes Bunyan combined disparate biblical elements—the entry of Christ into Jerusalem, the triumph of the conquering Christ of Revelation, Old Testament celebrations of the glory of Yahweh—to create a sense of splendor and festivity that takes the narrative into a higher key.

> Then he arose and entered *Mansoul*, he and all his servants. The Elders of *Mansoul* did also go dancing before him till he came to the Castle-gates. And *this* was the manner of his going up thither. He was clad in his Golden Armour, he rode in his Royal Chariot, the Trumpets sounded about him, the Colours were displayed, his ten thousands went up at his feet, and the Elders of *Mansoul* danced before him. (P. 295)

These same elders welcome the return of Emmanuel after the second defeat of Diabolus with words from the twenty-fourth Psalm: "*Lift up your heads, O ye Gates, and be ye lift up ye everlasting doors, and the King of Glory shall come in*" (p. 404). Yet they remain capable of ringing bells and otherwise behaving as people of Bunyan's own time. We are given enough realistic detail—including a military display in which Emmanuel's forces march and countermarch in the fashion of the New Model Army—to be able to believe in scenes that are clearly marvelous.

It was more difficult to represent the love of Christ, in ways that would appeal to his Puritan audience, without making him too familiar a figure to inspire reverence. Perhaps the best evidence of Bunyan's success at this is his handling of Emmanuel's reconciliation with Mansoul, which becomes a sustained drama of petitions and rebuffs culminating in Emmanuel's sudden act of forgiving the trembling prisoners who have been brought before him. Bunyan invokes Isaiah (61:3) with stunning effectiveness to suggest the miraculous nature of the transformation that Emmanuel works:

*Moreover the Prince stript the Prisoners of their mourning weeds, and
gave them beauty for ashes, the oyl of joy for mourning, and the garment
of praise for the spirit of heaviness.* (P. 288)

The striking thing about the scene is Bunyan's ability to use the metaphorical language of the Bible to suggest the quality of an act that is incomprehensible in human terms while preserving a convincing psychological
realism. He shows human nature strained to the breaking point by experiencing the glory of divine grace:

Yea, my Lord *Wilbewill* swounded out-right, but the Prince stept to him,
put his everlasting arms under him, imbraced him, kissed him, and bid
him be of good cheer, for all should be performed according to his word.
(P. 288)

By effectively bringing Christ into the human drama of *The Holy War*
Bunyan makes the prospect of consolation more vividly personal than it
ever becomes in *The Pilgrim's Progress*. The reader is made to share the
astonishment of the townspeople at the sudden and paradoxical reversal of
their situation when mercy supersedes the expected judgment and their
continuing wonder at the subsequent feast at which they eat "Angels food,"
representing the promises of the Word. On this occasion Emmanuel himself
expounds the "riddles" of Scripture so that the people understand the
meaning of such metaphors as the "lamb" and the "sacrifice:"

Oh how they were lightned! they saw what they never saw. They could
not have thought that such rarities could have been couched in so few and
such ordinary words. (P. 298)

Scenes of this sort suggest how far Bunyan had come from the fearful and
uncertain state he described in *Grace Abounding*. Heaven is domesticated
here, and God and man exist in comfortable harmony. The Bible itself has
lost its terror and its mystery.

Bunyan accentuates the character of Emmanuel's mercy and his leadership by opposing him to Diabolus. Perhaps the most interesting of the
numerous contrasts between the two have to do with their language.
Emmanuel's speech constitutes the standard by which truth is measured;
Diabolus uses his forensic skills to deceive the people with "Lying language"
(p. 215) and "Satanical Rhetorick" (p. 201), as Bunyan labels it in marginal
notes. Bunyan gave Diabolus an "orator," Ill-Pause, who uses his command
of words to delay the initial assault on Mansoul, and he made an oratorical
contest of the Diabolonian council summoned to plan a campaign against
Mansoul. Although Bunyan refers to the speech of one of the captains as an
oration, he tends to use such terms pejoratively. Diabolus's own sophistry
represents the greatest betrayal of the proper use of language in the work.

Bunyan says at one point that Diabolus has "a language, proper to himself, and it is the language of the infernal cave, or black pit" (p. 254). This "language of Diabolus" assumes various forms depending upon the occasion, but it invariably depends upon the assumption that Shaddai's rule will enslave the people of Mansoul and his will guarantee their liberty.

Diabolus gives the game away by his specious logic and by a tendency to exaggeration that the people of Mansoul finally learn to recognize for the blatant flattery it is:

> O! the desire of my heart, the famous town of Mansoul! how many nights have I watched, and how many weary steps have I taken, if perhaps I might do thee good: Far be it, far be it from me to desire to make a war upon you. (P. 374)

In the unlikely event that the reader should miss the falseness of Diabolus's exclamatory language, he would be set straight by a cluster of marginal citations of texts branding the devil as the enemy of man. Bunyan created a different style for Diabolus's communications with his followers, a satanic bombast that threatens to turn the Diabolonians into comic villains. The letters that pass between Diabolus and his agents in Mansoul are full of epic titles and grandiose avowals of evil designs that reflect an absurdly inflated sense of dignity. Diabolus becomes the "Great Father, and mighty Prince" and his captains "their mightinesses."

This pretentious correspondence can be contrasted with the simple petitions for forgiveness of the inhabitants of Mansoul and with official documents such as the commission to the captains to make war on Mansoul and the new charter granted the town by Emmanuel. Bunyan sought to enhance the authority of Emmanuel by clothing it in legal forms. The pardon that he issues is "written in Parchment, and sealed with seven Seals" (p. 288), and the charter translates scriptural language into quasi-legal terminology:

> Emmanuel Prince of Peace, and a great lover of the Town of Mansoul, I do in the name of my Father, and of mine own clemency, give, grant, and bequeath to my beloved Town of Mansoul,
> First, free, full, and everlasting forgiveness of all wrongs, injuries, and offences done by them against my Father, me, their neighbour, or themselves.
> Secondly, I do give them the holy Law, and my Testament, with all that therein is contained, for their everlasting comfort and consolation. (P. 319)

By casting the familiar promises into the form of a legal charter, Bunyan gave them a kind of validation that would have appealed to his more pragmatic readers. At the same time he took his revenge upon a legal system under which he was a consistent loser. His language implies that Scripture will displace ordinary statutes and contracts, as Emmanuel will supplant all secular authority.

Bunyan's most decisive revenge comes in the trials of the Diabolonians, which complete the identification of legal processes with the authority of God. It is easier to sympathize with martyrs convicted by the corrupt legal system of Vanity Fair than with victorious saints carrying out a divine mandate to "crucify" their enemies, yet it was natural and fitting that Bunyan in *The Holy War* expose worldly fraud through the workings of a superior kind of justice. The trials serve the critical function of finding out and publicly vindicating the truth. There could be no compromising with falsehood for Bunyan, because it challenged the authority of Scripture. No-truth is convicted for pulling down the image of Shaddai, Atheist for the ultimate falsehood of denying the existence of God. In the second round of trials Election-doubter and his fellows are sentenced to death for having "belyed the Word" (p. 422). Bunyan's court procedures provide some of the best drama in *The Holy War*, as when False-peace is caught out in an effort to deny his name, and thus invalidate the indictment, by Search-truth.

Emmanuel and his agents make formal speeches in a style that is high without becoming verbose and that draws much of its strength from Scripture. This dependence upon Scripture is proof of their truthfulness for Bunyan, as Diabolus's reliance upon the sword of his own tongue is a sign of his deceit. When the herald of Emmanual delivers a summons calling upon Mansoul to surrender, his words draw their authority from the fact that they are based upon those of God speaking to Job from the whirlwind. Emmanuel's speeches have an amplitude and force that are not always so directly derived from Scripture:

> Thou has also thy self (O! Thou Master of enmity) of spite, defaced my Fathers image in *Mansoul*, and set up thy own in its place; to the great contempt of my Father, the heightening of thy sin, and to the intolerable damage of the perishing Town of *Mansoul*. (P. 255)

Yet Emmanuel often echoes Scripture effectively, as in the conclusion of the address to Mansoul that follows the denunciation of Diabolus from which I have just quoted: "All my words are true, I am mighty to save, and will deliver my *Mansoul* out of his hand"[61] (p. 258). The first two phrases, taken almost verbatim from the Old Testament, serve as a final confirmation of Emmanuel's authority.

The long speech of Emmanuel with which Bunyan concluded *The Holy War* best illustrates his accomplishments in dramatizing Christ's role and epitomizes the character of the work itself. Bunyan achieved the difficult feat of making his speech appear simultaneously lofty and familiar, heightening Emmanuel's language by employing more repetitions than usual and by incorporating biblical rhythms and phrases yet expressing biblical promises and injunctions in an idiom that would appeal to his readers.

> O my Mansoul, *I have lived, I have died, I live, and will die no more for thee.... I will pray for thee, I will fight for thee, I will yet do thee good.* (P. 430)

The effect of the speech as a whole, and particularly of the last paragraph, is to suggest an intimacy between God and man that makes the Word seem unusually immediate and believable:

> *Remember therefore, O my* Mansoul, *that thou art beloved of me; as I have taught thee to watch, to fight, to pray, and to make war against my foes, so now I command thee to believe that my love is constant to thee.* ... Behold, I lay none other burden upon thee, than what thou hast already, hold fast till I come. (P. 431)

Emmanuel addresses the people in the marketplace, the symbolic center of their everyday lives. There is no sense of completeness here, as at the end of each part of *The Pilgrim's Progress*, no vision of transcendence. Emmanuel does describe the promise of heaven, in notably plain words. He will take down the town of Mansoul, "stick and stone," and transport it to his own country, where there will be no more plots, no more warfare, no more noise of the Diabolonian drum. But in the meanwhile Diabolonians remain hidden within the walls, and we are left with an injunction to be stalwart. Success will depend upon an ability to trust the Bible above the tangible world: "Nor must thou think always to live by sense, thou must live upon my Word" (p. 431).

If the conclusion of *The Holy War* is less rousing than that of *The Pilgrim's Progress*, it speaks more directly to the state of the warfaring Christian, in language that is colored by Scripture without being dominated by it. Emmanuel's final words recapitulate the action of *The Holy War* and embody the fundamental polarity of law and grace, anger and mercy, that runs through the work. In *Grace Abounding* Bunyan had felt the clash of these opposites as violent and capricious inner weather. In *The Holy War* they come together in the person of Emmanuel, reminding the people of Mansoul of his power and simultaneously demonstrating his love. Emmanuel remains the prince, flanked by his captains "in their state," but Bunyan's Puritan audience would have found him a comforting figure. He makes familiar and simple a divine design that explains the continued presence of the Diabolonian threat and the human capacity to resist it (" *'Twas I* that set Mr. Godlyfear *to work in* Mansoul. *'Twas I that stirred up thy* Conscience *and* Understanding" [p. 427]). We have moved from the bristling texts of *Grace Abounding* to the friendly teachers of *The Pilgrim's Progress*, Evangelist and Interpreter, to the embodiment of the Word itself in Emmanuel. If there is a loss of dramatic immediacy in the shift from the spiritual trials of the individual to the continuing warfare of mankind, it should be recognized nonetheless that Bunyan accomplished a remarkable feat in bringing the Word to life for his readers. Through the figure of Emmanuel he was able to make scriptural mysteries plain, "in ordinary words," and yet convey the wonder of the marvelous confrontation of God and man.

Notes

INTRODUCTION

1. William Haller, *The Rise of Puritanism* (New York, 1938); *Liberty and Reformation in the Puritan Revolution* (New York, 1955).

2. M. M. Knappen, *Tudor Puritanism* (Chicago, 1939); A. S. P. Woodhouse, ed., *Puritanism and Liberty*, 2d edition (Chicago, 1974 [first published 1938]); Perry Miller, *The New England Mind: The Seventeenth Century* (Boston, 1961 [first published 1939]).

3. Christopher Hill, *Puritanism and Revolution* (London, 1958); *Society and Puritanism in Pre-Revolutionary England*, 2d edition (New York, 1967 [first published 1964]); *The World Turned Upside Down* (London, 1972).

4. Michael Walzer, *The Revolution of the Saints* (Cambridge, Mass., 1965).

5. I am thinking of Joan Webber's chapters in *The Eloquent "I"* (Madison, 1968), on John Lilburne, Richard Baxter's autobiography, and the contrasts between Donne's *Devotions* and Bunyan's *Grace Abounding;* William Madsen's argument in *From Shadowy Types to Truth* (New Haven, 1968), against popular stereotypes, for the sensuous and imagistic quality of much Puritan writing; U. Milo Kaufmann's discussion of the Puritan tradition of "heavenly meditation" in his *The Pilgrim's Progress and Traditions in Puritan Meditation* (New Haven, 1966). Lawrence Sasek's earlier study, *The Literary Temper of the English Puritans* (Baton Rouge, 1961), also deserves mention, as does Harold Fisch's *Jerusalem and Albion* (London, 1964).

6. In his ambitious *Milton and the English Revolution* (New York, 1978 [first published 1977]). See also Boyd Berry's *Process of Speech: Puritan Religious Writing and Paradise Lost* (Baltimore, 1976). There have been, of course, numerous significant studies of Milton's prose in relation to contemporary writings, including Don M. Wolfe's *Milton in the Puritan Revolution* (New York, 1941), and Arthur Barker's *Milton and the Puritan Dilemma* (Toronto, 1942), as well as the introductions and commentary of the editors of the Yale edition of the prose.

7. Among them Henri Talon, *John Bunyan: The Man and His Works* (London, 1951); Roger Sharrock, *John Bunyan* (London, 1954); and R. M. Frye, *God, Man, and Satan* (Princeton, 1960), on Bunyan and Milton.

8. See *The American Puritan Imagination*, ed. Sacvan Bercovitch (Cambridge, 1974), and Bercovitch's *The Puritan Origins of the American Self* (New Haven, 1975).

9. For discussions of contemporary use of the term "Puritan" see especially Christopher Hill, *Society and Puritanism*, pp. 13–29, and Basil Hall, "Puritanism: The Problem of Definition," *Studies in Church History*, ed. G. J. Cuming (London, 1965), 2:283–96.

10. See Hill, *Society and Puritanism*, pp. 20–24.

11. See *The Protestant Mind of the English Reformation, 1570–1640* (Princeton, 1961). C. H. George put his case even more strongly in a subsequent article in which he suggests that Puritanism is a "bad concept" that should be abolished. "Puritanism as History and Historiography," *Past and Present* 41 (1968): 77–104.

12. See Nicholas Tyacke, "Puritanism, Arminianism, and Counter-Revolution," *The Origins of the English Civil War*, ed. Conrad Russell (London, 1973), pp. 119–43.

13. Such difficulties may be exaggerated by those who do not want to separate

Puritans and Anglicans. The burden of John F. H. New's *Anglican and Puritan* (Stanford, 1964) is that the theological differences are clearly discernible despite fundamental areas of agreement.

14. In addition to New see John Coolidge, *The Pauline Renaissance in England* (Oxford, 1970); David Little, *Religion, Order, and Law* (New York, 1969); J. Sears McGee, *The Godly Man in Stuart England* (New Haven, 1976).

15. See Woodhouse's introduction to *Puritanism and Liberty*, pp. 14ff. This practice differs from that of Hill, who stresses the tensions between radicals and orthodox Puritans tending to identify the former with secularism and the latter with Calvinist doctrine.

16. N. H. Keeble, ed., *The Autobiography of Richard Baxter* (London, 1974), p. xxvi.

17. Irène Simon describes the emergence of this norm and the discrediting of other sermon styles. See the chapter "The Reform of Pulpit Oratory in the Seventeenth Century" in the introduction to her *Three Restoration Divines: Barrow, Smith, Tillotson* (Paris, 1967).

18. *The Works of George Herbert*, ed. F. E. Hutchinson (Oxford, 1946), p. 233.

19. In his popular handbook of devotion, *Ancilla pietatis* (London, 1626), p. 108.

20. Ibid., p. 23. Barbara Lewalski cites Featley and Herbert, among others, as illustrating a centrist position on sermon style occupied by both Anglicans and Puritans. *Protestant Poetics and the Seventeenth-Century Religious Lyric* (Princeton, 1979), pp. 222ff.

21. *Works*, p. 235.

22. *The Arte of Prophesying. Workes* (London, 1616), p. 670.

23. See also Isaiah: "For as the rain cometh down, and the snow from heaven, and returneth not thither, but watereth the earth, and maketh it bring forth and bud, that it may give seed to the sower, and bread to the eater: so shall my word be that goeth forth out of my mouth" (55:10–11).

24. In the *Observations upon the Articles of Peace* (1649) he insisted that the extirpation of "Popery and Prelacy, then of Heresy, Schism, and prophaness" promised in the Solemn League and Covenant "can be no work of the Civil sword, but of the spirituall which is the word of God." *Complete Prose Works of John Milton*, ed. Don M. Wolfe (New Haven, 1953), 3:324.

25. Quoted by Paul Christianson, *Reformers and Babylon* (Toronto, 1978), pp. 87–88.

26. John Preston, *The New Creature* (London, 1633), p. 166.

27. See 2 Cor. 4:3–4; also Ps. 119:105,130.

28. Samuel Butler, *Hudibras*, ed. John Wilders (Oxford, 1967), p. 7.

29. See especially A. G. Dickens, *The English Reformation* (London, 1964), and Patrick Collinson, *The Elizabethan Puritan Movement* (London, 1967).

CHAPTER ONE

1. John Foxe, *The Acts and Monuments of John Foxe*, ed. Rev. Josiah Pratt (London, 1877), 6:596.

2. John Jewel, *An Apology of the Church of England*, ed. J. E. Booty (Ithaca, New York, 1963), p. 20.

3. Ibid., p. 76.

4. Ibid., p. 135.

5. W. H. Frere and C. E. Douglas, eds., *Puritan Manifestoes* (London, 1954), p. 92.

6. Jewel, *Apology*, p. 138.

7. Ibid.

8. See John Brown, *The History of the English Bible* (Cambridge, 1912), p. 34, for an account of such incidents. Margaret Deanesly, *The Lollard Bible* (Cambridge, 1920),

chap. 14, gives a scholarly assessment of the use of Wycliffite Bibles in the early sixteenth century and of efforts to suppress them. The author of the General Prologue to the second version of the Wycliffite Bible (1395) effectively described the need that the translation was meant to serve: "For though covetous clerks be wooed by simony, heresy, and many other sins to dispise and stop holy writ, as much as they may: yet the lewid people crieth after holy writ, to con and keep it, with great cost and peril of their life." Quoted by Deanesly, p. 258.

9. Foxe, *Acts and Monuments*, 4:250.

10. From Tyndale's preface to his translation of the Pentateuch, *Doctrinal Treatises* (Cambridge: Parker Society, 1847), pp. 393–94.

11. Tyndale, "The Obedience of a Christian Man," *Doctrinal Treatises*, p. 328.

12. See E. Harris Harbison, *The Christian Scholar in the Age of the Reformation* (New York, 1965), pp. 59ff., and P. Albert Duhamel, "The Oxford Lectures of John Colet," *Journal of the History of Ideas* 14 (1953): 493–510.

13. John C. Olin, ed., *Desiderius Erasmus: Christian Humanism and the Reformation* (New York, 1965), p. 105. Craig R. Thompson has traced the evolution of Erasmus's arguments in favor of translating Scripture into the vernacular, showing how he qualified them in response to conservative critics without abandoning his basic position. "Scripture for the Ploughboy and Some Others," *Studies in the Continental Background of English Renaissance Literature: Essays Presented to John L. Lievsay* (Durham, 1977), pp. 3–28.

14. *The Enchiridion of Erasmus*, trans. Raymond Himelick (Gloucester, Mass., 1970), p. 52. Sir Thomas Elyot used the same example to make the point that Scripture should be "reverently touched, as a celestial jewell or relike" (*The Boke named the Governour*, ed. H. H. S. Croft [London, 1880], 1:94).

15. "Cyclops; or, The Gospel Bearer," trans. Craig R. Thompson, *The Colloquies of Erasmus* (Chicago, 1965), p. 419.

16. Erasmus, *Enchiridion*, p. 52.

17. John B. Payne, *Erasmus: His Theology of the Sacraments* (1970), chap. 3, demonstrates that Erasmus moved away from his early enthusiasm for Origen and by the time he wrote *Ecclesiastae* (1535) advocated a middle way between a literal reading of Scripture and extreme allegorizing.

18. E. G. Rupp, A. N. Marlow, P. S. Watson, B. Drewery, eds., *Luther and Erasmus: Free Will and Salvation* (London, 1969), pp. 37ff.

19. Ibid., p. 40.

20. Ibid., p. 129.

21. Ibid., p. 132.

22. E. G. Rupp, *The Righteousness of God: Luther Studies* (London, 1953), p. 233.

23. Rupp, *Luther and Erasmus*, p. 109.

24. Ibid., p. 110.

25. For an example of this viewpoint in England see John Owen's *Of the Divine Originall, Authority, Self-Evidencing Light and Power of the Scriptures* (London, 1659). Owen sees "every *Letter* and *Tittle*" of the Bible as divinely inspired (p. 14).

26. J. K. S. Reid, *The Authority of the Scripture* (London, 1957), pp. 101–2.

27. Quoted by Rupp, *The Righteousness of God*, p. 229, from Luther's commentary on the first twenty-one psalms (1581–1521).

28. Ibid., p. 233.

29. S. L. Greenslade, ed., *The Cambridge History of the Bible* (Cambridge, 1963), vol. 3. Quoted by Roland Bainton in "The Bible in the Reformation," p. 23.

30. Foxe, *Acts and Monuments*, 5:117–18.

31. Tyndale, *Doctrinal Treatises*, p. 317.

32. Ibid., p. 22. E. G. Rupp has shown the substantial indebtedness of this work to Luther's preface to the New Testament. See his *Studies in the Making of the English Protestant Tradition* (Cambridge, 1947), p. 50.

33. Tyndale, "Prologue to Genesis," *Doctrinal Treatises*, p. 398.

34. Tyndale, "Obedience," *Doctrinal Treatises*, p. 324.

35. William Tyndale, *An Answer to Sir Thomas More's Dialogue* (Cambridge: Parker Society, 1850), p. 136.

36. Ibid., pp. 309–10.

37. Tyndale, "Parable of the Wicked Mammon," *Doctrinal Treatises*, p. 55.

38. Ibid., p. 78.

39. Tyndale, "Epistle to the Romans," *Doctrinal Treatises*, p. 493.

40. William Clebsch, *England's Earliest Protestants, 1520-1535* (New Haven, 1964), passim, and L. J. Trinterud, "A Reappraisal of William Tyndale's debt to Martin Luther," *Church History* 31 (1962): 24–45, argue for a decisive turn toward the law in the later Tyndale and represent this as a significant departure from Luther. E. G. Rupp has questioned the views of Clebsch and Trinterud, while admitting that Tyndale's work from 1532 on shows a strong ethical bias. Rupp views Tyndale's stress on election and on the work of the Spirit as evidence of the influence of Rhineland theologians. See "Patterns of Salvation in the First Age of the Reformation," *Archiv für Reformationsgeschichte* 57 (1966): 52–66.

41. Tyndale, "Prologue to Exodus," *Doctrinal Treatises*, p. 417.

42. Much of Tyndale's vigorous translation subsequently found its way into the Authorized Version of 1611. J. F. Mozley claims that 90 percent of his New Testament survived intact. *William Tyndale* (London, 1937), p. 108.

43. Foxe, *Acts and Monuments*, 4:667.

44. In 1535, Miles Coverdale brought out a complete English Bible, incorporating Tyndale's work supplemented by his own, with a fulsome dedication to Henry, but this failed to win the approval of the bishops. Cranmer helped to secure a royal license in 1537 for the "Matthew" Bible, an amalgam of Tyndale and Coverdale. In 1536 and again in 1538 Cromwell issued injunctions that included the command, not enforced until 1538, that a copy of the Bible in English be placed in all the churches. On Cromwell's key role in promulgating the English Bible, see A. G. Dickens, *The English Reformation* (London, 1967), pp. 183–96. On the early history of the English Bible, see Charles G. Butterworth, *The Literary Lineage of the King James Bible, 1340-1611* (Philadelphia, 1941); F. F. Bruce, *The English Bible* (Oxford, 1961); Alfred W. Pollard, *Records of the English Bible* (London, 1911).

45. See Harold R. Willoughby, *The First Authorized English Bible and the Cranmer Preface* (Chicago, 1942), pp. 11–20, for a discussion of the iconography of the title page.

46. Elizabeth C. Eisenstein, *The Printing Press as an Agent of Change* (Cambridge, 1979), 1:353. Eisenstein describes Roman Catholic policy devised at Trent as having the effect of holding the new functions of printing in check, not only by rejecting the vernacular Bible but by imposing new restrictions on lay reading and "by developing new machinery such as the Index and Imprimatur to channel the flow of literature along narrowly prescribed lines" (p. 355).

47. Stephen Neill comments: "Nothing is more striking in the Reformation than the recovery of the almost forgotten doctrine of the Holy Spirit. Of Cranmer's special interest in this doctrine the Prayer Book itself, with its constant references to the Holy Spirit, is evidence." *Anglicanism* (London, 1958), p. 79.

48. *Miscellaneous Writings and Letters of Thomas Cranmer* (Cambridge: Parker Society, 1846), p. 131. The homilies are "Of Salvation," "Of the True, Lively, and Christian Faith," and "Of Good Works."

49. G. W. Bromiley, *Thomas Cranmer, Theologian* (London, 1956), p. 22. Bromiley comments that "in most issues [Cranmer] could insist that his teaching was catholic and patristic as well as biblical" (p. 98).

50. James K. McConica, *English Humanists and Reformation Politics* (Oxford, 1965), charts the influence of Erasmus in England in the first two decades of the English Reformation.

51. "Of Ceremonies." See Douglas Harrison, ed., *The First and Second Prayer Books of Edward VI* (London, 1968), pp. 286–88.

52. Willoughby, *Authorized English Bible*, p. 47.

53. Ibid., p. 46.

54. Ibid., p. 45.

55. Ibid., p. 44.

56. Translated by John Tomkys in 1579 as *A most godly and learned Discourse of the woorthynesse, authoritie, and sufficiencie of the holy Scripture.*

57. Introduction to G. E. Duffield, ed., *The Work of William Tyndale* (London, 1964), p. xxx.

58. *A Dialogue Concerning Heresies* (1528). More defended the principle of authorized vernacular translation while condemning the two translations that made Scripture accessible to ordinary Englishmen in his day and stressing the dangers of lay reading. He cites with approval Jerome's and Gregory Nazianzen's rebukes of the common people for "meddling" with Scripture, elaborating upon Nazianzen's use of the example of Moses on Sinai to suggest that the people should not approach Scripture directly: "And as for the high secret mysteries of God and hard texts of holy scripture, let us know that we be so unable to ascend up so high on that hill, that it shall become us to say to the preachers appointed thereto, as the people saith unto Moses, "Hear you God, and let us hear you." W. E. Campbell and A. W. Reed, eds., *The English Works of Sir Thomas More* (London and New York, 1931), 2:244.

59. Willoughby, *Authorized English Bible*, p. 44. In a letter to young Edward VI Cranmer argued the value of being nourished from childhood by the "sweet milk" of "God's holy word," which he saw as leading children "to God, to the obedience of their Prince, and all virtue and honesty of life." *Miscellaneous Writings*, p. 419.

60. Henry Gee and William John Hardy, *Documents Illustrative of English History* (London, 1896), p. 276.

61. Pollard, *Records*, p. 236.

62. Tyndale, *Doctrinal Treatises*, p. 134.

63. A proclamation issued by Bishop Bonner of London, one of the chief villains in Foxe's account of the Marian prosecution, reflects these abuses. See Pollard, *Records*, p. 256.

64. Foxe, *Acts and Monuments*, 5:452.

65. See E. G. Rupp, *Six Makers of the English Reformation, 1500–1700* (London, 1957), pp. 28–29, and Lacey Baldwin Smith, *Tudor Prelates and Politics* (Princeton, 1953), pp. 242–43.

66. See Harrison, ed., *First and Second Prayer Books of Edward VI*, p. 3.

67. Willoughby, *Authorized English Bible*, p. 45.

68. John Griffiths, ed., *The Two Books of Homilies* (Oxford, 1859), p. 9.

69. *The First tome or volume of the Paraphrase of Erasmus upon the newe testamente*, 1548, "The preface unto the Kings Majesty," aiii (verso).

70. Erasmus, *Enchiridion*, p. 56.

71. See the conclusion of his preface to Edward.

72. R. F. Jones summarizes contemporary arguments for and against translation of the Bible. *The Triumph of the English Language* (Stanford, 1953), pp. 53–67.

73. *A Reply to M. Harding's Answer*, in John Ayre, ed., *The Works of John Jewel* (Cambridge: Parker Society, 1850), 2:678.

74. Ibid., p. 683.

75. Pollard, *Records*, p. 347.

76. Ayre, *Works of John Jewel*, 4:1164, 1171, 1172–73.

77. Ibid., 4:1166.

78. Pollard, *Records*, p. 349.

79. Ayre, *Works*, 4:1188.

80. Pollard, *Records*, pp. 375–76.

81. Ibid.

82. Lloyd E. Berry, ed., *The Geneva Bible* (Madison, 1969), "Introduction to the Facsimile Edition," p. 14.

83. Thomas Fuller, *The Appeal of Injured Innocence* (London, 1659).

84. See John Coolidge, *The Pauline Renaissance in England* (Oxford, 1970), chap. 2. Coolidge traces the evolution of the figure of the house of God in Old and New Testaments.

85. See Jer. 23:29, Heb. 4:21, Eph. 6:17.

86. Richard Greenham, *The Workes...William Laud* (London, 1601), p. 73.

87. Pollard, *Records*, p. 348.

88. Richard Hooker, *Of the Laws of Ecclesiastical Polity*, ed. Christopher Morris (London, 1958), 1:222 (I. xv. 4).

89. Ibid., 2:77 (V. xxi. 3).

90. Ibid., 1:214 (I. xiii. 3).

91. Frere and Douglas, *Puritan Manifestoes*, p. 91.

92. John Ayre, ed., *The Works of John Whitgift* (Cambridge: Parker Society, 1851), 1:187.

93. Ibid., p. 43.

94. William Pierce, ed., *The Marprelate Tracts* (London, 1911), p. 88.

95. Ibid., p. 326.

96. H. C. Porter traces the origins of the phrase in the course of discussing Protestant theory and practice of interpretation. "The Nose of Wax: Scripture and the Spirit from Erasmus to Milton," *Transactions of the Royal Historical Society*, 5th series, 14 (1964): 155–74.

97. Hooker, *Laws*, 1:246 (II. vii. 1).

98. Ibid., p. 316 (III. viii. 10). See H. C. Porter's lucid discussion of the Cartwright-Whitgift disputes and of Hooker's view of Scripture. "Hooker, the Tudor Constitution and the Via Media," in W. Speed Hill, ed., *Studies in Richard Hooker* (Cleveland, 1972), pp. 77–116.

99. Ayre, *Works of John Whitgift*, 1:190.

100. Cartwright derives these from 1 Cor. 10:32, 1 Cor. 14:40, 1 Cor. 14:26, and Rom. 14:6–7. See Coolidge, *Pauline Renaissance*, pp. 4–11. See also W. D. J. Cargill Thompson, "The Philosopher of the Politic Society," in Hill, *Studies in Richard Hooker*, pp. 24ff; and H. F. Scott Pearson, *Thomas Cartwright and Elizabethan Puritanism, 1535–1603* (Cambridge, 1925), pp. 88ff.

101. Coolidge, *Pauline Renaissance*, p. 9.

102. Ibid., pp. 21–22.

103. Hooker, *Laws*, 1:138–39 (Preface, viii. 11).

104. John Calvin, *Institutes of the Christian Religion*, ed. John T. McNeill (Philadelphia, 1960), vol. 1, chap. 7, passim.

105. William Fitzgerald, ed., *A Disputation on Holy Scripture* (Cambridge: Parker Society, 1849), pp. 279–80. Whitaker spoke for the Anglican church, against the Catholic

position, but it should be remembered that he represented the extreme Calvinist wing of the church. As the chief author of the controversial Lambeth Articles he came into sharp conflict with Lancelot Andrewes.

106. Ibid., p. 290.

107. Ibid., p. 335.

108. Ibid.

109. Quoted in Ronald S. Wallace, *Calvin's Doctrine of the Word and Sacrament* (London, 1953), p. 102. See also *Institutes*, 1.7.5: "we feel that the undoubted power of his divine majesty lives and breathes there. By this power we are drawn and inflamed, knowingly and willingly, to obey him, yet also more vitally and more effectively than by mere human willing or knowing."

110. G. W. Bromiley, ed. and trans., *Zwingli and Bullinger* (London, 1953), p. 71.

111. Reid, *Authority*, p. 251. Reid argues in opposition to some scholars that Calvin did not believe in the literal, verbal inspiration of Scripture. See pp. 29–55, passim. The complex issue of the relationship between Word and Spirit was resolved in various ways by the early reformers. Bucer showed himself aware of the hazards of trusting to the Spirit in praying for help in keeping "this middle course of spiritual freedom between the slavery of the letter and the license of a perverse spirit" (W. P. Stephens, *The Holy Spirit in the Theology of Martin Bucer*, [Cambridge, 1970], p. 151). As Stephens demonstrates, a belief that Christ works through "his vivifying Spirit" (p. 108) is at the center of Bucer's theology.

112. Frere and Douglas, *Puritan Manifestoes*, p. 15.

113. Hooker, *Laws*, 1:320 (III. viii. 13–15).

114. In fact, his skepticism about the use of such images can be seen in a passage from his "Sermon on the Certainty and Perpetuity of Faith in the Elect," *Laws*, 1:4: "The reason which is taken from the power of the Spirit were effectual, if God did work like a natural agent, as the fire doth inflame, and the sun enlighten, according to the uttermost ability which they have to bring forth their effects. But the incomprehensible wisdom of God doth limit the effects of his power to such a limit as seemeth best unto himself."

115. From *A Relation of the Conference between William Laud and Mr. Fisher the Jesuit*, *The Workes of...William Laud*, ed. William Scott and James Bliss, (Oxford, 1847–60), 2:97.

116. G. R. Potter and Evelyn M. Simpson, eds., *Sermons* (Berkeley and Los Angeles, 1953–62), 1:205. Elsewhere he says that "The *Spirit* of God *inanimates* the Scriptures, and makes them *his* Scriptures, the *Church actuates* the Scriptures and makes them *our* Scriptures" (*Sermons*, 6:282). Donne sees the Spirit as acting primarily through the ordinances of the church.

117. From *The Devout Soul* (1643) in Wynter, ed., *The Works of Joseph Hall* (New York, 1969) (a reprint of the 1863 edition) 6:527.

118. John Goodwin, *The Divine Authority of the Scriptures Asserted* (London, 1648), p. 134.

119. Ibid., pp. 141, 150.

120. For a discussion of Augustine's influence upon Protestant preaching and interpretation see Dennis Quinn, "Donne's Christian Eloquence," *English Literary History* 27 (1960): 276–97.

121. William Perkins, *The Arte of Prophesying*, *Workes* (London, 1616), p. 652.

122. Quoted by Larzer Ziff, *Puritanism in America* (New York and London, 1973), p. 51.

123. See Paul S. Seaver, *The Puritan Lectureships* (Stanford, 1970), for a thorough account of this struggle, with particular reference to the growth and function of lectureships. The story of the development of Puritan preaching has been told a number of

times, with varying emphases. See especially William Haller, *The Rise of Puritanism* (New York, 1938), and Christopher Hill, *Society and Puritanism in Pre-Revolutionary England* (New York, 1964).

124. Quoted in Hooker, *Laws*, 2:96.

125. Ibid., p. 58 (V. xviii. 3). Hooker also regarded catechising as a kind of preaching.

126. Ibid., p. 78 (V. xxi. 3).

127. See Heiko Obermann, "Preaching and the Word in the Reformation," *Theology Today* 18 (1961): 26–27. The phrase is from the *Confessio Helvetica Posterior*, which Obermann sees as consolidating a general belief in "the *ex opere operato* presence of God's Word in the preached Word."

128. Quoted by Obermann, p. 26.

129. Quoted by Stephens, *Holy Spirit*, p. 176.

130. Perkins, *The Arte of Prophesying*, *Workes*, p. 670. *The Calling of the Ministerie*, *Workes* (London, 1609), 3:456.

131. Joseph Haroutunian and Louise P. Smith, trans., *Calvin: Commentaries* (London, 1958), p. 107.

132. Thomas Hooker, *The Preparation of the Heart*, in *The Soules Implantation* (London, 1637), p. 66.

133. Ibid., pp. 67–68. Compare Jeremy Taylor on the way faith is aroused. One need only share a "humble, willing, and docile mind...for persuasion enters like a sunbeam, quietly, and without violence" (Reginald Heber, ed., *The Rule and Exercises of Holy Living, the Whole Works of...Jeremy Taylor* [London, 1861], 3:148). Donne speaks of Scripture as having an "orderly, sweet, and powerful working upon the reason" (*Sermons*, 3:358).

134. *The Arte of Prophesying*, chaps. 7 and 8.

135. *The Faithfull Shepheard* (London, 1607), p. 71. See chaps. 9, 10, and 11 passim.

136. *A Directory for the Publike Worship of God* (London, 1644), pp. 39, 40. *Reliquiae Liturgicae*, ed. Peter Hall (Bath, 1847), vol. 3.

137. Evelyn M. Simpson, ed., *Essays in Divinity* (Oxford, 1952), pp. 40–41.

138. Robert Boyle, *Some Considerations Touching the Style of the Holy Scriptures* (London, 1663), p. 78.

139. For a discussion of Boyle's religion see M. S. Fisher, *Robert Boyle: Devout Naturalist* (Philadelphia, 1945), chap. 8. Fisher sees the beginnings of higher criticism in Boyle's belief that not all parts of the Bible constitute divine revelation.

CHAPTER TWO

1. William Haller, who has done more than anyone else to call attention to the imaginative qualities of Puritan preaching in England, gives several pages to Sibbes's sermons. See *The Rise of Puritanism* (New York, 1937), pp. 160–63, and passim for commentary on Sibbes's life and influence.

2. Samuel Clarke, *Lives of Thirty-two English Divines*, 3d edition (London, 1677), p. 144.

3. Haller, *Rise of Puritanism*, pp. 19–23.

4. A. B. Grosart, "Memoir of Richard Sibbes, D.D.," from *The Complete Works of Richard Sibbes, D.D.*, ed. Grosart (Edinburgh, 1862–64).

5. Christopher Hill, *Society and Puritanism*, 2d edition (New York, 1967), p. 84.

6. According to Thomas Fuller, *Fuller's Worthies of England*, ed. P. A. Nuttall (London, 1840), 3:185.

7. Sibbes, *Works*, 1:cxv. Hereafter references to this edition will be cited in the text by volume and page number.

8. Isabel M. Calder, *Activities of the Puritan Faction of the Church of England, 1625-33* (London, 1957), p. 47. See also Christopher Hill's account of the activities and influence of the Feoffees, *Economic Problems of the Church* (Oxford, 1956), pp. 245-74.

9. Quoted in F. J. Powicke, *A Life of the Reverend Richard Baxter* (London, 1924), p. 283. Cf. John Preston, *The New Creature* (London, 1633), p. 165: "What doe we, when we dresse up a Sermon never so well? it is but the rigging of the sailes, and what will all this doe without wind? Is not the Spirit the wind?"

10. *The Saints Everlasting Rest* (London, 1650), p. 368.

11. Ibid., p. 398.

12. *The Sermons of John Donne*, ed. G. R. Potter and Evelyn Simpson (Berkeley and Los Angeles, 1953-62), 7:134. Hereafter references to this edition will be cited in the text by volume and page number. I owe this example to Russell Chambers, "An Angel in the East: A Study of John Donne's Ministry of the Word" (Ph.D. diss., University of Michigan, 1974).

13. Sibbes's text is Matthew 12:20: "A bruised reed shall he not break, and smoking flax shall he not quench, till he send forth judgment into victory."

14. Perry Miller, *The New England Mind: The Seventeenth Century* (Boston, 1961 [first published 1939]), p. 332.

15. In discussing the conversion experience Miller recognizes the appeal of Puritan sermons to the affections as well as to the understanding and uses the term "logic suffused with grace" to suggest a fusion of these approaches. His primary concern, however, is with the rational aspects of such sermons. Miller, *New England Mind*, pp. 286ff.

16. Sibbes, *Workes*, 3:374. Elsewhere he comments that "the authority the word hath is from itself" (2:493).

17. Norman Pettit, *The Heart Prepared* (New Haven, 1966). See pp. 66-75 for a detailed discussion of Sibbes's understanding of preparation in relation to that of such figures as Perkins and Preston.

18. See Coolidge's discussion of the difference between conformist and nonconformist senses of edification. *The Pauline Renaissance in England* (Oxford, 1970), pp. 45-50 and passim. Pettit, *Heart*, p. 48, quotes Richard Greenham's assertion that he tried "to edify the heart and conscience...to quicken affections to embrace true godliness."

19. I am indebted to Geoffrey Nuttall's discussion of Sibbes, *The Holy Spirit in Puritan Faith and Experience* (Oxford, 1946). See especially pp. 35-39.

20. See Sibbes, *Works*, 4:248ff., for a discussion of spiritual sight. William Madsen, *From Shadowy Types to Truth* (New Haven, 1968), pp. 155ff., and Winfred Schleiner, *The Imagery of John Donne's Sermons* (Providence, 1970), pp. 137-55, discuss the tradition of describing spiritual knowledge in terms of the eye of the soul.

21. Madsen, *Shadowy Types*, pp. 77-81. See also the important discussion of Sibbes's view of the imagination by U. Milo Kaufmann, *The Pilgrim's Progress and Traditions in Puritan Meditation* (New Haven, 1966), pp. 142ff.

22. Bernard, *Faithfull Shepheard*, pp. 65-66; Perkins, *Workes* (London, 1613), 2:659.

23. Benjamin Keach, *Tropologia* (London, 1682), sig. A₂. For a discussion of biblical eloquence as a model for preachers see Barbara Lewalski, *Protestant Poetics* (Princeton, 1979), pp. 217-26.

24. Augustine, *On Christian Doctrine*, trans. D. W. Robertson (New York, 1958), p. 139. The verse quoted is Jer. 23:29, which characterizes the Word as a fire and a hammer. Luther connected the power he found in the language of the Psalms with the earnestness of the authors: "What is the greatest thing in the Psalter but this earnest speaking amid these storm winds of every kind?" In his view, no Cicero could portray hope and fear so well. "Preface to the Psalter," *Luther's Works* (Philadelphia, 1960), 35:253-57.

25. Keach, *Tropologia*, sig. A₂.

26. John Calvin, *Institutes of the Christian Religion*, ed. John T. McNeill, (Philadelphia, 1960), 1:81.

27. Ibid., 1:82.

28. See, for example, Sibbes's *Works*, 2:57, 494.

29. Philip Schaff, ed., *The Creeds of the Evangelical Protestant Churches* (London, 1877), p. 603.

30. Perkins, *The Arte of Prophesying*, *Workes* (London, 1616), p. 670. Perkins described Scripture itself as "full of majestie in the simpleness of the words" (p. 650).

31. Lawrence Sasek, *The Literary Temper of the English Puritans* (Baton Rouge, 1961), documents a range of attitudes toward style among Puritans. At one extreme, Joseph Caryl urged preachers to imitate biblical eloquence and use oratory in the service of God, though "with sobriety and holy gravity" (Sasek, p. 56).

32. John Donne, *Devotions upon Emergent Occasions* (Ann Arbor, 1959), p. 124.

33. John Donne, *Sermons*, 6:55.

34. Ibid., 6:56, 2:170.

35. Ibid., 1:253.

36. Bernard, *Faithfull Shepheard*, pp. 65–66; *David's Musick* (London, 1616).

37. Haller, *Rise of Puritanism*, p. 143. See particularly chap. 4, "The Rhetoric of the Spirit."

38. Donne, *Devotions*, pp. 126–27.

39. See, for example, Donne's variations upon the phrase "floods of great waters," from Psalm 32. He considers a range of possible senses: tribulations, in the first instance, but also baptism, contrite tears, heresies and persecutions that threaten the church and, finally, the "inundation" of Christ's blood (*Sermons*, 9:328–33). When Donne invokes the familiar metaphor (*"Mundus Mare"*) in another sermon, he proceeds to draw out of it numerous subsidiary metaphors after first announcing: "The world is a Sea in many respects and assimilations" (2:306). Rather than use it to explore the tempests of the soul, he seizes upon aspects that reinforce a more general point about man's dependence upon God in a threatening and transient world. The sea is "bottomlesse to any line," it ebbs and flows, it will not quench our thirst, it contains "greater fish" that devour the smaller, it offers no permanent place of habitation.

40. See Winfred Schleiner's discussion of Augustine's sense of the Bible as *serenissimum speculum*, and of Donne's adaptation of the figure in *Imagery*, pp. 149–50, 235.

41. Donne also uses imagery of light to describe the unity of Scripture: "As the Essentiall word of God, the Son of God, is Light of light, so the written Word of God is light of light too, one place of Scripture takes light of another" (5:39). Compare George Herbert's more diffident approach to the "secrets" of the Word in "The Holy Scriptures (II):"

> Oh that I knew how all thy lights combine,
>   And the configurations of their glory!
> Seeing not only how each verse doth shine,
>   But all the constellations of the story.

Puritan preachers regularly bring together comparable verses from different parts of the Bible (Perkins had urged such "collation" as a means of clarifying the sense of the text). They do not celebrate the unity of Scripture in the manner of a Donne or a Herbert, however, or show the same degree of interest in exploring "configurations" of scriptural metaphors.

42. *Donne's Prebend Sermons* (Cambridge, Mass., 1971), pp. 40–41. See also Dennis Quinn, "Donne's Christian Eloquence," *English Literary History* 27 (1960), pp. 276–97.

Quinn comments: "Because of the sacramental nature of the words of the Bible, Donne's emphasis falls upon the form, the manner, the style of Scriptures, rather than the matter" (p. 286).

43. Donne, *Sermons*, 8:351.

44. See Stanley Stewart, *The Enclosed Garden* (Madison, 1966), for an account of the exegetical tradition and of literary uses of the Song of Songs in the seventeenth century.

45. John Calvin, *Commentary on the Book of Psalms*, trans. James Anderson (Edinburgh, 1845), 1:xxxvii. See also the "Argument" that precedes the psalms in the Geneva Bible, which describes them as offering "most present remedies against all tentations, and troubles of minde and conscience."

46. See Barbara Lewalski's discussion of this attitude in her article, "Typology and Poetry," *Illustrious Evidence*, ed. Earl Miner (Berkeley and Los Angeles, 1975), pp. 48–51.

47. Donne, *Sermons*, 9:296. Lancelot Andrewes exemplifies an Anglican habit of treating David's kingship as a pattern for Stuart monarchs. The Psalms furnished him with texts for a group of sermons celebrating James's miraculous deliverances, first from the conspiracy of the Gowries and then from the infamous Gunpowder Plot. Evidences of the divine protection of David provide the warrant for rejoicing in the victories of the Lord's anointed, in England as in Israel. *The Works of Lancelot Andrewes* (Oxford, 1854), vol. 4. See Sears McGee, *The Godly Man in Stuart England* (New Haven, 1976), p. 238, for a discussion of differences between the Puritan and the Anglican David.

48. In the background of *The Soul's Conflict* is Augustine's famous observation at the beginning of the *Confessions*: "Our heart is restless until it rests in thee." Sibbes frequently echoes Augustine and often cites him.

CHAPTER THREE

1. F. J. Powicke, "Story and Significance of the Rev. Richard Baxter's 'Saints Everlasting Rest'," *Bulletin of the John Rylands Library* 5 (1919–20), discusses the composition of the work and its history.

2. Richard Baxter, *The Practical Works* (London, 1707), 1:xxi.

3. Richard Baxter, *The Saints Everlasting Rest* (London, 1650), sig. A₂.

4. Louis Martz and U. Milo Kaufmann, the critics who have said most about Baxter's meditation, focus on the fourth part exclusively. See Martz, *The Poetry of Meditation* (New Haven, 1962), 2d ed., chap. 4 (also Martz's introduction to *The Poems of Edward Taylor*, ed. Donald E. Stanford [New Haven, 1960], pp. xxiii–xxix) and Kaufmann, *The Pilgrim's Progress and Traditions in Puritan Meditation* (New Haven, 1966), passim.

5. Barbara Lewalski, *Donne's "Anniversaries" and the Poetry of Praise* (Princeton, 1973), chap. 3, and *Protestant Poetics and the Seventeenth-Century Religious Lyric* (Princeton, 1979), chap. 5. See also Norman S. Grabo, "The Art of Puritan Meditation," *Seventeenth-Century News* 26 (1968): 7–9.

6. Kaufmann, *Traditions in Puritan Meditation*, pp. 133ff.

7. Martz has argued the indebtedness of Hall's *The Arte of Divine Meditation* (1607) to the *scala meditationis* of Johan Wessel Gansfort, which Hall had found reprinted in the *Rosetum* of Johannes Mauburnus. Martz, *The Poetry of Meditation*, pp. 62, 331ff. Frank Huntley minimizes this influence, arguing that Hall explicitly rejected the complex method implied by this scale. In *Bishop Joseph Hall: 1574–1656* (Cambridge, 1979), p. 77.

8. *Bishop Joseph Hall*, pp. 59–61.

9. *The Godly Preachers of the Elizabethan Church* (London, 1965), passim. M. M. Knappen makes a similar observation about Richard Rogers. *Two Puritan Diaries* (Chicago, 1933), pp. 78–79.

10. Lewalski, *Protestant Poetics*, pp. 148ff.

11. *Seven Treatises* (London, 1603), p. 233.

12. Ibid. Lewalski draws the majority of her illustrations of Protestant meditation from writers who could be characterized as Puritans, among them Rogers, Baxter, Richard Greenham, Richard Sibbes, Thomas Gataker, Thomas Hooker, and Edmund Calamy.

13. Kaufmann, *Traditions in Puritan Meditation*, pp. 133–34, quotes Sibbes on the reason for keeping heaven "daily in our eye:" "The life of a Christian is wondrously ruled in this world, by the consideration, and meditation of the life of another world" (*A Glance of Heaven* [London, 1638], p. 88).

14. John Calvin, *Institutes of the Christian Religion*, ed. John T. McNeill (Philadelphia, 1960), 3:9. See Ronald S. Wallace, *Calvin's Doctrine of the Christian Life* (London, 1959), pp. 88ff., for a discussion of Calvin's views on heavenly meditation.

15. John Calvin, Commentary on John 6:39, *Calvin's Commentaries: The Gospel according to St. John, 1–10*, trans. T. H. L. Parker (London, 1959), p. 162.

16. John Calvin, *Commentaries on...Philippians, Colossians, and Thessalonians*, trans. John Pringle (Edinburgh, 1851), p. 206.

17. Arthur Dent, *The Plaine Mans Path-way to Heaven* (London, 1605), 7th ed., p. 85.

18. Robert Bolton, *Some Generall Directions for a Comfortable Walking with God* (London, 1638), 5th ed., p. 65. Gordon Wakefield, *Puritan Devotion* (London, 1957), p. 152, sees Bolton as anticipating Baxter's soliloquies.

19. Ibid., p. 62.

20. See Kaufmann's sixth chapter, "Two Divergent Traditions in Puritan Meditation," *Traditions in Puritan Meditation*, pp. 118–50. Kaufmann suggests that Hall modified the system that he found in Mauburnus to emphasize the logical elaboration of the subject of meditation.

21. Joseph Hall, *The Arte of Divine Meditation* (London, 1606), p. 29.

22. This technique is so widespread that it cannot be seen as characterizing any particular kind of meditation.

23. Joseph Hall, *Soliloquies* (London, 1651), p. 330. See also *The Soules Farewell to Earth, and Approaches to Heaven*, published with *Soliloquies*, and *The Devout Soul; or, Rules of Heavenly Devotion* (1650). Hall's soliloquies bear some striking resemblances to the soliloquies of Baxter in *The Saints Everlasting Rest*, though Hall tends to be more concerned with the attributes of God and the nature of union with God and Baxter with the joys of fruition.

24. John Downame, *A Guide to Godlynesse* (London, 1629), p. 533.

25. Kaufmann, *Traditions in Puritan Meditation*, p. 121.

26. Downame, *Guide*, pp. 545–46.

27. Ibid., p. 534.

28. Not all the writers I have mentioned were so earthbound as Downame. Ambrose suggests Baxter, and may well have been influenced by him, in meditations upon the soul's love of Christ and upon the eternity of heaven.

29. Hall, *Arte*, p. 473. Baxter urges his readers to use their sabbaths as "steps to glory" (*The Saints Everlasting Rest*, p. 705), and refers to the ordinances (sacraments) as "stairs" (p. 676), but he does not use this traditional figure in connection with meditation itself.

30. Cf. Baxter's *Poetical Fragments* (London, 1681), sig. A₄: "Reason is a sleepy half-useless thing, till some Passion excite it."

31. *A Christian Directory* (London, 1673), p. 155.

32. Lewalski, *Donne's "Anniversaries,"* pp. 84–92.

33. Joan Webber has suggested that Baxter was unable to realize a literary persona in *Reliquiae Baxterianae*. She sees the stylistic inconsistencies of that work as interesting for the way they mirror Baxter's humanness and his immersion in the conflicts of his age and

argues that Baxter has no style, in contrast to more artful writers like Robert Burton or Sir Thomas Browne. See *The Eloquent "I"* (Madison, 1968), pp. 115–48, passim. These remarks must be qualified for *The Saints Everlasting Rest*, though I would not use the term "persona" of that work because it smacks of the "playing" that Baxter took pains to denounce. The style of *The Saints Everlasting Rest* is not so consistent or contrived as, say, Donne's, but it is nonetheless distinctive and clearly reflects Baxter's intelligence and his passionate concern for the souls of his readers. It is a plain style that relies heavily upon repetition, imperatives, exclamations, and questions. Baxter wrote an aggressive prose calculated to shake his readers out of the lethargy that he imagined to be man's natural condition, and at times an enthusiastic, headlong prose. For a very thorough discussion of Baxter's sense of style see N. H. Keeble, "Some Literary and Religious Aspects of the Works of Richard Baxter," (D.Phil. thesis, Oxford University, 1973), chap. 4.

34. In *A Priest to the Temple, The Works of George Herbert*, ed. F. E. Hutchinson (Oxford, 1941), p. 225.

35. Richard Baxter, *Gildas Salvianus: The Reformed Pastor* (London, 1656), p. 78.

36. Ibid., p. 277.

37. Ibid., p. 278.

38. Ibid., p. 394.

39. Quoted by Geoffrey Nuttall, *Richard Baxter and Philip Dodderidge* (London, 1951), p. 14.

40. Baxter, *Reformed Pastor*, p. 278.

41. Webber, *The Eloquent "I,"* pp. 128–34.

42. Quoted by Webber, *The Eloquent "I,"* p. 133.

43. Richard Baxter, *The Reformed Pastor*, p. 123.

44. Quoted by Geoffrey Nuttall, *Richard Baxter* (London, 1965), p. 53.

45. Quoted by Webber, *The Eloquent "I,"* p. 116.

46. Baxter, *Reformed Pastor*, p. 408.

47. Richard Baxter, *Poetical Fragments* (London, 1681), p. 40.

48. Nuttall, *Richard Baxter*, p. 124.

49. Baxter, *Reformed Pastor*, p. 263.

50. See *The Saints Everlasting Rest*, pp. 142–43. Baxter confesses to some difficulty in understanding exactly how the Spirit and the Word cooperate in this work.

51. See Herbert's "Bunch of Grapes."

52. The Catholic practice of reconstructing historical scenes by the application of the senses naturally led to considerable specificity. In the meditation on the life of Christ attributed to Bonaventura, for example, one finds a very full dramatization of the crucifixion, complete with a description of the crowd. See Bonaventura, *The Life of Christ*, trans. W. H. Hutchings (London, 1881), p. 249. By dividing the events of the Passion into stages to be the subject of a sequence of meditations Ignatius invites a similarly detailed kind of imagining. See *The Spiritual Exercises of St. Ignatius*, trans. Anthony Mottola (New York, 1964), exercises for the third week.

53. The Catholic historian of religion Louis Bouyer faults Baxter for making the action of the Spirit so necessary to an understanding of Scripture and thus to meditation. His norm is Ignatius. See *Orthodox Spirituality and Protestant and Anglican Spirituality* (London, 1969), p. 159.

54. John Milton, *Paradise Lost*, 12.313–14.

55. Quoted by Geoffrey Nuttall, *Richard Baxter*, p. 5.

56. Nuttall, *Baxter and Dodderidge*, p. 27n.

57. Baxter, *Poetical Fragments*, no page.

CHAPTER FOUR

1. Lewis H. Berens, *The Digger Movement in the Days of the Commonwealth* (London, 1906), pp. 37–38. Berens reprints the account of the interview that appears in Bulstrode Whitelocke's *Memorial of English Affairs* (1682).

2. Winstanley himself preferred the term "True Levellers," which appears in the title of his manifesto, *The True Levellers Standard Advanced*, 1649.

3. Gerrard Winstanley, *A New-Yeers Gift for the Parliament and Armie*, 1650.

4. *The Works of Gerrard Winstanley*, ed. George H. Sabine (New York, 1965), pp. 434–35. Page numbers cited in the text refer to this edition.

5. Winthrop S. Hudson, "The Economic and Social Thought of Gerrard Winstanley," *Journal of Modern History* 18 (1946): 1–21. Hudson argues convincingly that the digging should be regarded primarily as an "eschatological sign" of the sort given by Old Testament prophets (he cites Ezekiel in particular as a model for Winstanley). Winstanley's expectation of an age of the Spirit marks him as one of the numerous spiritual descendants of Joachim of Fiore, the influence of whose theory of three ages of history (identified with Father, Son, and Holy Spirit) has been traced by Marjorie Reeves in her massive study, *The Influence of Prophecy in the Later Middle Ages* (Oxford, 1969). See also Norman Cohn, *The Pursuit of the Millennium* (London, 1957) and Ernest Tuveson, *Millennium and Utopia* (Berkeley, 1949). For studies of millenarian thought in Winstanley's times see Peter Toon, ed., *Puritans, the Millennium and the Future of Israel: Puritan Eschatology* (Cambridge, 1970); Bryan Ball, *A Great Expectation* (Leiden, 1975); and Paul Christianson, *Reformers and Babylon* (Toronto, 1978).

6. Winstanley's group did spawn imitations in several other counties. K. V. Thomas, "Another Digger Broadside," *Past and Present* 42 (1969): 57–68, discusses the extent of Digger activity.

7. Winstanley received extensive treatment in studies by L. H. Berens, a disciple of Henry George (*The Digger Movement*, 1906), and the German Marxist Eduard Bernstein (*Cromwell and Communism*, 1930 [first published 1908]). The most important subsequent studies are by D. W. Petegorsky (in *Left-Wing Democracy in the English Civil War*, 1940); G. H. Sabine (the long introduction to the indispensable edition that he published in 1940); Christopher Hill (*The World Turned Upside Down*, 1972); and T. Wilson Hayes, *Winstanley the Digger* (Cambridge, Mass., 1979). Hill, who has probably done more than anyone else to publicize Winstanley, published in 1973 a Penguin edition of selections from the works, with a substantial introduction. Hayes's ambitious study appeared when my chapter was in final draft. It offers the fullest account available of the evolution of Winstanley's thought, with extensive reference to the three early tracts not included in Sabine's edition.

8. Winstanley characterizes his work as declaring "a full Commonwealths Freedome, according to the Rule of Righteousness, which is Gods Word" (509) and cites the call of Hugh Peters, Cromwell's chaplain, to seek principles of government in Scripture as a warrant for publishing it. The biblical authority for his conception was Paul's reference in Ephesians (2:12) to the "commonwealth of Israel."

9. Paul Elmen has criticized what he sees as a Marxist overemphasis upon economic explanations of the Diggers. Elmen's focus is on the biblical origins of Winstanley's ideas and his continuing concern with man's spiritual needs. See "The Theological Basis of Digger Communism," *Church History* 23 (1954): 207–18. For an extreme statement of the opposing position, which tends to discount or ignore religious elements in assessing Winstanley's thought, see C. H. George, "Gerrard Winstanley: A Critical Retrospect," in C. Robert Cole and Michael E. Moody, eds., *The Dissenting Tradition* (Athens, Ohio, 1975). George sees Winstanley as moving from mysticism to "rational socialism" and argues that the Bible has only an "ornamental" relation to his thought.

10. Christopher Hill, while emphasizing Winstanley's secularism, has written suggestively on his mythic use of biblical materials, comparing him with Blake in this regard. See the introduction to his Penguin edition, *Winstanley: The Law of Freedom and Other Writings*, pp. 54–59. M. H. Abrams (in *Natural Supernaturalism* [New York, 1971], pp. 52 ff.) has commented upon the general similarities between Winstanley's and Blake's uses of biblical imagery. Hayes (passim) offers extensive commentary upon Winstanley's biblical imagery, also with reference to Blake.

11. The definitive study of the relationship of Word and Spirit in the religious writing of the period is Geoffrey Nuttall's *The Holy Spirit in Puritan Faith and Experience* (Oxford, 1946). See especially pp. 20–34.

12. Sabine discusses these figures in his account of Winstanley's predecessors, pp. 21–35. Hayes discusses Saltmarsh and Everard in particular, stressing the influence of Everard's hermeticism upon Winstanley. See especially *Winstanley the Digger*, pp. 66 ff. and 179 ff.

13. John Everard, *Some Gospel-Treasures Opened* (London, 1653), p. 329. This collection of sermons was published posthumously.

14. Ibid., pp. 284, 311.

15. See Nuttall, *Holy Spirit*, pp. 27–28.

16. Quoted by Nuttall, *Holy Spirit*, p. 69.

17. Jeremiah describes himself as having to speak out because God's word was like a fire in his bones (Jer. 20:9).

18. Jackson Cope has discussed the blurring of literal and metaphoric in Fox's *Journal*, which he sees as exemplified by a description of the Scottish landscape that refers to the "thick, cloddy earth of hypocrisy and falseness." See his "Seventeenth-Century Quaker Style," *PMLA* 71 (1956): 725–54.

19. See Joan Thirsk, ed., *The Agrarian History of England and Wales, IV, 1500–1640* (Cambridge, 1967); cited by Robert W. Kenny in the useful introduction to his edition of *The Law of Freedom in a Platform* (New York, 1973).

20. Christopher Hill has written several pages of commentary on Winstanley's prose style. See *Winstanley: The Law of Freedom and Other Writings*, pp. 59–66.

21. See Rev. 12:4, which describes "a great red dragon" casting down a third of the stars of heaven with his tail.

22. Winstanley, like other millenarian writers of the period, used the language of Revelation (Rev. 11:2, 12:14) to locate his historical moment: "The Lord he gives this beast a toleration to rule 42 months, or a time, times, and the dividing of time...but now the 42 months are expiring, we are under the half day of the Beast, or the dividing of time." In *Fire in the Bush* Winstanley used the formula "time, times, and dividing of times" to refer both to historical periods and to the spiritual development of the individual. He saw the "dividing of times" as characterized by "variety of Churches, and differences in Religion" and also by the warfare of Michael and the dragon within the soul (485–86).

23. See Keith Thomas, "The Date of Gerrard Winstanley's *Fire in the Bush*," *Past and Present* 42 (1968): 160–62. Others have argued for an earlier date, primarily on grounds that the work sounds so like others from the Digger period. See especially George, "Gerrard Winstanley," pp. 192–94.

24. From verses printed on the title page, reproduced by Hill. *Winstanley: The Law of Freedom and Other Writings*, p. 273.

25. Everard, *Gospel-Treasures*, p. 608.

26. Quoted by Christopher Hill, *The World Turned Upside Down*, p. 165. Hill's sympathetic and provocative discussion of the Ranters takes up much of the book. See also A. L. Morton, *The World of the Ranters* (London, 1970).

27. Hill's view has been attacked in a recent article by Lotte Mulligan, John K. Graham, and Judith Richards: "Winstanley: A Case for the Man as He Said He Was," *Journal of Ecclesiastical History* 28 (1977): 57–75. The authors, challenging all those who stress Winstanley's modernism, and Hill in particular, insist that Winstanley expected the inner transformation that he sought to be brought about by a transcendent God. They cite Winstanley's belief that God spoke to him and his expectation that Christ would appear "glorified with thousand thousands attending upon him" (Sabine, 471).

28. *The World Turned Upside Down*, p. 120.

29. Winstanley pictures fallen man as literally and figuratively corrupting the earth with his decaying body and his "venimous and stinking unrighteousnesse" (113).

30. He subtitled *The Fire in the Bush* "The great battell of God Almighty, between Michaell the seed of life, and the great dragon, the curse fought within the spirit of man."

CHAPTER FIVE

1. John Milton, *The Reason of Church Government, Complete Prose Works of John Milton*, ed. Don M. Wolfe (New Haven, 1953), 1:803. Hereafter references to the Yale edition of Milton's prose will be cited in the text by volume and page number.

2. Stephen Marshall, Edmund Calamy, Milton's former tutor Thomas Young, Matthew Newcomen, William Spurstow.

3. *A Modest Confutation* (London, 1642), p. 2.

4. See Thomas Kranidas, *The Fierce Equation* (The Hague, 1965), chaps. 1 and 2, and "Milton and the Rhetoric of Zeal," *Texas Studies in Language and Literature* 6 (1965): 423–32; Keith W. Stavely, *The Politics of Milton's Prose Style* (New Haven, 1975); D. M. Rosenberg, "Satirical Techniques in Milton's Polemical Prose," *Satire Newsletter* 8 (1971): 91–97, and "Style and Meaning in Milton's Anti-Episcopal Tracts," *Criticism* 15 (1973): 43–57; Michael Lieb, "Milton's *Of Reformation* and the Dynamics of Controversy," *Achievements of the Left Hand* (Amherst, 1974), ed. Shawcross and Lieb, pp. 55–82; Joel Morkan, "Wrath and Laughter: Milton's Ideas on Satire," *Studies in Philology* 69 (1972): 475–95; James Egan, "The Satiric Wit of Milton's Prose Controversies," *Studies in the Literary Imagination* 10 (1977): 97–104.

5. See especially Kranidas, *Fierce Equation*, pp. 66–68; Morkan, "Wrath and Laughter," passim.

6. Milton, *Prose Works*, 1:625. Milton states at the outset of *Christian Doctrine* that one must look for doctrine "in the Holy Scriptures alone with the Holy Spirit as guide" (6:127).

7. See *Of Reformation* (1:568), for a denunciation of the "crabbed" and "abstruse" style of the fathers. Its antithesis, not surprisingly, is "the sober, plain, and unaffected stile of the Scriptures."

8. See Kranidas, *Fierce Equation*, pp. 59 ff., for a discussion of Anglican decency and Milton's attacks upon it.

9. He does defend his interpretation of a particular text in *Animadversions* by appealing to the "Law of Method," which demands that "clearest and plainest expressions be set formost" (1:709).

10. Stanley Fish argues that Milton's real aim in *The Reason of Church Government* was to discredit the use of reason. While his analysis of Milton's rhetorical strategy is useful, the underlying argument ignores assumptions about proper and improper uses of reason that inform *The Reason of Church Government* and other antiprelatical tracts. See *Self-Consuming Artifacts* (Berkeley, 1972), pp. 265–302.

11. John Coolidge observes that for Puritans the Gospel had a power like that of Arthur's shield. *The Pauline Renaissance in England* (Oxford, 1970), p. xi. James Nohrnberg sees the unveiling of Arthur's shield as "a powerful symbol for the manifestation of

God's Word." *The Analogy of "The Faerie Queene"* (Princeton, 1976), p. 207.

12. For the opposite point of view see Richard Hooker, *Of the Laws of Ecclesiastical Polity*, ed. Christopher Morris (London, 1958), 2:417 (V.lxxvii.1): "The power of the ministry of God...raiseth men from the earth and bringeth God himself down from heaven, by blessing visible elements it maketh them invisible grace."

13. The concluding line of the sonnet, "On the New Forcers of Conscience under the Long Parliament."

14. In another military metaphor Milton announces his aim to reduce the people of God "to their firme stations under the standard of the Gospell" (1.627). For his attraction to the Pauline sense of "church-discipline" as necessary to Christian warfare see 1.758.

15. "On the New Forcers of Conscience."

16. See *Prose Works*, 2.82, and 338 and the section on Scripture in *Christian Doctrine*, especially 6.582–83. For a discussion of Milton's hermeneutics in the light of seventeenth-century practice see George Conklin, *Biblical Criticism and Heresy in Milton* (New York, 1949), pp. 24–40. H. R. MacCallum's useful article "Milton and the Figurative Interpretation of the Bible," *University of Toronto Quarterly* 31 (1962): 397–415, places Milton in the Protestant tradition of opposition to allegorical interpretation and stresses his conservatism with regard to figurative interpretation and the use of typology.

17. See Sirluck's introduction to the Yale edition, especially pp. 153–58. Arthur Barker, *Milton and the Puritan Dilemma* (Toronto, 1942), p. 104, notes that Milton describes the will of God revealed in the Law as "commensurate to right reason." Milton regarded the moral principles established by the Law as remaining valid, although he saw the whole Mosaic law as abrogated by the Gospel.

18. See Theodore L. Huguelet, "The Rule of Charity in Milton's Divorce Tracts," *Milton Studies* 6 (1974): 199–214. Huguelet traces the appeal to charity in exegesis to Augustine and demonstrates that various reformers, including Grotius, continued the tradition. Yet he finds that Milton's rule was essentially a concept of his own.

19. See also *Prose Works*, 2:678, for a contrast between the "written letter" and "the unerring paraphrase of Christian love and Charity." In *Of Reformation* Milton had linked insensitivity to "inward acts of *worship*" with an inability to apprehend the inner life of Scripture: "Men came to scan the *Scriptures*, by the Letter, and in the Covenant of our Redemption, magnified the external signs more than the quickning power of the Spirit" (1:522).

20. Milton of course descends to particulars in developing his argument, noting, among other things, that Christ's words must be understood in terms of their context, as a rebuke to the licentiousness of the Pharisees, and that Christ often used *"hyperbolies."*

21. See Sirluck's explanation of how Milton revised his position on the relationship of the Old Testament and the New: 2:147, 154–58.

22. See Milton's comment on the Hebraisms of the New Testament, 2:671: "The New Testament, though it be said originally writt in Greeke, yet hath nothing neer so many *Atticisms* as *Hebraisms, & Syriacisms* which was the Majesty of God" (2:671).

23. See Barker, especially chaps. 5 and 6, for a lucid account of the nature of this shift.

24. See Michael Fixler, *Milton and the Kingdoms of God* (Evanston, 1964), especially chap. 3, for a thorough discussion of the evolution of Milton's apocalyptic hopes. See also Fixler's excellent article, "Ecclesiology," in *A Milton Encyclopedia*, ed. William B. Hunter, Jr., particularly for his discussion of Milton's sense of the authority of the Holy Spirit.

25. For an extended discussion of Milton's attitudes toward prophecy and his sense of himself as prophet see William Kerrigan, *The Prophetic Milton* (Charlottesville, 1974), especially chap. 3. See also J. A. Wittreich, *Visionary Poetics* (San Marino, Calif., 1979).

26. A. S. P. Woodhouse, *Puritanism and Liberty* (Chicago, 1974 [first published

1938]), p. 65 n.; Barker, *Milton and the Puritan Dilemma*, p. 285.

27. Barker, *Milton and the Puritan Dilemma*, pp. 106, 118, 81.

28. A. S. P. Woodhouse, *The Poet and His Faith* (Chicago, 1965), p. 105.

29. Although Milton observes the conventional distinction between faith (the knowledge of God) and love (the worship of God) in structuring *Christian Doctrine*, he notes that the division is artificial: "Although these two parts are distinguished in kind, and are divided for the purpose of instruction, in practice they are inseparable" (6:129).

30. In *Christian Doctrine* Milton quotes from John 16:13 more than once: "Howbeit when he, the Spirit of truth, is come, he will guide you into all truth."

31. See Barker, *Milton and the Puritan Dilemma*, chap. 17, for a discussion of Milton's understanding of regeneration and its divergence from Calvin's and that of orthodox Puritanism. In the same chapter Barker analyzes Milton's rejection of Calvin's understanding of predestination.

32. Northrop Frye makes a useful distinction between "practical" reason, which finds an outlet in action, and "speculative" reason, which merely wanders, guided by no controlling vision. *The Return of Eden* (Toronto, 1965), p. 96.

33. See Mary Ann Radzinowicz, *Toward "Samson Agonistes": The Growth of Milton's Mind* (Princeton, 1979), passim, for a lucid discussion of the ways in which the heroes of Milton's major poems grow in understanding through the exercise of reason. I find her excessively skeptical of Milton's claims to inspiration (see pp. 350–64) and more insistent than Milton upon the "rationality" of the Spirit (see p. 279 n.). Radzinowicz adopts and extends Woodhouse's distinction between an inner light "mysterious and in effect arbitrary in its revelations" (like that of the Quakers) and an inner light that "might be regarded as one with rectified reason." See *The Heavenly Muse*, pp. 140–41. While there is some warrant for such a dichotomy, I believe that it leads to an oversimplified view of Milton's sense of the operation of the Spirit. Identifying the Spirit too closely with reason drains it of its revelatory power.

34. Alden Sampson, *Studies in Milton* (New York, 1913), pp. 181–82, comments on the reactions of William Ellery Channing and Bishop Sumner. Sampson goes on to try to demonstrate Milton's affinities with George Fox, especially with regard to their sense of an inner light. Christopher Hill's *Milton and the English Revolution* (New York, 1978 [first published 1977]) is by far the most ambitious effort to date to link Milton with radical thought. While Hill's efforts to place Milton's works in the context of radical ideas circulating when he wrote are important and useful, he tends to ignore Milton's kinship with aspects of Puritan tradition in England. Hill also makes Milton's approach to Scripture seem unduly conservative by contrasting it solely with that of the extreme radicals. To say that Milton insisted upon the authority of the Bible in order "to protect the institutions of society against the anarchy of individual consciences" (Hill, p. 316) is to slight his repeated use of Scripture as a weapon against institutionalized religion.

35. Chiefly from Hill. Barker offers a careful analysis of the radical tendencies in Milton's late tracts, with particular attention to the relationship of his views to those of other writers on the Puritan left. I differ from him in making more of continuities with the earlier prose and in emphasizing the role of the Spirit.

36. In discussing his blindness in the *Second Defense of the English People* Milton claimed to experience "an inner and far more enduring light" (4.1.590). One can recognize that Milton does not oppose the teachings of the Spirit to reason without having to conclude that "the inner light remained for him that intellectual ray" (Barker, *Milton and the Puritan Dilemma*, p. 258). The early Quakers tended to distinguish the inner light from reason and conscience. They found it necessary to test its authenticity, however, by such standards as moral purity and self-consistency. They might also check the leadings of the Spirit against biblical standards of conduct. See Hugh Barbour, *The Quakers in*

Puritan England (New Haven, 1964), pp. 179–81.

37. Hooker, *Laws*, 1:102, 324.

38. Ibid., 2:37.

39. Ibid., 1:114.

40. *The Works of John Milton* (New York, 1931–42), 6:24.

41. "Scripture only can be the final judge or rule in matters of religion and then only in the conscience of every Christian to himself." Milton defined conscience as "that full perswasion whereby we are assur'd that our beleef and practise, as far as we are able to apprehend and probably make appeer, is according to the will of God and his Holy Spirit within us." Frank Allen Patterson, ed., *The Works of John Milton*, (New York, 1931–40), 6:7, 5. In *The Reason of Church Government* Milton describes God as enjoining action "by his Secretary conscience" (3:342). In *Paradise Lost* the Father asserts, "I will place within them as a guide / My Umpire *Conscience*" (3:194–95). The language suggests that Milton saw the conscience of the Christian as informed by the Holy Spirit, also described as guiding man.

42. Milton, *Prose Works*, 6:28. Milton had anticipated this position in *Areopagitica:* "Neither is God appointed and confined...lest we should devote ourselves to set places, and assemblies, and outward callings of men" (2:466).

43. See Barker, *Milton and the Puritan Dilemma*, pp. 313–14.

44. Milton, *Prose Works*, 6:79.

45. "On the Late Massacre in Piedmont."

46. From John Saltmarsh, *Sparkles of Glory*, 1647. Quoted by William Haller, *Liberty and Reformation in the Puritan Revolution* (New York, 1955), p. 199. Haller notes Milton's kinship with Saltmarsh.

47. See Milton's chapter on the Holy Spirit in *Christian Doctrine* (bk. 1, chap. 6). He allows for various uses of the term "spirit" in Scripture: to refer to the power of Father or Son, to impulses from God, to the light of truth by which God leads his people, and to spiritual gifts, as well as to "the actual person of the Holy Spirit" (6:285). As part of his antitrinitarian campaign Milton argues that the third person is meant relatively seldom by references to spirit and that the Holy Spirit is inferior to both Father and Son. The burden of his argument is that the Spirit is not God but rather a "minister of God." Milton's discussion in *Christian Doctrine* has to do with the essence of the Holy Spirit. His insistence upon interpreting the term in a "broader sense" than usual does not imply a restrictive view of the power and influence of the Spirit in the roles of comforter, sanctifier, and guide to divine truth. It simply reflects his conviction that "The Spirit does everything in the name of the Father and the Son" (6:294).

48. *The Return of Eden* (Toronto, 1965), p. 96.

49. Milton still associates truth with "light from above, from the fountain of light" (*PR*, 4.289), although he no longer implies that men must make an extraordinary effort to kindle their sight at this light.

50. The critical importance of "rousing motions" from God in guiding Samson's actions confirms this direction. Hill asserts (p. 447) that "Samson was as entirely dependent on the motions of the spirit as Quakers, Ranters, and other extreme radicals." This overstates the case, but the resemblance is significant.

51. J. B. Broadbent, *Some Graver Subject* (New York, 1960), p. 230, links Milton's two uses of Ezekiel's chariot and sees the victorious Son of *Paradise Lost* as representing the truth associated with the beams of the Gospel in the prose.

52. See 2 Peter 3:13.

53. Emory Elliott has recently discussed the poem's concern with the proper understanding of Scripture, in the course of an article dealing primarily with biblical allusions, "Milton's Biblical Style in *Paradise Regained*," *Milton Studies* 6 (1974): 227–41.

54. Barbara Lewalski notes that the Son's understanding of Scripture is dependent upon the illumination of the Spirit. *Milton's Brief Epic* (Providence, 1966), p. 162.

55. I agree with Frye and Lewalski that Christ's final words to Satan are ambiguous and should be regarded both as a rebuke to Satan for presuming to tempt the Father and a recognition and assertion of his own divinity. Frye, *Return of Eden*, pp. 140–41; Lewalski, *Milton's Brief Epic*, pp. 316–18.

CHAPTER SIX

1. I omit Bunyan's other major work, *The Life and Death of Mr. Badman*, because it is less dependent upon Scripture than the others and, to my mind at least, not so significant an accomplishment.

2. Roger Sharrock has noted that Bunyan is least traditional in the central part of the work and that his account of his vicissitudes is unique in its "freedom from rationalization into stock Calvinist formulae." *Grace Abounding to the Chief of Sinners* (Oxford, 1962), p. xxxii. Sharrock divides the work according to what he sees as four conventional divisions in the autobiography of the period: before conversion (sections 1–36), conversion (27–252), calling (253–305), and ministry (319–39). See pp. xxx–xxxi. In an earlier article, "Spiritual Autobiography in *The Pilgrim's Progress,*" *Review of English Studies* 24 (1948): 16, Sharrock distinguishes six stages in the progress of the conversion described in *Grace Abounding*, beginning with the conviction of sin and culminating in final assurance of grace. Dean Ebner, *Autobiography in Seventeenth-Century England* (The Hague, 1971), pp. 22–71, sees *Grace Abounding* as conforming to four Calvinist stages of spiritual enlightenment, which he derives from various theological writings of the period. His stress is on the Calvinism of Bunyan's and other Baptist autobiographies.

3. The relationship of Luther's commentary to *Grace Abounding* has never been explored in any detail. Roger Sharrock calls the "vehement emotionalism" of Bunyan's "moments of justification" Lutheran rather than Calvinist. *John Bunyan* (London, 1968), p. 34. In his valuable study of Bunyan's theology Richard Greaves finds Bunyan to have been significantly influenced by Luther, especially by the polarity of divine wrath and divine grace that receives so much of Luther's attention in the commentary on Galatians. See *John Bunyan* (Abingdon, Berkshire, 1969), passim.

4. Quotations are taken from Sharrock's edition of *Grace Abounding*.

5. *A Commentarie of Master Doctor Martin Luther upon the Epistle of S. Paul to the Galatians*, 9th ed. (London, 1635), A_2 verso.

6. *A Commentarie*, fol. 88.

7. Ibid., fol. 266, verso.

8. Augustine, *Confessions*, trans. E. B. Pusey (New York, 1949), p. 167.

9. *A Commentarie*, fol. 35.

10. Ibid., fol. 152, verso.

11. Ibid., fol. 231, verso.

12. See also Bunyan, *Grace Abounding*, secs. 96, 228.

13. *A Commentarie*, fol. 190, verso.

14. Ibid., fol. 190, verso.

15. Ibid., fol. 243, verso.

16. Sharrock notes the indebtedness of Bunyan to Luther's discussion of righteousness in his commentary on Galatians 5:5. *Grace Abounding*, pp. 144, 149–50.

17. Elizabeth Bruss sees Bunyan demonstrating a new capacity for Ramistic analysis at this point in the narrative, as he subjects the text to "a rigorous series of proofs and applications." *Autobiographical Acts* (Baltimore, 1976), p. 48.

18. Edward Dowden, *Puritan and Anglican* (London, 1904), p. 237.

19. *The Works of John Bunyan*, ed. George Offor (Glasgow, 1859), 3:721. Hereafter cited as *Works*.

20. Bunyan, *Works*, 3:409.

21. In *The Holy City* Bunyan shows a typically Puritan tendency to qualify his response to figurative language: "Yet consider that these are but metaphorical and borrowed expressions, spoken to our capacities" (*Works*, 3:424). He was to take a bolder line in the verses in which he justified *The Pilgrim's Progress*.

22. Bunyan, *Works*, 3:432.

23. Ibid., p. 421.

24. Ibid.

25. Bunyan, *Works*, 3:420.

26. Ibid., p. 419.

27. William York Tindall discusses the nature of Bunyan's millenarianism as it is manifested in *The Holy City* and such late works as his commentary on the first ten chapters of Genesis and the tract, *Of Antichrist and his Ruin*, both published posthumously in 1692. See *John Bunyan: Mechanick Preacher* (New York, 1934), chap. 6.

28. Bunyan, *Works*, 3:398.

29. John Bunyan, *The Pilgrim's Progress*, ed. J. B. Wharey, 2d ed. rev. by Roger Sharrock (Oxford, 1960), p. 4. Quotations from *The Pilgrim's Progress* are taken from this edition.

30. In *"The Pilgrim's Progress" and Traditions in Puritan Meditation* (New Haven, 1966). See especially pp. 3–15. Kaufmann suggests that Bunyan's efforts to prove that his metaphors are unambiguous (*logos*) arise from a need to satisfy the expectations of his audience; Kaufmann finds that other aspects of his Apology, especially the concluding lines, reveal a sense of his narrative as *mythos*, appealing to his audience in nonrational ways. My intention is to extend Kaufmann's argument, though without using his terms.

31. Bunyan, *Works*, 3:437.

32. See Brainerd Stranahan, "Bunyan and the Bible: Uses of Biblical Materials in the Imaginative Structure of *The Pilgrim's Progress*," (Ph.D. diss., Harvard, 1965) for a very full discussion of Bunyan's biblical sources. Stranahan notes the high frequency of references to Hebrews in *The Pilgrim's Progress* and *Grace Abounding*.

33. Bunyan, *Works*, 3:382.

34. Such readers would have seen references linking the pilgrims with the saving history of the Israelites as putting the authority of the Word behind the metaphor of the journey. The Shining Ones confirm Christian's identity as a spiritual descendant of Abraham when they prepare him for entering the New Jerusalem: "You are going to *Abraham*, to *Isaac*, and *Jacob*, and to the Prophets" (p. 159). Secret tells Christiana before she sets out that God "will feed thee with the Fat of his House, and with the Heritage of *Jacob* thy Father" (p. 179). Christian interprets his journey in the light of Old Testament history, identifying himself as "of the Race of *Japhet*, whom God will perswade to dwell in the Tents of *Shem*" (p. 46), thereby associating himself with the favored line that will have dominion over Canaan according to God's promise to Noah in Genesis 9:27. When he loses his roll, he recalls the trials of the Israelites: "Thus it happened to *Israel* for their sin, they were sent back again by the way of the Red-Sea" (p. 44). Bunyan again invokes the Exodus in part 2 when he describes the seal with which Interpreter marks the children of Christiana as "the contents and sum of the Passover which the Children of Israel did eat when they came out from the Land of Egypt" (p. 208).

35. Bunyan, *Works*, 3:382.

36. Martin Gardner, ed., *The Annotated Alice* (New York, 1960), p. 88.

37. Stanley Fish's claim, in *Self-Consuming Artifacts* (Berkeley and Los Angeles,

1972), chap. 4, that *The Pilgrim's Progress* offers an illusory kind of progress seems to me fundamentally mistaken. My reading implicitly questions two key assumptions upon which Fish's argument depends. The first is that Bunyan continually frustrates expectations aroused in the reader by the linear form of his work and hence disqualifies the work "as a vehicle of the insight it pretends to convey" (p. 225). This position depends upon the unstated assumption that Bunyan was interested only in exposing his reader's limitations. To maintain it Fish must ignore Bunyan's climactic celebration of the joys of Beulah and of the New Jerusalem and the various signs that point to these joys along the course of Christian's journey. What Fish pictures as deceptive linear form was the sustaining metaphor of Puritan spiritual life in Bunyan's time. The other major assumption that I would question is that "in *The Pilgrim's Progress* there is an inverse relationship between visibility and reliability" (p. 240). This depends upon the further assumption that all Christian's experiences should be regarded as occurring in the "carnal" world in which Christians must learn to distrust the evidence of their senses. Such assumptions will work for Vanity Fair but not for the Delectable Mountains or for Beulah, landscapes from which Christian derives sensuous enjoyment that is a sign of spiritual progress. Some of what I have to say, particularly about the subjectivity of the individual way of faith, complements Fish's discussion, but where he looks to a tension between normal habits of perception and the demands of faith to explain the dynamics of the work I look primarily to Bunyan's understanding and use of the Bible.

38. Roger Sharrock, *John Bunyan: The Pilgrim's Progress* (London, 1966), p. 26. See also Kaufmann, pp. 106–17, on the unity of Puritan religious experience.

39. "The Origins of Puritanism," *Church History* 20 (March 1951): 54.

40. William Perkins, in *A Golden Chaine* (*Works*, Cambridge, 1603), speaks of the four major stages as degrees of the "declaration of Gods love."

41. Bunyan, *Christ a Complete Saviour.* Cited by Greaves, p. 49.

42. See John Calvin, *Institutes of the Christian Religion*, ed. John T. McNeill (Philadelphia, 1960), 2:607: "First, he [the Spirit] has been given to us for sanctification in order that he may bring us, purged of uncleanness and defilement, into obedience to God's righteousness.... Second, we are purged by his sanctification in such a way that we are besieged by many vices and much weakness so long as we are encumbered with our body. Thus it comes about that, far removed from perfection, we must move steadily forward, and though entangled in vices, daily fight against them."

43. Kaufmann, *Pilgrim's Progress and Traditions*, p. 115.

44. Mark Twain, *Adventures of Huckleberry Finn*, ed. E. S. Bradley, R. C. Beatty, and E. H. Long (New York, 1961), p. 83.

45. See *A Relation of the Imprisonment of Mr. John Bunyan*, in *Works*, 1:50–52.

46. Henri Talon has commented on the dreamlike quality of Bunyan's landscapes. He describes the country through which Christian travels as a "dream land," a "country of the soul," which becomes "real" for Christian. See "Space and the Hero in *The Pilgrim's Progress*," *Etudes Anglaises* 14 (1961): 124–30. The article constitutes part of the introduction to Talon's anthology of Bunyan's works, *God's Knotty Log* (New York, 1961).

47. Both Kaufmann and Roland M. Frye have commented on Christian's education in scriptural truth. In *God, Man, and Satan* (Princeton, 1960) Frye argues: "Throughout, there is a deepening of understanding on Christian's part, a vitally progressive revelation" (p. 138).

48. See Kaufmann, *Pilgrim's Progress and Traditions*, pp. 133 ff., for a discussion of the "heavenly-mindedness" of much Puritan meditation and the use of the senses in evoking the joys of heaven. William Madsen, in *From Shadowy Types to Truth* (New Haven, 1968), pp. 166 ff., argues that critics have neglected the imagistic, and sensuous, character of much Puritan writing.

49. In *The Strait Gate* Bunyan exhorts his readers to "strive for the faith of the Gospel, for the more we believe the Gospel, and the reality of the things of the world to come, with the more stomach shall we labour to possess the blessedness" (*Works*, 1:369).

50. Ibid., 3:540.

51. Ibid., 3:552.

52. See John Calvin, *Institutes*, 1:595. See also 1:600; 2:1307, 1456.

53. See, for example, Exod. 3:8, 13:5; Lev. 20:24; Num. 14:8; Deut. 8:7–9, 11:8–12; Josh. 1:13–15.

54. Bunyan, *Works*, 3:567. The phrase, a composite of Gal. 5:22–23 and Phil. 1:11, appears in Bunyan's elaboration of the parable of the fig tree in Luke 13: *The Barren Fig Tree; or, The Doom and Downfall of the Fruitless Professor.*

55. The most influential critics of Bunyan have regarded *The Holy War* as too elaborately contrived to be judged an artistic success. See Sharrock, *John Bunyan* (London, 1968), pp. 118–37, and Henri Talon, *John Bunyan: The Man and His Works*, trans. Barbara Wall (London, 1951), pp. 240–56. In the introduction to his useful modern edition James Forrest makes more substantial claims for the work.

56. Sharrock comments on the political allegory of the latter part of *The Holy War*, noting that it points to such events as efforts by Charles II in 1681 to pack the Bedford corporation. See *John Bunyan*, pp. 125–28.

57. E. M. W. Tillyard, *The English Epic and its Backgrounds* (London, 1954), pp. 397–406.

58. Bunyan, *The Life and Death of Mr. Badman and The Holy War*, ed. John Brown (Cambridge, 1905), p. 184. Quotations from *The Holy War* are taken from this text.

59. Forrest has a helpful discussion of possible allegorical levels. See Bunyan, *The Holy War*, ed. James F. Forrest (New York, 1968), xii–xv.

60. Greaves sees the influence of Luther in Bunyan's opposition of Mount Gracious and Mount Justice in Emmanuel's siege of Mansoul. *John Bunyan*, pp. 27–28.

61. The second is from Isa. 63:1, the first most probably from 2 Sam. 7:28.

Index